高山滑雪竞赛规则

（2021）

汉英对照

张越　安娜　宫建　等　译

国家体育总局冬季运动管理中心
中国滑雪协会
审定

人民体育出版社

图书在版编目（CIP）数据

高山滑雪竞赛规则 : 2021 : 汉英对照 / 张越等译 ; 国家体育总局冬季运动管理中心 , 中国滑雪协会审定 . -- 北京 : 人民体育出版社 , 2022
ISBN 978-7-5009-6141-3

Ⅰ . ①高… Ⅱ . ①张… ②国… ③中… Ⅲ . ①高山滑雪—竞赛规则—世界— 2021 —汉、英 Ⅳ . ① G863.114

中国版本图书馆 CIP 数据核字 (2021) 第 277390 号

*

人民体育出版社出版发行
北京新华印刷有限公司印刷
新　华　书　店　经　销

*

880 × 1230　32 开本　15 印张　442 千字
2022 年 1 月第 1 版　2022 年 1 月第 1 次印刷
印数：1—2,000 册

*

ISBN 978-7-5009-6141-3
定价：100.00 元

社址：北京市东城区体育馆路 8 号（天坛公园东门）
电话：67151482（发行部）　　邮编：100061
传真：67151483　　邮购：67118491
网址：www.sportspublish.cn

编委会

序

推动我国冰雪运动跨越式发展是实现第二个百年奋斗目标的重要组成部分。壬寅虎年新春佳节之际，第 24 届冬季奥林匹克运动会将在北京、张家口隆重举行，这将是我国建设体育强国的又一生动展现和良好契机。

高山滑雪是冬季奥林匹克运动中极具观赏性的项目，被誉为冬奥会皇冠上的明珠，并以其跨度大、速度快、风景美、参与度高而被世界各地的运动爱好者们所喜爱。

我国冰雪运动尚处于起步阶段，群众基础、运动水平、规则意识都需要有一个长期培养提高的过程，特别是在竞赛规则方面，无论是在国际竞赛制度设计中的话语权重方面，还是国内裁判员、教练员、运动员对规则的理解和把握方面，都有待提高。希望本书的出版能为我国裁判员、运动员、教练员、竞赛官员等更好地学习、掌握和运用高山滑雪竞赛规则，为广大爱好者更好地参与、欣赏高山滑雪，提升滑雪技能提供指导和帮助。

本书由具有丰富高山滑雪竞赛经验的体育界专家与具有精深法学理论和实践功底的法律界专家联手翻译、审定。编译时严格遵循原文含义，坚持“信、达、雅”的翻译标准，在完整准确把握国际雪联最新竞赛要求的前提下，结合中文语言表达习惯，力求准确、严谨、流畅、简洁。全书叙事清楚，目标明确，语言朴实，逻辑严谨，要言不烦。望大作早日出版，服务冬奥，补白科研，完成夙愿。期待海坨展翅，踏雪寻梅。

参与本书翻译工作的主要成员中大多是即将参加冬奥会的裁判员（NTO）、教练员，他们日常工作本已繁忙，但仍旧克服困难夜以继日地译稿，在火车上、地铁上，甚至是出差期间都在看稿，他们相互鼓励、共同切磋、乐在其中，成效也比较显著。

北京冬奥会召开前夕，本书正式出版，既是为北京2022年冬奥会献上的厚礼，也将为提高我国高山滑雪竞技水平，促进大众冰雪运动普及，强化中国在国际体育竞赛中的话语权作出其应有的贡献。希望我国体育界及社会各界以冬奥会的成功举办及本书的正式出版为开端，进一步关注体育法治事业，共同推动我国冰雪运动在法治化、规范化轨道上高质量发展。

国务院参事

中国政法大学法学院院长

体育法博士生导师

前言

为了更好地贯彻落实习近平总书记关于大力开展冰雪运动的讲话精神和党中央、国务院关于大力发展冰雪运动的要求，丰富干部职工冬季文体生活，进一步激发和促进司法部机关干部职工参与冰雪运动的热情，更好地为推广冰雪运动贡献司法行政力量，2021 年年初，司法部机关工会经部领导同志同意，组织成立了司法部机关冰雪运动协会，司法部机关及在京直属事业单位在职工会会员积极踊跃参加，并已组织多项活动。在此期间，具有较高滑雪和英语水平、较深厚法学功底和丰富的立法、执法监督、行政复议工作经验的译者，结合自己的工作实际，在 2013 年译本的基础上，完成国际雪联最新的 2021 年 7 月版《国际雪联竞赛规则（ICR）》第四编《高山滑雪竞赛规则》（以下简称“《规则》”）编译工作，并于 2021 年 8 月以司法部机关工会、司法部冰雪运动协会向冬季运动管理中心递交了《关于国际雪联滑雪竞赛规则（2021）有关事项的报告》，报请审定该规则译稿，以期对推动我国高山滑雪水平有所裨益。冬季运动管理中心收到报告，即组织中国滑雪协会有关同志对译稿进行全面审定。期间，我们又联系了人民体育出版社，就本书的出版、赞助、分发等事宜做好准备。冬季运动管理中心批复后，本书正式进入出版流程，在人民体育出版社的大力支持下，以最快的速度完成了本书的审查、把关工作，确保本书在北京冬奥会开幕之前可以如期交到每一位参加北京冬奥会高山滑雪项目的国内外裁判（NTO）和有关官员手中。

高山滑雪国际竞赛的组织与裁判须依据《国际雪联竞赛规则（ICR）》开展。《规则》包括竞赛通则、高山滑雪竞赛通则、各比赛项目的特殊规则三部分。其中与竞赛相关的其他有关要求，须按照《规则》的规定执行其他的具体规则，如《国际雪联反兴奋剂规则》。

为兼顾国内外读者方便使用，促进我国高山滑雪运动国际化，本书采用中英文双页对照排版模式。在本书译审过程中，我们也发现了《规则》原文中存在的一些前后表述、标点不统一等明显的错误，为了保证本书符合我国图书编辑质量要求而作了相应调整。此外，本书特别编制了《高山滑雪常用术语英汉对译表》作为附录，针对常用术语，特别是一些容易混淆概念的理解、区分做了详细阐释说明。

本书在翻译、校订、整理、出版和法律风险评估等过程中，得到了各方的大力协助和支持。在此，衷心感谢国务院参事焦洪昌老师百忙之中参加本书译审工作；感谢国家体育总局冬季运动管理中心的领导同志们的大力支持；感谢亲自审校本书的高山滑雪国家队领队和两任教练；感谢承担本书急迫而繁重的双语译校工作的各位编辑；感谢为本书出版提供了精神和物质帮助的各位支持者。

本书编译过程中难免错漏，敬请中外读者批评指正。

Table of Content

目　录

1st Section

第一部分

2nd Section

第二部分

3rd Section

第三部分

1st Section
第一部分

200 Joint Regulations for all Competitions

200.1 All events in the FIS Calendar must be held under the applicable FIS Rules.

200.2 Organisation and Conduct

Rules and instructions for the organisation and conduct of the various competitions are to be found in their respective rules.

200.3 Participation

Competitions listed in the FIS Calendar are only open to all properly licensed competitors entered by their National Ski Associations in accordance with current quotas.

200.4 Special Regulations

The FIS Council can authorise a National Ski Association to adopt rules and regulations to organise national or international competitions with different grounds for qualification but only provided that they do not go beyond the limits laid down in the present rules.

200.5 Control

All competitions listed in the FIS Calendar must be supervised by a Technical Delegate of the FIS.

200 竞赛通则

200.1 《国际雪联竞赛日历》中的所有比赛均须依照相应的《国际雪联滑雪竞赛规则》举办。

200.2 组织与实施

组织与实施各类比赛的规则和工作指南参见各自的相关规则。

200.3 参赛

《国际雪联竞赛日历》中的各项比赛，仅允许各国家滑雪协会根据其当前的配额，指派正式注册的运动员参赛。

200.4 特别规定

国际雪联理事会可以授权某国家滑雪协会采用规则和规定，组织不同参赛资格的国内或者国际比赛，但是不能超出国际雪联现行规则限定的范围。

200.5 监督

《国际雪联竞赛日历》中的所有比赛均须接受国际雪联技术代表的监督。

200.6 Every legal sanction imposed and published in respect of a competitor, official or trainer will be recognised by the FIS and the National Ski Associations respectively.

201 Classification and Types of Competitions

201.1 Competitions with Special Rules and/or Limited Participation

National Ski Associations affiliated with the FIS - or clubs belonging to these National Ski Associations with the approval of their association - may invite neighbouring National Ski Associations or their clubs to their own competitions. These competitions must not be promulgated or announced as international competitions, and the limitation must be made clear in the announcement.

201.1.1 Competitions with special rules and/or limited participation or including non-members may be held under special competition rules as approved by the FIS Council. Any such rules must be published in the announcement.

201.2 Competitions with Non–Members of the FIS

The FIS Council can authorise one of its member National Ski Associations to invite a non-member organisation (military etc.) to competitions, or accept invitations from such an organisation.

200.6 对运动员、官员或者教练员实施并公布的法律制裁，应当取得国际雪联和国家滑雪协会的双重确认。

201 比赛分类与类型

201.1 适用特别规则或者特别参赛限制的比赛

国际雪联所属各国家滑雪协会或者这些国家滑雪协会授权其所属俱乐部，可以邀请邻近的国家滑雪协会或其俱乐部参加他们自行组织的比赛。但是这些比赛不得公布或宣称是国际比赛，并且应当在赛事公告中明确参赛限制的具体情形。

201.1.1 可以根据国际雪联理事会批准的特别比赛规则，举办适用特别规则、参赛限制或者有非国际雪联成员参加的比赛。任何此类特别规则均须在赛事公告中公布。

201.2 有非国际雪联成员参加的比赛

国际雪联理事会可授权其某一成员国家滑雪协会邀请非成员的组织（如军队等）参加比赛，或者接受此类组织的参赛邀请。

201.3 Classification of Competitions

201.3.1 Olympic Winter Games, FIS World Ski Championships and FIS World Junior Ski Championships

201.3.2 FIS World Cups

201.3.3 FIS Continental Cups

201.3.4 International FIS Competitions (FIS Races)

201.3.5 Competitions with Special Participation and/or Qualifications

201.3.6 Competitions with Non-Members of the FIS

201.4 FIS Disciplines

A discipline is a branch of a sport and may comprise one or several events. For example Cross-Country Skiing is a FIS Discipline, whereas the Cross-Country Sprint is an Event.

201.4.1 Recognition of Disciplines in the International Ski Federation

New disciplines, comprising one or several events, widely practised in at least twenty-five countries and on three continents may be included as part of the programme of the International Ski Federation.

201.3 比赛分类

201.3.1 冬季奥林匹克运动会、国际雪联世界滑雪锦标赛和国际雪联世界青少年滑雪锦标赛

201.3.2 国际雪联世界杯

201.3.3 国际雪联洲际杯

201.3.4 国际雪联国际比赛（国际雪联比赛）

201.3.5 适用特别参赛条件或者资格的比赛

201.3.6 有非国际雪联会员参加的比赛

201.4 国际雪联竞赛分项

竞赛分项是某项体育运动（大项）的分支，可能包含一至数项比赛项目（小项）。例如，越野滑雪是国际雪联的一个竞赛分项，而短距离越野滑雪则是其中的一个比赛项目(小项)。

201.4.1 国际雪联认证的竞赛分项

包含一至数个比赛项目的新的国际雪联竞赛分项，应至少在3个大洲、25个国家广泛开展，方可获得国际雪联认证并纳入其竞赛项目目录。

201.4.2 Exclusion of Disciplines from the International Ski Federation

If a discipline is no longer practised in at least twelve National Ski Associations on at least two continents the FIS Congress may decide to exclude the discipline from the programme of the International Ski Federation.

201.5 FIS Events

An event is a competition in a sport or in one of its disciplines. It results in a ranking and gives rise to the award of medals and/or diplomas.

201.6 Types of Competitions

International competitions consist of:

201.6.1 Nordic Events

Cross-Country, Roller Skiing, Ski-Jumping, Ski-Flying, Nordic Combined, Team Competitions in Nordic Combined, Nordic Combined with Roller Skiing or In-line, Team Ski-Jumping, Ski-Jumping on plastic jumping hills, Popular Cross-Country races

201.6.2 Alpine Events

Downhill, Slalom, Giant Slalom, Super-G, Parallel, Combined, KO, Team Competitions

201.6.3 Freestyle Ski Events

Moguls, Dual Moguls, Aerials, Ski Cross, Halfpipe, Slopestyle, Big Air, Team Competitions

201.4.2 国际雪联对竞赛分项除名

若某一国际雪联竞赛分项的开展范围不足 2 个大洲、12 个国家滑雪协会，国际雪联代表大会可决定将其从国际雪联竞赛项目目录中除名。

201.5 国际雪联比赛项目（小项）

比赛项目是某个运动项目或者其竞赛分项中的一项比赛。其结果形成排名并颁发奖牌或者证书。

201.6 比赛类型

国际雪联的国际滑雪比赛包括：

201.6.1 北欧滑雪项目

越野滑雪、滑轮滑雪、跳台滑雪、北欧两项、北欧两项团体赛、滑轮滑雪北欧两项或直排滑轮滑雪北欧两项、跳台滑雪团体赛、夏季跳台滑雪、大众越野滑雪赛

201.6.2 高山滑雪项目

滑降、回转、大回转、超级大回转、平行式比赛、全能比赛、淘汰赛、团体比赛

201.6.3 自由式滑雪项目

雪上技巧、双人雪上技巧、空中技巧、障碍追逐、U 形场地技巧、坡道障碍技巧、大跳台、团体比赛

201.6.4 Snowboard Events
Slalom, Parallel Slalom, Giant Slalom, Parallel Giant Slalom, Halfpipe, Snowboard Cross, Big Air, Slopestyle, Team Competitions

201.6.5 Telemark Events

201.6.6 Firngleiten

201.6.7 Speed Skiing Events
Speed 1 (S1), Speed 2 (S2), Speed 2 Junior (S2J)

201.6.8 Grass Ski Events

201.6.9 Combined Events with other Sports

201.6.10 Youth, Masters, Para Snow Events, etc.

201.7 FIS World Championship Programme

201.7.1 To be included in the programme of the FIS World Championships, events must have a recognised international standing both numerically and geographically, and have been included for at least two seasons in the World Cup before a decision about their admission can be considered.

201.7.2 Events are admitted no later than three years before specific FIS World Championships.

201.6.4 单板滑雪项目
回转、平行回转、大回转、平行大回转、U形场地技巧、障碍追逐、大跳台、坡道障碍技巧、团体比赛

201.6.5 泰勒马克滑雪项目

201.6.6 费恩格累顿滑雪项目

201.6.7 速度滑雪项目
速度1（S1）、速度2（S2）、青少年速度2（S2J）

201.6.8 草地滑雪项目

201.6.9 与其他运动结合的比赛项目

201.6.10 青年赛、大师赛、残疾人雪上比赛等。

201.7 国际雪联世界锦标赛竞赛项目目录

201.7.1 任何比赛项目（小项）必须在开展范围的数据统计和地理分布两方面均获得国际公认，并且至少已经有两个赛季纳入世界杯赛项目，方可考虑将其纳入国际雪联世界锦标赛竞赛项目目录。

201.7.2 比赛项目（小项）纳入国际雪联世界锦标赛比赛项目目录至少三年后，方可成为其正式比赛项目。

201.7.3 A single event cannot simultaneously give rise to both an individual and a team ranking.

201.7.4 Medals may only be awarded at the FIS World Championships and FIS Junior World Championships in all disciplines (Alpine, Nordic, Snowboard, Freestyle Ski, Grass Skiing, Rollerski, Telemark, Speed Skiing) when there are a minimum of 8 nations participating in team competitions and 8 nations represented in an individual event.

202 FIS Calendar

202.1 Candidature and Announcement

202.1.1 Each National Ski Association is entitled to present its candidature for the organising of the FIS World Ski Championships in accordance with the published Rules for the Organisation of World Championships.

202.1.2 For all other competitions, the registrations for inclusion in the International Ski Calendar have to be made to FIS by the National Ski Association according to the Rules for the FIS Calendar Conference published by the FIS.

202.1.2.1 The applications of the National Ski Associations (NSA) are entered by using the FIS Calendar program in the members section of the FIS website: www.fis-ski.com by 31st August (31st May for the Southern Hemisphere).

201.7.3 单个比赛项目（小项）的比赛成绩不能同时累计个人和团体排名。

201.7.4 在国际雪联世界锦标赛和国际雪联青少年世界锦标赛中，只有每个竞赛分项所包含的团体比赛项目均有至少 8 个国家、个人项目均有代表至少 8 个国家的运动员参加比赛时，国际雪联竞赛分项（高山滑雪、北欧两项、单板滑雪、自由式滑雪、草地滑雪、滑轮滑雪、泰勒马克式滑雪、速度滑雪）才可以颁发奖牌。

202 国际雪联竞赛日历

202.1 候选资格与公布

202.1.1 各国家滑雪协会均有权依据公布的《世界锦标赛组织规则》申请承办国际雪联世界滑雪锦标赛。

202.1.2 拟举办其他所有比赛的国家滑雪协会必须根据国际雪联公布的《国际雪联竞赛日历会议规则》，向国际雪联申请注册以纳入《国际滑雪竞赛日历》。

202.1.2.1 国家滑雪协会（NSA）的办赛申请必须于 8 月 31 日（南半球为 5 月 31 日）前，在国际雪联官网 www.fis-ski.com 中的国际雪联成员专区通过竞赛日历填报程序完成递交。

202.1.2.2 Allocation of competitions

Allocation of the competitions to the National Ski Associations is made through the electronic communication process between FIS and the National Ski Associations. In the case of FIS World Cup competitions, the calendars are subject to the approval of the Council, on proposal of the respective Technical Committee.

202.1.2.3 Homologations

Competitions that appear in the FIS Calendar may only take place on competition courses or jumping hills homologated by the FIS.

The homologation certificate number must be indicated when applying for the inclusion of competition in the FIS Calendar. In a number of Snowboard, Freestyle Skiing, Free Ski disciplines and events the course or facility is built up for each competition that therefore does not have a permanent homologation. The course or facility approval process is therefore defined in the respective rules.

202.1.2.4 Publication of the FIS Calendar

The FIS calendar is published by FIS on the FIS website www.fis-ski.com.It will be updated to reflect cancellations, postponements and other changes continuously by FIS.

202.1.2.5 Postponements

In case of the postponement of a competition listed in the FIS Calendar, the FIS has to be informed immediately and a new invitation must be sent to the National Ski

202.1.2.2　　比赛分配

国际雪联通过与各国家滑雪协会之间的电子通信流程，向国家滑雪协会分配比赛。国际雪联世界杯应根据相关技术委员会的提议，由国际雪联理事会批准纳入竞赛日历。

202.1.2.3　　认证

《国际雪联竞赛日历》中列出的比赛只能在经国际雪联认证的赛道或跳台上进行。

申请将比赛列入《国际雪联竞赛日历》时必须提供认证编号。在许多单板滑雪、自由式滑雪、自由滑雪的分项和小项中，赛道或设施是为每个比赛而建立的，没有一个永久的认证。因此，赛道或设施的批准过程由各自的规则确定。

202.1.2.4　　公布《国际雪联竞赛日历》

《国际雪联竞赛日历》由国际雪联在国际雪联官网 www.fis-ski.com 上公布。国际雪联根据取消、延期及其他变动情况，持续更新《国际雪联竞赛日历》。

202.1.2.5　　延期

《国际雪联竞赛日历》中的比赛需要延期的，须立即通知国际雪联并向各国家滑雪协会重新发出邀请，否则该比赛不能累计国际雪联积分。

Associations, otherwise the competition cannot be considered for FIS points.

202.1.2.6 Calendar Fees

In addition to the annual subscription, a calendar fee is set by the FIS Congress and is due for each year and for each event listed in the FIS Calendar. For additional events, a 50% surcharge will be made in addition to the regular calendar fee for applications submitted 30 days before the date of the competition. The calendar fee for a competition that has to be rescheduled remains the responsibility for payment in full of the original organising National Ski Association.

At the beginning of the season, each NSA will receive an invoice for 70 % of its total invoice from the previous season. This amount will be debited from its FIS account. At the end of the season each NSA will receive a detailed invoice for all registered competitions during the season. The balance will be subsequently debited or credited to the NSA account at FIS.

202.1.3 Appointment of Race Organiser

In the event that the National Ski Association appoints a race organiser, such as an affiliated ski club, it shall do so using the form Registration Form National Ski Association and Organiser or by means of a similar written agreement. An application by a National Ski Association for inclusion of an event on the International Ski Calendar shall mean that the necessary agreement to organise the event has been established.

202.1.2.6 赛事费

除了每年缴纳会费外，需缴纳由国际雪联代表大会确定的赛事费。赛事费对每项纳入《国际雪联竞赛日历》的比赛项目按年收取。对于额外增加的比赛项目，在比赛日前 30 天提出申请的，在正常赛事费基础上加收 50% 的费用。对于重新安排的比赛，原主办国家滑雪协会仍需全额缴纳赛事费。

在赛季初，各国家滑雪协会均会收到 1 张占上赛季发票总金额 70% 的发票。这笔费用将从各国家滑雪协会在国际雪联的账户中扣除。在赛季结束时，各国家滑雪协会均会收到本赛季所有注册比赛的详细发票。差额部分将从各国家滑雪协会在国际雪联的账户中多退少补。

202.1.3 指定赛事组织者

国家滑雪协会指定赛事组织者（如所属的滑雪俱乐部），应采用《国家滑雪协会和组织者登记表》或类似书面协议的形式。国家滑雪协会申请将某一比赛纳入《国际滑雪竞赛日历》，意味着已达成组织该项比赛的必要协议。

202.2 Organisation of Races in other Countries

Competitions which are organised by other National Ski Associations may only be included in the FIS Calendar when the National Ski Association of the country concerned where the competitions will be organised gives its approval.

203 Licence to participate in FIS Races (FIS Licence)

A licence to participate in FIS races is issued by a National Ski Association to competitors who fulfil the criteria for participation through registering the competitor with FIS in the respective discipline(s).

203.1 The FIS licence year begins on July 1st and finishes on June 30th of the following year.

203.2 To be eligible for participation in FIS events, competitors must have a licence issued by their National Ski Association. Such a licence shall be valid in the Northern and Southern hemispheres for the licence year only.
The validity of a licence can be limited to participation in one specific country or in one or more specific events.

203.2.1 The National Ski Association must guarantee that all competitors registered with a FIS License to participate in FIS races accept the Rules of the International Ski Federation, in particular the provision which foresees the exclusive competence of the Court of Arbitration for Sport as the court of appeal in doping cases.

202.2 **在其他国家组织比赛**

只有赛事举办地的国家滑雪协会同意在其国内举办比赛时，这项由其他国家滑雪协会组织的比赛才能纳入《国际雪联竞赛日历》。

203 国际雪联参赛许可证（国际雪联许可证）

国家滑雪协会为运动员在相应的国际雪联竞赛分项中注册，并向符合参赛标准的运动员核发参加国际雪联比赛的参赛许可证。

203.1 国际雪联参赛许可证有效期从 7 月 1 日起到次年 6 月 30 日止。

203.2 为取得参加国际雪联赛事的资格，运动员必须持有其所属国家滑雪协会颁发的国际雪联参赛许可证。该许可证仅在许可年度参加北半球和南半球的赛事时有效。

许可证的有效范围可以限定为只参加在特定国举办的赛事或 1 个或多个特定的比赛项目。

203.2.1 国家滑雪协会必须保证所有由其注册获得国际雪联参赛许可证的运动员都能在参加国际雪联比赛时遵守《国际雪联滑雪竞赛规则》，特别是规定体育仲裁法庭享有对兴奋剂申诉案件的专属管辖权的条款。

203.3 A National Ski Association may only issue a FIS licence to participate in FIS races when competitors have proven their nationality and therefore eligibility by submitting a copy of their passport and signed the Athletes Declaration in the form approved by the FIS Council and returned it to their National Ski Association. All forms from under-age applicants must be counter signed by their legal guardians. Both the copy of the passport and signed Athletes Declaration must be made available to FIS on request.

203.4 During the FIS licence year, a competitor may only participate in International FIS competitions with a FIS licence to participate in FIS races issued by one National Ski Association.

203.5 **Application for a change of FIS Licence Registration**

All applications to change licence registration from one member National Ski Association to another are subject to consideration by the FIS Council at its Meetings in the spring (applications may only be submitted by 1st May each year). In principle an application to change licence registration will not be granted unless competitors demonstrate their personal association with the new nation.

Prior to submitting an application to change licence registration, competitors must possess the citizenship and passport of the country for which they wish to compete.

203.3 国家滑雪协会仅在运动员证明其国籍并满足下列资格条件后，方可核发准予其参加国际雪联比赛的国际雪联参赛许可证：运动员应提交其护照复印件、以国际雪联理事会批准的形式签署《运动员宣言》并将其返给国家滑雪协会。未成年申请人递交的所有申报必须与其法定监护人会签。护照复印件和所签署的《运动员宣言》要在国际雪联要求时随时提交。

203.4 特定的国际雪联参赛许可年度内，运动员只能凭一个国家滑雪协会颁发的国际雪联参赛许可证参加国际雪联的国际比赛。

203.5 **申请转会**

所有更改国际雪联参赛许可证上注册的国家滑雪协会的申请，将在春季会议时由国际雪联理事会审议（变更申请必须在每年的 5 月 1 日前提交）。原则上，要变更参赛许可证上此项注册信息，运动员必须证明其本人与新的注册国的关系，否则将不被批准。

在提交变更参赛许可证注册信息申请前，运动员必须拥有其希望代表参赛的国家的国籍和护照。此外，运动员在提出变更注册的国家滑雪协会的申请前，

In addition, competitors must have had their principal legal and effective place of residence in the new country for a minimum of two (2) years immediately prior to the date of the request to change registration to the new country/National Ski Association. An exception to the two year residency rule may be waived if the competitor was born in the territory of the new country, or whose mother or father is a national of the new country. Applications will not be accepted if a parent has obtained a passport for the new country, but is not resident, and/or there is no family ancestry.

Furthermore, competitors are required to submit a detailed explanation with the application about their personal circumstances and the reason for requesting a change of licence registration.

203.5.1 If competitors have already participated in FIS calendar events for a National Ski Association, they must have the written agreement to be released from the former National Ski Association in addition to the citizenship, passport and residency requirements in art. 203.5 before the new National Ski Association may submit a request to FIS for a change of registration.

If such a written agreement is not given, competitors may not participate in any FIS calendar events for a period of twelve months from the end of the last season in which they competed for their present National Ski Association, nor may they be issued with a licence to participate in FIS races by the new National Ski Association.

必须在新国家拥有其主要的合法且有效的居所至少满两年。对该两年居留规定的例外是，运动员出生在新国家的领域内，或其母亲或父亲是新国家的公民。如果申请人父母一方已获得新国家的护照但不是其居民或者在新国家没有家族血统，则不会接受其申请。

此外，运动员还必须随申请书一并提交有关其本人境况，以及申请更改参赛许可证注册国的原因的详细说明。

203.5.1 如果运动员已经代表某国家滑雪协会参加过《国际雪联竞赛日历》中的比赛，那么除具备本规则第203.5条所列国籍、护照和居住要求外，还必须获得原国家滑雪协会放行的书面同意后，新国家滑雪协会才可以向国际雪联提交注册变更请求。

未获得该同意书的，自运动员代表所属国家滑雪协会参赛的上个赛季结束后的12个月内，该运动员不得参加《国际雪联竞赛日历》中的任何比赛，也不能获得由新国家滑雪协会核发的参加国际雪联比赛的参赛许可证。

These rules are also valid when a competitor has more than one nationality and would like to change National Ski Association licence registration.

203.5.2 The FIS Council reserves the right in its absolute discretion, to grant or to decline to grant, a change of licence notwithstanding the fulfilment of the aforementioned conditions where it deems it is contrary to the spirit of the rule and in the best interests of the International Ski Federation to do so (e.g. to decline to grant a change of licence if a member National Ski Association tries to "import" a competitor).

203.5.3 In the event that a competitor does not fulfil all the criteria required to apply for a change of National Ski Association licence registration, the onus shall be on the competitor to demonstrate in writing to the satisfaction of the FIS Council that exceptional circumstances exist and it is in the best interests of the International Ski Federation to grant the change.

203.5.4 Competitors will retain their FIS points if they change their National Ski Association under the condition that the former National Ski Association granted the release of the competitor.

203.5.5 In the event that any of the documents for an application to change licence registration submitted by the National Ski Association (letter of release from the former

运动员拥有一个以上国籍并希望变更参赛许可证上注册的国家滑雪协会，上述规则同样适用。

203.5.2 虽然符合前述条件，但如果国际雪联认定其申请行为违背了规则的精神，且所作决定（如认定成员国家滑雪协会试图引进“归化”运动员而拒绝批准）符合国际雪联的最大利益，则国际雪联理事会保留批准或拒绝批准转会的绝对自由裁定权。

203.5.3 如果运动员未能满足申请转会所需全部条件，需提交书面材料证明其存在特殊情况且同意转会符合国际雪联最大利益，以说服国际雪联理事会。

203.5.4 运动员所属前国家滑雪协会同意放行的，更改所属国家滑雪协会后原有国际雪联积分仍予以保留。

203.5.5 国家滑雪协会提交的申请转会文件（前国家滑雪协会同意放行函、护照、居住证明材料）造假的，国际雪联理事会将制裁该运动员及新国家滑雪协会。

National Ski Association, passport, residency papers) are found to be false, the FIS Council will sanction the competitor and the new National Ski Association.

204 Qualification of Competitors

204.1 A National Ski Association shall not support or recognise within its structure, nor shall it issue a licence to participate in FIS or national races to competitors who:

204.1.1 Have conducted themselves in an improper or unsportsmanlike manner or has not respected the FIS medical code or anti-doping rules ;

204.1.2 Accept or have accepted, directly or indirectly, any money-payments for the participation at competitions ;

204.1.3 Accept or have accepted a prize of a higher value than fixed by article 219 ;

204.1.4 Permit or have permitted their names, titles or individual picture to be used for advertising, except when the National Ski Association concerned, or its pool for this purpose, is party to the contract for sponsorship, equipment or advertisements.

204.1.5 Knowingly compete or have competed against any skier not eligible according to the FIS Rules, except if:

204 运动员参赛资格

204.1 国家滑雪协会既不得在其组织体系内支持或承认，也不得向下列运动员颁发参加国际雪联或其国内比赛的参赛许可证：

204.1.1 有不正当或缺乏运动员风范的举止，或不遵守国际雪联的医事法典或反兴奋剂规则者；

204.1.2 直接或间接接受或接受过参赛费者；

204.1.3 接受或接受过价值超过本规则第 219 条规定的奖励者；

204.1.4 允许或曾允许将自己的姓名、头衔或个人照片用于广告宣传的，但所属的国家滑雪协会或其滑雪联营者为有关赞助、竞赛器材或广告等合同的一方当事人时除外。

204.1.5 故意与违反国际雪联规定的不适格滑雪运动员进行比赛或曾经比赛的，除非有下列情形：

204.1.5.1 The competition is approved by the FIS Council, is directly controlled by the FIS or by a National Ski Association, and the competition is announced "open".

204.1.6 Have not signed the Athletes Declaration;

204.1.7 Are under suspension.

204.2 With the issuance of a licence to participate in FIS competitions and entry the National Ski Association confirms, that valid and sufficient accident insurance for training and competition is in place for the competitor and assumes full responsibility.

205 Competitors Obligations and Rights

Competitors whatever their age, gender, race, religion or belief, sexual orientation, ability or disability have the right to participate in snow sports in a secure environment and protected from abuse.

FIS encourages all member nations to develop policies to safeguard and promote the welfare of children and young persons.

205.1 The competitors are obliged to make themselves familiar with the appropriate FIS Rules and must comply with the additional instructions of the Jury. Competitors must also follow the FIS rules regulations.

205.2 Competitors are not permitted to use doping. (see FIS

204.1.5.1 比赛经国际雪联理事会批准、由国际雪联或某国家滑雪协会直接监管并且比赛宣称为“公开”赛的。

204.1.6 尚未签署《运动员宣言》者；

204.1.7 处于禁赛期者。

204.2 国家滑雪协会为运动员核发参加国际雪联比赛的参赛许可证并准许其加入国家滑雪协会，即视为为运动员投保了有效且充分的训练和比赛的意外伤害保险并承担全部责任。

205 运动员的义务和权利

运动员无论年龄、性别、种族、宗教或信仰、性取向、有无残疾，均享有在安全的环境中参加雪上运动并免受侵犯的权利。

国际雪联鼓励所有成员的所属国制定保护和促进儿童和青少年福祉的政策。

205.1 运动员有义务熟悉其参赛项目相关的《国际雪联滑雪竞赛规则》，必须遵从仲裁委员会的具体指令。运动员还必须遵从依据国际雪联竞赛规则实施的管理。

205.2 运动员不得使用兴奋剂（参见《国际雪联反兴奋剂

Anti-Doping Rules and Procedural Guidelines).

205.3 As stated in the Athletes Declaration, competitors have the right to inform the Jury of safety concerns they may have regarding the training and competition courses. More details are given in the corresponding discipline rules.

205.4 Competitors who do not attend the prize-giving ceremonies without excuse lose their claim to any prize including prize money.

In exceptional circumstances, competitors may be represented by another member of their team, but this person has no right to take their place on the podium.

205.5 Competitors must behave in a correct and sportsmanlike manner towards members of the Organising Committee, volunteers, officials and the public.

205.6 Support for the Competitors

205.6.1 Competitors registered with FIS by their National Ski Association to participate in FIS races may accept:

205.6.2 Full compensation for travel cost to training and competition;

205.6.3 Full reimbursement for accommodation during training and competitions;

205.6.4 pocket money;

规则》及《国际雪联反兴奋剂程序指南》)。

205.3 如《运动员宣言》中所述，运动员有权向仲裁委员会报告训练和比赛赛道可能存在的安全问题。相应的国际雪联竞赛分项规则中对此有更详细规定。

205.4 运动员无正当理由不参加颁奖仪式的，将失去对包括奖金在内的任何奖励的请求权。

在例外情况下，获奖运动员可由其队友代表，但该代表无权代其登上领奖台。

205.5 运动员必须以正确的、符合运动员风范的方式对待组委会成员、志愿者、官员和公众。

205.6 运动员的参赛保障

205.6.1 运动员经其国家滑雪协会在国际雪联注册参加国际雪联比赛的，即可享受如下赛事保障：

205.6.2 全额报销参加训练和比赛的交通费；

205.6.3 全额报销训练和比赛期间的住宿费；

205.6.4 零用金；

205.6.5 Compensation for loss of income according to decisions of their National Ski Association;

205.6.6 Social security including insurance for training and competition;

205.6.7 Scholarships.

205.7 A National Ski Association may reserve funds to secure their competitors' education and future career after retiring from active competitive skiing.
The competitors have no claim to these funds which shall be dispensed only according to the judgement of their National Ski Association.

205.8 Gambling on Competitions

Competitors, trainers, team officials and technical officials are prohibited from betting on the outcome of competitions in which they are involved.
Reference is made to the FIS Rules on the Prevention of the Manipulation of Competitions.

206 Advertising and Sponsorship

In the context of this rule advertising is considered as the presentation, of signage or other visibility at the venue informing the public of the name of a product or service to achieve awareness of a company or an organisation and its brand name, activities, products or service. On the other hand Sponsorship provides a company with the

205.6.5 其国家滑雪协会确定的误工费；

205.6.6 包括训练和比赛保险在内的社会保险；

205.6.7 奖学金。

205.7 国家滑雪协会可以建立储备基金，用于保障其所属运动员从竞技滑雪退役后的教育和未来职业。

运动员对此类基金没有当然的请求权，国家滑雪协会有权自主决定基金的分配。

205.8 **赌赛**
禁止运动员、教练员、随队官员和技术官员对其参与比赛的结果下注。

参见《国际雪联预防操纵比赛规则》。

206 广告与赞助

在本规则中，广告被视为展示在场馆的标识或其他可视化物件，意在告知公众产品或服务的名称，使之对公司或组织及其品牌名称、活动、产品或服务有所认知。另外，赞助为公司提供了与竞赛或一系列赛事活动直接联系起来的机会。

opportunity to have a direct association with the competition or series of events.

206.1 Olympic Winter Games and FIS World Championships

All Advertising and Sponsorship rights to the Olympic Winter Games and FIS World Championships belong to the IOC and to the FIS respectively and are subject to separate contractual arrangements.

206.2 FIS Events

For all FIS Events the FIS Advertising Rules define the advertising opportunities in the competition area and are subject to the approval of the FIS Council. For the FIS World Cup Events the FIS Advertising Rules form an integral part of the FIS Organisers Agreement with the National Ski Associations and Organisers.

206.3 Member National Ski Associations

Each FIS affiliated National Ski Association that organises events in its country which are included in the FIS calendars, has the authority as the owner of the event advertising rights to enter into contracts for their sale.

In the case of FIS World Cup competitions these rights shall be defined in the Organiser Agreement upon approval of the FIS Council and considering the National Ski Associations responsibilities.

In cases where a National Ski Association organises events outside its own country these FIS Advertising rules also apply.

206.1 **冬季奥林匹克运动会与国际雪联世界锦标赛**

冬季奥林匹克运动会和国际雪联世界锦标赛的所有广告和赞助权分别属于国际奥委会和国际雪联，并分别受各自合同的安排约束。

206.2 **国际雪联比赛**

对于国际雪联的所有比赛，《国际雪联广告规则》规定了比赛场地内的广告投放条件，并由国际雪联理事会批准。就国际雪联世界杯而言，该规则是与国家滑雪协会和组织方签订的《国际雪联组织方协议》的必要组成部分。

206.3 **成员国家滑雪协会**

国际雪联所属各国家滑雪协会在其国内组织《国际雪联竞赛日历》中的比赛，有权作为比赛广告权的所有者签订广告销售合同。

就国际雪联世界杯而言，此类广告权应在国际雪联理事会批准并考虑国家滑雪协会责任的《国际雪联组织方协议》中予以明确。

国家滑雪协会在其国外组织比赛的，此类国际雪联广告规则同样适用。

206.4 Title and Presenting Sponsorship Rights

In the case of FIS series approved by the FIS Council, FIS markets the rights of the title/presenting sponsor (alternative naming possible) package. For the FIS World Cup series these are marketed to appropriate sponsors that promote the image and values of the discipline concerned. The revenue generated from the sale of the title/presenting sponsor rights is invested by FIS to provide a professional organisation.

206.5 Use of Markings and supports

All Advertising and commercial markings and supports used shall comply with the technical specifications set forth in the applicable FIS Advertising Rules.

206.6 Advertising Packages

Location, number, size and form of the advertising are specified in the FIS Advertising Rules for each discipline. Detailed information including graphical illustrations is laid out in the discipline-specific Marketing Guides which are published on the FIS Website. The Marketing Guides are reviewed and updated as necessary by the Committee for Advertising Matters and approved by the FIS Council prior to their publication.

206.7 Sponsorships by commercial betting companies

206.7.1 FIS will not allocate Title / Presenting Sponsor rights to commercial betting companies.

206.4 **冠名和协办赞助商权利**

对于国际雪联理事会批准的国际雪联系列赛，国际雪联会出售冠名或者协办赞助商（实际命名可能会有变化）套餐权利。国际雪联世界杯系列赛的套餐权利，将会出售给适当的赞助商以提升相关国际雪联竞赛分项的形象和价值。

因出售冠名或者协办赞助商权利而获得的收益，国际雪联用于提供更为专业的比赛组织服务。

206.5 **标识与支撑物的使用**

所有广告和商业标识所使用的支撑物均应符合相关的《国际雪联广告规则》中的技术规范。

206.6 **广告套餐**

《国际雪联广告规则》为每个国际雪联竞赛分项规定了广告的位置、数量、尺寸和形式。在国际雪联官网上发布的国际雪联各具体竞赛分项的《营销指南》中，列出包括示意图在内的详细信息。《营销指南》由广告事务委员会在必要时审查更新，经国际雪联理事会批准后公布。

206.7 **商业博彩公司的赞助**

206.7.1 国际雪联不会将冠名或者协办赞助商权利授予商业博彩公司。

206.7.2 Sponsorships of events by commercial betting companies is permitted subject to 206.7.3 below.

206.7.3 Advertising of commercial betting companies or other betting activities on or with the athletes (head sponsors, competition suits, starting bibs) is prohibited with the exception of lotteries and companies operating nonsports betting only.

206.8 A National Ski Association or its pool may enter into contracts with a commercial firm or organisation for financial sponsorship and or the supply of goods or equipment if the specific company or organisation is acknowledged as an Official Supplier or Sponsor by the National Ski Association. Advertising using photographs, likeness or names of FIS competitors with any sportsman not eligible according to either the FIS eligibility rules or the eligibility rules of the IOC, is forbidden.

Advertising with or on competitors with tobacco or alcohol products or drugs (narcotics) is forbidden.

206.9 All compensation under such contracts must be made to the National Ski Association or its ski pool which shall receive the compensation subject to the regulations of each National Ski Association. Competitors may not directly receive any part of such compensation except as stated in art.205.6. The FIS may at any time call for a copy of the contract.

206.7.2 商业博彩公司可以依据下文第 206.7.3 条赞助比赛活动。

206.7.3 禁止在有关运动员或着装方面（主赞助商、比赛服、出发号码布）为商业博彩公司或其他博彩活动做广告，仅经营非体育博彩的彩票和公司除外。

206.8 被国家滑雪协会确认为官方供应商或赞助商的特定公司或组织，国家滑雪协会或其滑雪联营者可与该商业公司或组织签订合同，以获得资金赞助或者商品或竞赛器材供应。禁止采用国际雪联运动员与任何依据国际雪联资格规则或国际奥委会资格规则不适格的运动员在一起的照片、肖像或姓名进行广告宣传。

禁止在有关运动员或在运动员着装上做烟草、酒类产品或毒品（麻醉品）的广告。

206.9 此类合同中规定的所有赔偿必须付给根据各国家滑雪协会的规定应获得赔偿的国家滑雪协会或其滑雪联营者。除本规则第 205.6 条规定的例外以外，运动员不能直接接受此类赔偿的任何部分。国际雪联可随时要求提供此类合同副本。

206.10 Equipment goods supplied to and used by the national team must, with reference to markings and trademarks, conform with the specifications stated in art. 207.

207 Competition Equipment and Commercial Markings

207.1 Competition Equipment at FIS Events

Only the competition equipment, according to the FIS rules on advertising, provided by the National Ski Association, complete with the commercial markings approved by the National Ski Association, may be worn in FIS World Cup and FIS World Ski Championships competitions. Obscene names and/or symbols on clothing and equipment are forbidden.

207.1.1 At FIS World Ski Championships, FIS World Cup and all events on the FIS Calendar, a competitor is not allowed to take equipment (skis/board, poles, ski boots, helmet, glasses) to the official ceremonies involving anthems and/or flag raising. Holding/carrying equipment on the victory podium after conclusion of the whole ceremony (handing over trophies and medals, national anthems) for press photos, pictures, etc. is however permitted.

207.1.2 **Winners presentation / Equipment on the podium**

At FIS World Ski Championships and all events of the FIS Calendar, a competitor is allowed to take the following equipment on the podium:

206.10 提供给国家队并由国家队使用的竞赛器材等物资所涉及的商业标识和注册商标，必须符合本规则第207条的具体规定。

207 竞赛器材与商业标识

207.1 国际雪联比赛中的竞赛器材

依据国际雪联的广告规则，只有国家滑雪协会提供的竞赛器材，配以国家滑雪协会批准的商业标识，方可在国际雪联世界杯和国际雪联世界滑雪锦标赛中穿戴。禁止在服装和器材上使用淫秽名称或者符号。

207.1.1 在国际雪联世界滑雪锦标赛、国际雪联世界杯和《国际雪联竞赛日历》中的其他各项比赛中，运动员均不得携带竞赛器材（滑雪板/单板、滑雪杖、雪鞋、头盔、眼镜）参加包含奏国歌或者升旗环节的正式仪式。但在整个仪式（颁发奖杯和奖牌、奏唱国歌）结束后，为拍摄新闻特写、照片等，允许在颁奖台上手持或者携带竞赛器材。

207.1.2 颁奖台上的获奖者及竞赛器材展示

在国际雪联世界滑雪锦标赛和《国际雪联竞赛日历》中的各项比赛中，允许参赛运动员在颁奖台上携带以下器材：

- Skis / Snowboards;
- Footwear: The athletes may wear their boots on their feet, but are not allowed to wear them anywhere else (such as around their neck). Other shoes cannot be taken on the podium during presentation except if they are worn on the feet;
- Poles: not on/around skis, normally in the other hand;

- Goggles: either worn or around the neck;
- Helmet: if worn only on the head and not on another piece of equipment, e.g. skis or poles;
- Ski straps: maximum of two with name of the producer of skis;eventually one can be used for a wax company;
- Nordic Combined and Cross-Country Ski Poles Clips. A clip can be used to hold the two poles together. The clip can be the width of the two poles, though not wider than 4 cm. The length (height) can be 10cm. The long side of the clip is to be parallel to the poles. The commercial marking of the pole manufacturer can cover the entire surface of the clip;
- All other accessories are prohibited: waist bags with belt, phones on neck-bands, bottles, rucksack/backpack, etc.

207.1.3 An unofficial presentation (flower ceremony) of the winner and the winner's ceremony immediately after the event in the event area with the national anthem even before the protest time has expired, is allowed at the organiser's own risk. Visible wearing of the starting bibs is mandatory.

- 滑雪板 / 单板；
- 鞋类：运动员可以穿着雪鞋，但不允许挂在其他任何地方（如脖子上）。运动员不能携带其他鞋子上颁奖台，除非穿在脚上；
- 滑雪杖：不得环绕或者放在滑雪板上面，一般拿在另一只手上；
- 护目镜：可以戴着或者挂在脖子上；
- 头盔：如果穿戴，只能戴在头上，不得置于其他竞赛器材（如滑雪板或滑雪杖）之上；
- 滑雪板捆扎带：带有滑雪板生产商名称的最多 2 条，有 1 条可用于蜡制品企业；
- 北欧两项和越野滑雪滑雪杖夹：可以用夹子把两根滑雪杖夹在一起。雪杖夹可以有两根滑雪杖宽，最宽 4 厘米。长度（高度）可达 10 厘米。雪杖夹的长边应与滑雪杖平行。滑雪杖制造商的商业标识可以覆盖整个的雪杖夹表面；
- 所有其他配件均在禁止之列：带腰带的腰包、用颈带挂在脖子上的手机、瓶子、帆布背包 / 背包等。

207.1.3 可以在比赛一结束甚至抗议期限尚未届满时，立即在比赛区举行获胜者的非正式展示（献花仪式）以及颁奖典礼并奏国歌，但风险由组织方承担。出席此类仪式必须明显地佩戴出发号码布。

207.1.4 Visible wearing of the starting bib of the event or other outerwear of the NSA is mandatory in the restricted corridor (including the leader board and TV interview locations).

207.2 Commercial Markings

Specifications about the size, the form and the number of commercial markings on equipment and clothing as well as the by-laws for commercial markings and for advertising are to be reviewed by the Committee for Advertising Matters and approved by the FIS Council each spring for the following competition season and published by the FIS.

207.2.1 The rules governing commercial markings and advertising on equipment and clothing as well as the relevant by-laws published in the Specifications for Commercial Markings on Equipment, must be followed.

207.2.2 Any competitor who breaches the advertising rules is subject to sanction, as provided for in art. 223.1.1. An offence for which a sanction may apply and a penalty be imposed is defined as conduct that is in violation or non–observance of competition rules.

207.2.3 If a National Ski Association fails to enforce these rules with on their own competitor(s) or for any reason prefers to refer the case to the FIS, the FIS may take immediate steps to suspend a competitor's licence. The competitors concerned and/or their National Ski Association have the right to make an appeal before a final decision is taken.

207.1.4 在限制通道（包括名次显示牌前和电视采访区）内必须明显地佩戴比赛的出发号码布或身着国家滑雪协会的外套。

207.2 商业标识

有关竞赛器材与服装上的商业标识的尺寸、形式和数量的具体规定，以及商业标识和广告的补充规定等，均应由广告事务委员会进行审查，由国际雪联理事会于每年春季批准并由国际雪联予以公布，用于随后到来的赛季。

207.2.1 必须遵守规范竞赛器材和服装上的商业标识与广告的规则以及公布在《竞赛器材上的商业标识的具体规定》中的相关补充规定。

207.2.2 任何违反广告规则的运动员都将受到制裁，本规则第 223.1.1 条对此有具体规定。可以适用制裁并予以处罚的违规行为，是指违反或不遵守竞赛规则的行为。

207.2.3 国家滑雪协会未能对其所属运动员实施此类规则，或者因故更倾向于将案件移送国际雪联，国际雪联可以立即采取措施暂时吊销运动员的参赛许可证。涉事运动员或者其所属国家滑雪协会有权在最终决定作出前提出申诉。

207.2.4 If an advertiser uses the name, title or individual picture of a competitor in connection with any advertisement, recommendation or sale of goods without the approval or knowledge of the competitor, the competitor may give a "power of attorney" to their National Ski Association or to the FIS to enable them, if necessary, to take legal action against the company in question. If the competitor concerned fails to do so, the FIS shall judge the situation as if the competitor had given permission to the company.

207.2.5 The FIS Council shall be informed of infractions or breaches of these rules that have taken place with regard to the qualification of competitors, sponsorship and advertising and support for the competitors, and shall review what measures to take to deal with cases.

208 Exploitation of Electronic Media Rights

208.1 General Principles

208.1.1 **Olympic Winter Games and FIS World Championships**
All Media rights to the Olympic Winter Games and FIS World Championships belong to the IOC and to the FIS respectively, and are subject to separate contractual arrangements.

208.1.2 **Rights owned by the member National Ski Associations**
Each FIS affiliated National Ski Association that organises events in its country which are included in the

207.2.4 广告客户未经运动员同意或知晓，即将其姓名、头衔或个人照片用于商品的广告、推销或销售中，该运动员可向其所属国家滑雪协会或国际雪联发出“授权委托书”，以便在必要时得以对涉事公司采取法律行动。如果涉事运动员未这样做，国际雪联可推定该运动员已经默许涉事公司这样做。

207.2.5 在运动员资格、赞助和广告以及运动员参赛保障等方面，如有违反本规则的行为发生，应通报国际雪联理事会，由其酌情采取措施处理此类事件。

208 电子媒体版权的开发利用

208.1 一般原则

208.1.1 冬季奥林匹克运动会和国际雪联世界锦标赛

冬季奥林匹克运动会和国际雪联世界锦标赛的所有媒体版权分别属于国际奥委会和国际雪联，同时受各自的合同安排约束。

208.1.2 国际雪联成员国家滑雪协会拥有的权利

国际雪联所属各国家滑雪协会在其国内举办《国际雪联竞赛日历》中的比赛的，有权作为电子媒体版权

annual FIS calendars, has the authority as the owner of the electronic media rights to enter into contracts for the sale of the electronic media rights on those events. In cases where a National Ski Association organises events outside its own country, these rules also apply, subject to bi-lateral agreement with the National Ski Association of the country where the event takes place.

208.1.3 Promotion

Contracts shall be prepared in consultation with the FIS with the intention of giving the widest promotion and exposure to the sports of skiing and snowboarding and considering the best interests of the National Ski Associations.

208.1.4 Access to events

For all competitions, admission of personnel and their equipment to the media areas will be limited to those having the necessary accreditation and access passes. Priority access will be given to rights holders and the system of accreditation and access control must avoid possible abuse by non-rights holders.

208.1.5 Control by the FIS Council

The FIS Council exercises control over the adherence to the principles of this Rule by National Ski Associations and all organisers. Should a contract or individual clauses thereof, create a major conflict of interest for the FIS, a member National Ski Association or its organiser, then

的所有者签订此类比赛电子媒体版权的销售合同。国家滑雪协会在国外组织的比赛，本规则同样适用，并受与比赛举办国的国家滑雪协会达成的双边协议的约束。

208.1.3 推广

拟订合同应与国际雪联协商，以期最大限度地宣传推广滑雪运动，同时兼顾国家滑雪协会的最大利益。

208.1.4 采访比赛

所有比赛的媒体区，均仅限具备必要注册和采访通行证的人员及其器材进入。权利持有者将获得优先出入权，注册和访问控制系统必须避免无权者闯入的可能。

208.1.5 国际雪联理事会的监督

国际雪联理事会对各国家滑雪协会和所有组织方遵守本规则确立原则的情况实施监督。合同或其个别条款与国际雪联、国家滑雪协会成员或其组织方的利益有重大冲突的，国际雪联理事会将对此进行评估。各涉事方要提供完整的信息，以便找到适当

this will be evaluated by the FIS Council. Full information will be provided so that the appropriate solution can be found.

208.2 Definitions

In the context of this rule the following definitions will apply:
"Electronic Media Rights" means the rights for Television, Radio, Internet and Mobile devices.
"Television rights" means the distribution of television images, both analogue and digital, comprising video and sound, by means of terrestrial transmitters, satellite, cable, fibre or wire for public and private viewing on television screens. Pay-per-view, subscription, interactive TV, video on demand services, IPTV or similar technologies, are also included in this definition.
"Radio rights" means the distribution and reception of radio programmes, both analogue and digital, over the air, by wire or via cable to devices, both fixed and portable.
"Internet" means access to images and sound through interconnected computer networks.
"Mobile and portable devices" means the provision of images and sound through a telephone operator and receivable on mobile telephone or other non fixed devices, such as Personal Digital Assistants.

208.3 Television

208.3.1 Standard of production and promotion of competitions

In the agreements concerning production with a TV

的解决方案。

208.2 定义

在本规则语境中适用如下定义：

“电子媒体版权”是指与电视、广播、互联网和移动设备有关的权利。

“电视权利”是指通过地面发射器、卫星、电缆、光纤或电线传送包括视频和音频在内的模拟和数字信号的电视图像，供公众和私人在电视屏幕上观看。该定义也包含按次计费、订阅、互动电视、视频点播服务、网络电视或类似技术。

“广播权利”是指通过无线、有线或电缆向固定和便携设备传送和接收模拟和数字信号的无线电节目的权利。

“互联网”是指通过互联计算机网络获取图像和声音。

“移动和便携式设备”是指通过电话运营商提供图像和声音，并可在移动电话或其他非固定设备（如个人数字助理）上接收。

208.3 电视

208.3.1 比赛内容的制作和推广标准

在与作为主转播商的电视组织或代理机构签订有关

organisation or agency acting as host broadcaster, the quality of TV transmissions for ski and snowboard events published in the FIS Calendar – especially for FIS World Cup competitions – must be considered. Of particular importance, while taking into consideration applicable national laws and rules affecting broadcasting, are:

a) Top quality and optimal production of a TV signal (for live or deferred transmission depending on the event) in which sport is the centrepiece.
b) Adequate consideration and appearance of venue advertising and event sponsors.
c) A standard of production in conformity with the FIS TV Production Guidelines and appropriate to current market conditions for the discipline and to the level of the FIS competition series. This means live coverage of the entire event including the winner presentation for live transmission (unless circumstances determine that a live production is not provided). This coverage shall be produced in a neutral way, shall not concentrate on any athlete or nation and shall show all competitors.
d) The live international signal of the host broadcaster must include appropriate graphics in English, particularly the official FIS logo, timing and data information and results, and international sound.
e) Where it is appropriate to the individual TV market, there should be live TV transmission in the country where the event takes place and in other countries with a high interest.

制作的协议时，必须考虑《国际雪联竞赛日历》中发布的滑雪和单板滑雪比赛（尤其是国际雪联世界杯比赛）的电视传输质量。特别重要的是，在考虑影响转播的相关国家法律和规章的同时，要确保：

a) 坚持以体育运动为中心的原则，务求电视信号的高质量和精工细作（电视信号实时还是延迟传输，视具体比赛项目而定）。
b) 适当兼顾场地广告和比赛赞助商，为其提供适度的出镜机会。
c) 遵循《国际雪联电视制作指南》的制作标准，适应国际雪联竞赛分项的当前市场条件及国际雪联系列赛的赛事等级。即整个比赛的实时报道必须全覆盖，包括实时传输优胜者展示场景（除非现场无法提供实时制作节目的条件）。这种全覆盖节目的制作应保持中立，不应聚焦于个别运动员或国家，而应展现所有参赛选手。

d) 主转播商的实时国际信号必须包括适当的英文图形，特别是国际雪联的官方标志、计时和数据信息和比赛成绩以及国际音频信号。

e) 在适合独家电视市场的情况下，应在举办赛事的国家及其他对此兴趣浓厚的国家进行电视直播。

208.3.2 Production and Technical costs

Except when otherwise agreed between the National Ski Association and the agency/company managing the rights, the cost of producing the television signal for the exploitation of the different rights will be borne by the broadcaster having acquired the rights in the country where the competition takes place or a production company mandated to produce the signal by the company owning the rights. In certain cases, the organiser or the National Ski Association may assume these costs.

For each of the different rights granted under this rule the technical expenses that are to be paid for by those organisations that have acquired the rights and which are seeking to access the television signal (original picture and sound without commentary), have to be agreed between the producing company or the agency/company managing the rights, as applicable. This also applies to any other production costs that may be requested.

208.3.3 Short extracts

Short extracts granting news access for non-rights holders are to be provided to television companies according to the following rules. It is noted that in a number of countries national legislation governs the showing of short extracts in news programmes.

These extracts may only be used in regularly scheduled news programmes and cannot be kept for archive purposes.

a) In those countries where legislation exists regarding

208.3.2 制作与技术费用

除非国家滑雪协会与经营相关权利的机构 / 公司另有协议，为开发利用不同权利而制作电视信号的成本应由在比赛举办国获得相应权利的转播商或由获得拥有权利的公司的授权负责制作信号公司承担。在某些情况下，组织方或国家滑雪协会也可以承担这些费用。

对于每一项根据本规则获得的不同权利，应由已经获得权利的组织及寻求获取电视信号（没有评论的原始图像和声音）的组织共同支付技术费用，如果可能的话，必须通过制作公司与经营此类权利的机构 / 公司达成的协议来兑现。该原则也适用于索要任何其他制作费用的情形。

208.3.3 短片集锦

可以根据如下规则，向非持权电视公司提供短片集锦，以使其获取新闻素材。值得指出的是，有些国家的国内立法对新闻节目中的短片集锦播映进行了规范。

这样的短片集锦只能用于按照固定时间安排播出的新闻节目，不能用于存档。

a) 在对体育赛事的新闻获取已经立法的国家，相关

news access to sporting events then this legislation will always hold precedence for reporting on FIS events.

b) In those countries where no legislation exists regarding news access by competing networks and provided that agreements between the company managing the rights and the primary rights holder take precedence then short extracts of a maximum of 90 seconds news access will be granted to competing networks by the agency/company managing the rights for transmission four hours after the rights holding network has shown the competition. The use of this material will cease 48 hours after the end of the competition. If the rights holding network delays its transmissions by more than 72 hours from the end of the competition, then competing networks can show extracts of a maximum of 45 seconds commencing 48 hours after and ending 72 hours after the event itself. Any request to exploit short extracts shall be addressed to the agency/company managing the rights which shall grant to the broadcasters access to the short extracts subject to agreement regarding the technical costs incurred to receive the material.

c) In those countries where no transmission rights have been purchased by a television company, all television organisations will be able to transmit short extracts of 45 seconds as soon as the material is available, subject to agreement with the agency/company managing the rights regarding the technical costs to be incurred to receive the material. Permission for the use of this material will expire after 48 hours.

立法在规范国际雪联比赛报道方面始终优先适用。

b) 在竞争性网站的新闻获取尚未立法的国家，如果经营转播权利的公司与主要持权转播商之间的协议居于优先地位，那么在持权网站转播比赛 4 小时后，经营转播权利的机构 / 公司有权向竞争性网站授予最长 90 秒的短片集锦新闻播放权。比赛结束 48 小时后，必须停止使用上述授权播放的材料。如果持权网站延误新闻传输自比赛结束后起算超过 72 小时，则竞争性网站可以在比赛结束后 48 小时至 72 小时，播出最长 45 秒的集锦。任何利用短片集锦的请求均应提交给管理转播权利的机构 / 公司，由其授予转播商使用短片集锦的权利，但要受就接收短片集锦材料产生的技术费用达成的协议的约束。

c) 在那些电视公司都没有购买转播权的国家，一旦短片集锦材料可用，所有电视机构都能立即播出 45 秒的短片集锦，但要遵守管理转播权利的机构 / 公司就接收短片集锦材料所产生技术费用与之达成的协议。允许使用短片集锦材料的期限至比赛结束 48 小时后到期。

d) Short extracts will be produced by the host broadcaster or the agency/company managing the rights and distributed by that agency/company, taking into consideration 208.3.2 above.

208.4 Radio

The promotion of FIS events through radio programmes will be encouraged by making available accreditation to the principle radio station(s) in each interested country. Access to the venue will be granted solely to those radio organisations that have obtained the necessary contractual authorisation from the rights holder, and will be only for the production of radio (audio) programmes. If accepted by national practice and the authorisation is granted, these programmes can also be distributed on the internet site of the radio station.

208.5 Internet

Unless the contract for the sale of the Electronic Media Rights on FIS events states otherwise, each television rights holder that also acquires the internet rights, will ensure that video streams from its website other than short extracts are geoblocked against access from outside its own territory. Regularly scheduled news bulletins containing material of FIS events may be streamed on the rights holding broadcaster’ s website, provided no changes are made to the bulletin as transmitted in the original programme.

Video and audio material produced in public areas where

d) 参考上述第 208.3.2 条，短片集锦由主转播商或经营转播权利的机构 / 公司制作，由经营转播权利的机构 / 公司负责分发。

208.4 **广播**

鼓励通过广播节目宣传国际雪联比赛，如向每个感兴趣国家的主要无线电台提供注册机会。仅允许从持权转播商处获得必要合同授权的广播组织，只能为了制作广播（音频）节目而进入场地。如果为所在国家的惯例所接受且已经获得授权，这些广播节目也可以在其电台的官网上发布。

208.5 **互联网**

除非出售有关国际雪联比赛电子媒体版权的合同另有约定，各电视持权转播商同时获得互联网转播权，并均应确保出自其官网的视频流（不包括短片集锦）具有地理锁区功能，以屏蔽来自境外的访问。如果原节目中播送的新闻简报未做更改，持权转播商可在其网站上流播包含国际雪联比赛材料的定期新闻简报。

在不需要注册、门票或其他访问许可就可以进入的

accreditation, tickets or other permissions are not required to gain access must not contain race footage. It is recognised that new technology provides members of the public with the possibility to produce unauthorised video recordings that may be posted on websites. Appropriate information advising that the unauthorised production and use of video material is prohibited and that legal proceeding could be taken, will be shown at all entrances and printed on entrance tickets.

All National Ski Associations and the rights holders/agencies will give permission for short extracts to be placed on the FIS website for noncommercial use subject to the following conditions:

a) When short extracts have not been acquired for Internet distribution the maximum duration of the news material from FIS competitions will be 30 seconds per discipline/per session and will be accessible on the FIS website until 48 hours after the end of the competition. The financial conditions relating to the provision of this material will be agreed between the FIS and the rights owner.

b) The material will be provided by the rights owner or host broadcaster as soon as possible, but at the latest six hours after the end of the competition.

208.6 Mobile and portable devices

In the cases where the rights for distribution by mobile and portable devices have been awarded, the rights purchaser/operator will be free to produce from the television signal

公共区域制作的视频和音频材料，不得包含比赛的连续镜头。新技术为公众提供了制作未经授权的视频录像的可能,这类资料可能会上传到网站上。为此，要在各入口处张贴并在门票上打印提示信息，告诫公众未经授权制作和使用视频材料是禁止的，可能会面临法律风险。

各国家滑雪协会和持权转播商和机构均获准将短片集锦上传到国际雪联官网上用于非商业用途，但必须符合以下条件：

a) 若短片集锦未获得互联网传播权，取自国际雪联比赛的新闻材料的最长时长为每一国际雪联竞赛分项或者每场比赛 30 秒，可以通过国际雪联官网访问，到比赛结束 48 小时后为止。与提供本材料有关的财务事宜由国际雪联和版权所有人商定。

b) 版权所有人或主转播商应尽快提供短片集锦材料，最迟不晚于比赛结束后 6 小时。

208.6 **移动与便携式设备**

已经被授予移动与便携式设备转播权利的权利购买方 / 运营商，可以免费从电视信号中撷取其认为最符合客户需求的内容。使用此类设备在全国范围进

the content it considers best meets the needs of its customers. Any live streaming of television programmes on a national basis using these devices shall not be altered from that available through other distribution channels.
In countries where no mobile distribution rights have been sold, short extracts or clips of a maximum duration of 20 seconds will be offered to operators when the material has been produced and for a period of 48 hours on the condition that the operators pay all related technical costs to the agency/company managing the rights.

208.7 Future developments

The principles contained in this Rule 208 shall be the basis for the exploitation of Electronic Media Rights to FIS events in the future. The FIS Council, on the recommendation of the National Ski Associations, the relevant commissions and experts, will establish the conditions considered appropriate to each new development.

209 Film Rights

All agreements regarding film productions of FIS competitions will be between the film producer and the National Ski Association or the company managing the related rights. All contractual arrangements regarding the exploitation of other media rights will be respected.

210 Organisation of Competition

行的任何电视节目流直播，均不能改编自通过其他传播渠道获得的电视节目。

在没有出售移动转播权利的国家，运营商向版权经营机构 / 公司支付所有相关技术费用的，短片集锦或持续时间最长为 20 秒的剪辑材料在制作完后提供给运营商，并可持续使用 48 小时。

208.7 **未来发展**

本规则 208 条中所包含的原则应成为未来开发利用国际雪联比赛的电子媒体版权的基础。国际雪联理事会将根据国家滑雪协会、相关委员会和专家的建议，确定适合每一新的发展的条件。

209 影片版权

所有关于国际雪联比赛的制片协议均应由制片方与国家滑雪协会或经营相关权利的公司签订。与其他媒体权利开发利用相关的所有合同安排都会得到遵守。

210 竞赛组织

211 Organisation

211.1 The Organiser

211.1.1 The Organiser of a FIS competition is the person or group of persons who make the necessary preparations and directly carry out the running of the competition in the resort.

211.1.2 If the National Ski Association itself is not the competition organiser, it may appoint an affiliated club to be the organiser.

211.1.3 The organiser must ensure that accredited persons accept the regulations regarding the competition rules and Jury decisions, and in World Cup races the organiser is obliged to obtain the signature of all persons who do not have a valid FIS season accreditation to this effect.

211.2 The Organising Committee

The Organising Committee consists of those members (physical or legal) who are delegated by the organiser and by the FIS. It carries the rights,duties and obligations of the organiser.

211.3 Organisers which hold competitions involving competitors not qualified under art. 203 - 204 have violated the International Competition Rules and measures are to be taken against them by the FIS Council.

211 组织

211.1 组织方

211.1.1 国际雪联比赛的组织方是为比赛做必要准备，并在比赛场地直接组织比赛运行的个人或团体。

211.1.2 国家滑雪协会本身不是比赛组织方的，可以指定一家所属俱乐部作为组织方。

211.1.3 组织方必须确保注册参赛人员服从有关竞赛规则和仲裁委员会的决定规制。在国际雪联世界杯比赛中，对于未获得国际雪联赛季资格有效注册的所有人员，组织方必须获得其承诺遵守上述规制要求的签名。

211.2 组委会

组委会由组织方和国际雪联委派的成员（自然人或法人）组成，享有组织方的权利、承担组织方的义务和履行组织方的职责。

211.3 组织方举办比赛容许不符合本规则第203条至第204条规定的选手参赛的，违反了《国际比赛规则》，国际雪联理事会将对其采取措施。

212 Insurance

212.1 The organiser must take out liability insurance for all members of the Organising Committee. The FIS shall provide its employees and appointed officials, who are not members of the Organising Committee (e.g. equipment controller, medical supervisor, etc.), with liability insurance when they are acting on behalf of the FIS.

212.2 Before the first training day or competition, the organiser must be in possession of a binder or cover notes issued by a recognised insurance company and present it to the Technical Delegate. The Organising Committee requires liability insurance with coverage of at least CHF 1 million; whereby it is recommended that this sum is at least CHF 3 million; this sum can be increased according to decisions of the FIS Council(World Cup etc.).
Additionally, the policy must explicitly include liability insurance claims by any accredited participant, including competitors, against any other participant including but not limited to officials, course workers, coaches, etc.

212.3 The Organiser respectively its' National Ski Association may request the FIS insurance broker to arrange cover for the competition (at the cost of the Organiser) if the organiser does not have the necessary insurance cover in place.

212.4 All competitors participating in FIS events must car ryaccident insurance, in sufficient amounts to cover accident,

212 保险

212.1 组织方必须为组委会全体成员投保责任保险。非组委会成员的国际雪联雇员、任命的官员（如竞赛器材核查员、医疗主管等）在代表国际雪联工作时，国际雪联应为其投保责任保险。

212.2 在第一个训练日或第一场比赛之前，组织者必须拿到由认可的保险公司签发的临时保单或保险单，并将其提交给技术代表。组委会需要的责任保险，保险金额至少为 100 万瑞士法郎；据此，建议保险金额至少为 300 万瑞士法郎；根据国际雪联理事会的决定，这一数额可以进一步增加（如世界杯等）。

此外，该保单保险范围必须明确覆盖比赛所有注册参与者（包括参赛运动员）针对任何其他参与者（包括但不限于官员、赛道工作人员、教练员等）提起的责任保险索赔。

212.3 如果组织方未能提供必要的保险，则组织方及其所属国家滑雪协会可以分别要求国际雪联保险经纪人为比赛安排保险事宜（费用由组织方承担）。

212.4 参加国际雪联比赛的所有运动员均须买好意外保险，保险金额足以覆盖事故、运输和救援费用，包括比

transport and rescue costs including race risks as well as an appropriate third-party liability insurance.

The National Associations are responsible for adequate insurance coverage of all their competitors sent and inscribed by them.

The National Ski Association or their competitors must be able to show proof of the respective insurance coverage at any time on request of the FIS, one of its representatives or the organising committee.

212.5 All trainers and officials inscribed and sent to FIS events by a National Association must carry accident and third-party liability insurance, in sufficient amounts to cover accident, transport and rescue costs from damages caused. The National Ski Association or their trainers and officials must be able to show proof of the respective insurance coverage at any time on request of the FIS, one of its representatives or the organising committee.

213 Programme

A programme must be published by the organisers for each competition listed in the FIS Calendar which must contain the following:

213.1 Name, date and place of the competitions, together with information on the competition sites and the best ways of reaching them;

赛风险以及适当的第三方责任保险。

国家滑雪协会负责为自己派遣和注册的运动员提供足够的保险。

国家滑雪协会或其运动员在国际雪联、国际雪联某一代表或组委会要求时必须能够随时出示各自保险范围的证明。

212.5 所有由国家协会注册并派遣参加国际雪联赛事活动的培训师和官员必须投保事故和第三方责任保险，保险金额足以支付事故、运输和因损害产生的救援费用。国家滑雪协会或其培训师和官员在国际雪联、国际雪联某一代表或组织委员会要求时必须能够随时出示各自保险范围的证明。

213 秩序册

组织方必须针对《国际雪联竞赛日历》中的每一比赛项目公布一份秩序册，其中必须包含以下内容：

213.1 比赛的名称、日期和地点，以及比赛场地的信息和最佳抵达方式；

213.2 Technical data on the individual competitions and conditions for participation;

213.3 Names of principal officials;

213.4 Time and place for the first team captains' meeting and the draw;

213.5 Timetable for the beginning of the official training and the start times;

213.6 Location of the official notice board;

213.7 Time and place for the prize-giving;

213.8 Final date of entry and address for entries, including telephone, telefax and e-mail address.

214 Announcements

214.1 The Organising Committee must publish an announcement for the event.
It must contain the information required by art. 213.

214.2 Organisers are bound by the rules and decisions of the FIS in limiting the number of entries. A further reduction in entries is possible under art.201.1 provided it is made clear in the announcement.

214.3 Postponements or cancellations of competitions and

213.2 各项比赛的技术数据和参赛条件；

213.3 主要官员姓名；

213.4 第一次领队会议和抽签的时间地点；

213.5 包括场地适应训练开始时间和出发时间的时间表；

213.6 官方公告牌的位置；

213.7 颁奖时间和地点；

213.8 报名的截止日期和地址，包括电话、传真和电子邮件地址。

214 公告

214.1 组委会必须发布比赛公告。

其中必须包含本规则第 213 条所要求的信息。

214.2 组织方在限制参赛人数方面受国际雪联规则和决定的约束。如果在公告中已明确说明，则可以根据本规则第 201.1 条进一步减少参赛人数。

214.3 推迟或取消比赛和秩序册变更必须立即通过电话、

programme alterations must be communicated immediately by telephone, e-mail or telefax to the FIS, all invited or entered National Ski Associations and the appointed TD. Competitions moved to an earlier date must be approved by the FIS.

215 Entries

215.1 All entries must be sent so that the Organising Committee receives them before the final date of entry. The organisers must have a final and complete list not later than 24 hours before the first draw.

215.2 National Ski Associations are not permitted to enter and draw the same competitors in more than one competition on the same date.

215.3 Only National Ski Associations are entitled to make entries for international competitions. Every entry should include:

215.3.1 Code number, name, first name, year of birth, National Ski Association;

215.3.2 An exact definition of the event for which the entry is made.

215.4 Entries for FIS World Championships (see Rules for the Organisation of FIS World Championships).

215.5 The entry of a competitor by the National Ski Association

电子邮件或传真通知国际雪联、所有受邀或参赛的国家滑雪协会和国际雪联指派的技术代表。提前举行比赛必须报经国际雪联批准。

215 报名

215.1 所有报名参赛信息都必须及时发送，以便组委会能在截止日期前收到。组织方必须在第一次抽签 24 小时前收到最终的、完整的参赛人员名单。

215.2 国家滑雪协会不得在同一比赛日组织同一批运动员报名参加一项以上的比赛和抽签。

215.3 只有国家滑雪协会有资格经办国际比赛的参赛报名。报名内容包括：

215.3.1 注册代码、姓、名、出生年份、所属国家滑雪协会；

215.3.2 确切说明报名参加的比赛项目。

215.4 国际雪联世界锦标赛报名（参见《国际雪联世界锦标赛组织规则》)。

215.5 运动员经国家滑雪协会办理的参赛报名，构成参赛

for a race shall constitute a contract solely between the competitor and the organiser and shall be governed by the Athletes Declaration.

216 Team Captains' Meetings

216.1 The time and location of the first team captains' meeting and of the draw must be shown in the programme. The invitations for all other meetings have to be announced to the team captains at their first meeting.
Emergency meetings must be announced in good time.

216.2 Representation by a substitute from another nation during discussions at team captains' meetings is not allowed.

216.3 The team captains and trainers must be accredited by the organisers according to quota.

216.4 Team captains and trainers must obey the ICR and the decisions of the Jury and must behave in a proper and sportsmanlike manner.

217 Draw

217.1 Competitors' starting order for each event and each discipline is decided according to a specific formula by draw and/or point order.

运动员与组织方之间签订的一对一合同，并受《运动员宣言》的约束。

216 领队会议

216.1 必须在秩序册中列明第一次领队会议和抽签的时间和地点。其他所有会议的邀请必须在第一次领队会议上向领队宣布。

紧急会议必须及时通知。

216.2 不允许由来自其他国家的代理人代替参会代表参加领队会议的讨论。

216.3 领队和教练员必须由组织方根据配额进行注册。

216.4 领队和教练员必须遵守《国际雪联滑雪竞赛规则》和仲裁委员会的决定，必须举止得体、行事具备运动员风范。

217 抽签

217.1 运动员在每一比赛项目和国际雪联竞赛分项中的出发顺序要根据特定程式通过抽签结合积分确定。

217.2 The competitors entered by a National Ski Association will only be drawn if provided written entries have been received by the organiser before the closing date.

217.3 If competitors are not represented at the draw by a team captain or trainer, they will only be drawn if it is confirmed by telephone, telegram, email or telefax by the beginning of the meeting that the competitors who are entered will participate.

217.4 Competitors who have been drawn and are not present during the competition must be named by the TD in the TD report, indicating if possible the reasons for absence.

217.5 Representatives of all the nations taking part must be invited to the draw.

217.6 If a competition has to be postponed by at least one day, the draw must be done again.

218 Creation and Distribution of Digital Content

218.1 Introduction

Information and data are an essential part of understanding and presenting sport, both as a means of measuring and reporting on athletic performance and communicating and promoting sport to the public. FIS, as the international body governing the sports of Skiing and Snowboarding, and

217.2 运动员通过国家滑雪协会报名后，必须确保组织方在截止日期前收到书面参赛报名表后方可参加抽签。

217.3 如果报名参赛的运动员没有领队或者教练代表其抽签，那么只有在抽签会议开始前通过电话、电报、电子邮件或传真确认参赛的，方可参加抽签。

217.4 已经抽签但未到场参赛的运动员，必须由技术代表在其报告中点名；如有可能，可以说明缺席的原因。

217.5 必须邀请所有参赛国家的代表参加抽签。

217.6 比赛推迟超过一天的，必须重新抽签。

218 数字内容的创作与传播

218.1 引言

信息和数据是理解和展示体育的一个重要部分，它既是衡量和报告运动成绩的一种手段，也是向公众宣传和推广体育的一种手段。国际雪联作为管理高山滑雪和单板滑雪运动的国际机构，在国家滑雪协会的合作下，受委托开发、管理和准确处理与他们

with the cooperation of its National Ski Associations, is entrusted for the development, management and accuracy of data related to their common activities.

As an important part of the promotion of Skiing and Snowboarding, FIS encourages National Ski Associations to provide their members, stakeholders and fans with data and information related to FIS activities.

All National Ski Associations are encouraged to provide general information relating to the events and competitions on the FIS calendar, for use by interested parties.

The purpose of this Rule is to define digital content and identify how it can be exploited.

218.2 Definition of Digital Content

Digital Content shall mean all information related to FIS activities, which is made available in a digital form.

Digital Content is comprised of two elements:

- Basic written digital content that is freely available, in the public domain and can be used without restriction. This includes documentary archives, reports, rules, official calendars, start and results lists including names of competitors,competition and venue information, running orders, statistics, rankings and standings and information regarding weather conditions;
- Specialist digital content which includes real time information provided by the Official Data and Timing Providers, athlete biographical information and performance data, event and other related content produced by stakeholders, including content on the social media

共同活动有关的数据。

作为推广高山滑雪和单板滑雪运动的一个重要部分，国际雪联鼓励各国家滑雪协会向其成员、利害关系方和粉丝提供与国际雪联活动相关的数据和信息。

鼓励所有国家滑雪协会提供与国际雪联日历上的活动和比赛有关的一般信息供有关方面使用。

本规则的目的是定义数字内容，并确定其如何能够被利用。

218.2 **数字内容的定义**

数字内容是指与国际雪联活动有关的所有信息，这些信息以数字形式提供。

数字内容由两个要素组成：

- 基本的书面数字内容，可以免费获得，可以在公共领域不受限制地使用。包括文献档案、报告、规则、官方日历，选手姓名、比赛和地点、比赛顺序、统计数据、排名和榜单的开始和结果的清单，以及有关天气的信息；

- 专业数字内容，包括官方数据和计时供应商提供的实时信息、运动员的传记信息和表现数据、赛事和其他由利害关系方制作的相关内容，包括运动员、赞助商和官员的社交媒体网站上的内容。此外，还包括所有有开发权的视频档案。

sites of athletes, sponsors and officials. Also included are all video archives for which exploitation rights are vailable.

Digital content includes all formats, together with any graphical, textual, video or other representations of such data, information and statistics.

218.3 Ownership of Digital Content

The ownership of digital content is determined by the relevant permissions and the contractual relationship, if any, under which such content has been produced and the conditions to be applied for its exploitation.

218.4 Use of Specialist Digital Content

The development of digital technology has made it possible for the consumer to have instant access to specialist digital content that enhances the viewing experience and interest in sport.

Access to moving pictures can stimulate interest in FIS competitions, and the inclusion of live timing and data feeds adds to the attraction of any video production. Use of the live timing and data feeds on World Cup and World Championships competitions is subject to obtaining the agreement of the owner of these feeds.

218.5 Access to Specialist Digital Content

Each party seeking to access specialist digital content must find an agreement with the owner/rights holder of the digital content and defining the terms and conditions

数字内容包括所有格式，以及这些数据、信息和统计数据的任何图形、文本、视频或其他表现形式。

218.3 数字内容的所有权

数字内容的所有权由相关的许可和合同关系决定，如果有的话，这些内容是根据这些许可和合同关系制作的，以及适用于其利用的条件。

218.4 专业数字内容的使用

数字技术的发展使消费者有可能即时获得专业的数字内容，提高其观看体验和对体育的兴趣。

获得动态图片可以激发人们对国际雪联比赛的兴趣，而加入现场计时和数据传输则可以增加视频制作的吸引力。使用世界杯和世锦赛比赛的实时计时和数据资料，必须获得这些资料所有者的同意。

218.5 获取专业的数字内容

寻求获取专业数字内容的每一方都必须与数字内容的所有者 / 权利人达成一份协议，并界定使用该内容的条款和条件。在所有情况下，特别是在个人数据

under which this content can be used. In all cases, and particularly with regard to personal data, a strict adherence to the GDPR or other equivalent law or regulation must be enforced.

The FIS shall advise anyone seeking to use specialist digital content, the name of the owner/rights holder and provide contact numbers.

Should individual owners/rights holders of specialist digital content consider it appropriate, their content could be bundled and offered centrally to the market using the FIS as their representative.

218.6 Review

In view of constant change and development in technology this rule will be kept under constant review and when appropriate updated on a regular basis.

219 Prizes

219.1 The detailed rules concerning the awarding of prizes will be published by the FIS. Prizes shall consist of mementos, diplomas, cheques or cash. Prizes for records are forbidden. The FIS Council decides in the autumn on the minimum respectively maximum values of the prize money approximately one and a half years before the competition season. The organisers have to inform the FIS by October 15th of the amount.

219.2 If two or more competitors finish with the same time or

方面，必须严格遵守 GDPR 或其他同等法律或法规。

国际雪联应告知任何寻求使用专业数字内容的人，所有人 / 权利人的姓名并提供联系电话。

如果专业数字内容的个别所有者 / 权利人认为合适，他们的内容可以捆绑起来，由国际雪联代表其集中向市场提供。

218.6 **审查**

鉴于技术的不断变化和发展，本规则将持续得到审查，并在适时更新。

219 奖励

219.1 有关奖品颁发的详细规则由国际雪联公布。奖品包括纪念品、获奖证书、支票或现金。禁止对打破纪录的奖励。国际雪联理事会于赛季前一年半左右的秋季，决定奖金的最低和最高限额。组织方必须在 10 月 15 日前将奖金额告知国际雪联。

219.2 两名或两名以上运动员用时或得分相同的，应给予

receive the same points, they shall be given the same placing. They will be awarded the same prizes, titles or diplomas. The allocation of titles or prizes by drawing lots or by another competition is not allowed.

219.3 All prizes are to be awarded no later than the final day of a competition or event series.

220 Team Officials, Coaches, Service Personnel, Suppliers and Firms' Representatives

In principle these regulations apply to all disciplines, taking into consideration the special rules.

220.1 The Organising Committee of an event must provide the Technical Delegate with a list of persons accredited to the competition.

220.2 It is forbidden for suppliers and for persons in their service to advertise inside the restricted area or to wear clearly visible commercial markings on their clothing or equipment which do not conform with art. 207.

220.3 Team officials accredited service personnel and suppliers receive from the FIS an official FIS accreditation in the Event concerned and must perform their specified function. The individual organisers are free to accredit additional company representatives or other important persons.

其相同的名次。他们应获得相同的奖品、头衔或获奖证书。不得通过抽签或重赛等方式决定头衔或奖品的分配。

219.3 所有奖励的颁发时间不得迟于比赛或系列赛的最后一天。

220 随队官员、教练员、服务人员、供应商和公司代表

此类规定原则上适用于国际雪联所有竞赛分项，同时也要兼顾特殊规则。

220.1 比赛组委会必须向技术代表提供一份注册参赛人员名单。

220.2 禁止供应商及其服务人员在禁区内做广告或者在其服装、竞赛器材上出现不符合本规则第 207 条规定的明显商业标识。

220.3 随队官员、注册服务人员和供应商获得国际雪联处核发的相关比赛的国际雪联正式注册证，并履行注册证中列明的职能。除正式注册证外，各组织方可自行为公司代表或其他重要人物办理注册证。

220.4 Only persons who have the official FIS accreditation or a special accreditation from the organiser for course or jumping-hill have access to the courses and jumping-hills (according to special rules of the discipline).

220.5 The Different Types of Accreditation

220.5.1 Technical Delegates, the Jury, and the persons mentioned in art. 220 with clearly visible accreditation have access to the courses and jumping-hills.

220.5.2 Servicemen attached to teams are permitted entry to start area and service area at the finish. They are not allowed entry to the courses or jumping-hills.

220.5.3 Company representatives accredited at the discretion of the organisers who do not have FIS accreditation are not permitted entry to the courses and restricted service areas.

221 Medical Services, Examinations and Doping

221.1 National Ski Associations are responsible for the fitness of their competitors to race. All competitors, male and female are required to undergo a thorough evaluation of their medical health. This evaluation is to be conducted within the competitor's own nation.

221.2 If requested by the FIS Medical Committee or its representative,competitors must undergo a medical examination

220.4 只有获得国际雪联正式注册证或组织方办理的赛道或跳台特别注册证的人员，才能进入赛道或跳台（依据国际雪联该竞赛分项的特别规则）。

220.5 注册证件的不同类型

220.5.1 技术代表、仲裁委员会和本规则第 220 条规定的佩戴显著注册证件的人员可以进入赛道和跳台。

220.5.2 随队服务人员可以进入出发区和终点服务区，但不得进入赛道或跳台。

220.5.3 由组织方酌情批准但未获得国际雪联注册证件的公司代表，不得进入赛道及受限服务区。

221 医疗服务、医学检查与兴奋剂检测

221.1 各国家滑雪协会要对其参赛运动员的身体状况是否适宜参加比赛负责。所有运动员不分男女，都必须接受对其健康状况的全面评估。健康评估在运动员本国进行。

221.2 国际雪联医疗委员会或其代表提出要求的，运动员必须在比赛前或者比赛后接受医学检查。

before or after the competition.

221.3 Doping is forbidden. Any offence under these FIS Anti-Doping Rules will be punished under the provisions of the FIS Anti-Doping Rules.

221.4 Doping controls may be carried out at any FIS competition (as well as out of competition). Rules and procedures are published in the FIS Anti-Doping Rules and FIS Procedural Guidelines.

221.5 Gender of the Competitor

If any question or protest arises as to the gender of the competitor, FIS shall assume responsibility for taking the necessary steps to determine the gender of the competitor.

221.6 Medical Services Required from Event Organisers

The health and safety of all those involved in a FIS competition is a primary concern of all event Organisers. This includes the competitors as well as volunteers, course workers and spectators.

The specific composition of the medical support system is dependent on several variables:

- The size, level, type of the event being held (World Championships, World Cup, Continental Cup, FIS-level, etc.) together with the local medical standards of care and geographic locations and circumstances;

221.3 禁止使用兴奋剂。任何违反《国际雪联反兴奋剂规则》的行为，都会依照该规则予以惩处。

221.4 国际雪联的任何比赛都可以实施兴奋剂检查（比赛之外也不例外）。兴奋剂检查的规则和程序公布在《国际雪联反兴奋剂规则》和《国际雪联反兴奋剂程序指南》。

221.5 **运动员的性别**

对运动员性别有任何疑问或抗议的，由国际雪联负责采取必要措施确定该运动员的性别。

221.6 **比赛组织方应当提供的医疗服务**

包括运动员以及志愿者、赛道工作人员和观众在内的所有参与国际雪联比赛者的健康和安全，是全体比赛组织者的首要关注点。

医疗保障系统的具体组成取决于以下几个可变因素：

- 所举办比赛的规模、级别、类型（国际雪联世界锦标赛、世界杯、洲际杯、国际雪联级别赛等）及当地医疗标准、地理位置和环境；

- The estimated number of competitors, support staff and spectators;
- The scope of responsibility for the Event Medical Organisation (competitors, support staff, spectators) should also be determined.

The Organiser / The Chief of Medical and Rescue Services must confirm with the race director or technical delegate that the required rescue facilities are in place before starting the official training or competition. In the event of an incident, or issue that prevents the primary medical plan from being utilized, the back-up plan must be in place before recommencing the official training or competition.

The specific requirements concerning facilities, resources, personnel and team physicians are contained in the respective discipline rules and the FIS Medical Guide.

222 Competition Equipment

222.1 A competitor may only take part in a FIS competition with equipment which conforms to the FIS Regulations. Competitors are responsible for the equipment that they use (skis, snowboard, bindings, ski boots, suit, etc.). It is their duty to check that the equipment they use conforms to the FIS specifications and general safety requirements and is in working order.

222.2 The term competition equipment encompasses all items of equipment which the competitor uses in competitions.

- 运动员、支持人员和观众的估计人数；

- 还应确定赛事医疗组织的责任范围（运动员、支持人员、观众）。

组织方及医疗救援服务主管必须在场地适应训练或比赛开始前向竞赛指导或技术代表确认所需的救援器材已到位。如果发生事故或出现首要医疗计划实施受阻，必须在场地适应训练或比赛重新开始前制订备用计划。

有关设施、资源、人员和随队医生的具体要求包含在相应的国际雪联竞赛分项的竞赛规则和《国际雪联医疗指南》中。

222 竞赛器材

222.1 运动员参加国际雪联比赛只能携带符合国际雪联规定的竞赛器材。运动员对其所用竞赛器材（滑雪板、单板、固定器、滑雪鞋、滑雪服等）负责，有义务确保自己所用竞赛器材符合国际雪联具体规定和一般安全要求并处于正常工作状态。

222.2 “竞赛器材”这一术语涵盖了运动员在比赛中所使用的所有器材，包括服装以及具有技术功能的器材。整

This includes clothing as well as apparatus with technical functions. The entire competition equipment forms a functional unit.

222.3 All new developments in the field of competition equipment must be approved in principle by the FIS.
The FIS does not take any responsibility for the approval of new technical developments, which at the time of introduction may contain unknown risk to the health or cause an increase in the risk of accidents.

222.4 New developments must be submitted by May 1st, (Grass Ski August 1st) at the latest, for the following season. The first year new developments can only be approved provisionally for the following season and must be finally confirmed prior to the subsequent competition season.

222.5 The Committee for Competition Equipment publishes equipment by-laws after approval by the FIS Council (definitions or descriptions of the equipment items which are allowed).
In principle unnatural or artificial aids which modify the performance of the competitors and/or constitute a technical correction of the individual's physical predisposition to a defective performance, as well as competition equipment which impact the health of the competitors or increase the risk of accidents are to be excluded.

套竞赛器材构成一个功能单元。

222.3 竞赛器材领域的所有革新改进，原则上都必须得到国际雪联的批准。

新技术发展的引入可能包含未知的健康风险或导致事故风险增加，国际雪联并不因批准新技术发展而承担任何相应的责任。

222.4 供新赛季使用的新开发竞赛器材最迟须在 5 月 1 日（草地滑雪项目为 8 月 1 日）前提交。新开发竞赛器材首年使用时只能获得在该赛季使用的临时批准，并且必须在该赛季的下一赛季开始前得到最终确认。

222.5 经国际雪联理事会批准后，竞赛器材委员会发布竞赛器材补充规定(获准的竞赛器材名录定义或说明)。

原则上不得使用非自然或人为的辅助手段来改变运动员的表现和（或）构成对个人身体素质缺陷表现倾向的技术修正，也不得使用影响运动员健康或增加事故风险的竞赛器材。

222.6 Controls

Before and during the competition season or on submission of protests to the Technical Delegate at the competition concerned, various controls can be carried out by members of the Committee for Competition Equipment or official FIS Equipment Controllers. Should there be a well-founded suspicion that regulations were violated, the equipment items must be confiscated immediately by the controllers or Technical Delegates in the presence of witnesses and be forwarded sealed to the FIS, which will submit the items to a final control by an officially recognised institution. In cases of protest against items of the competition equipment, the losing party will bear the investigation costs.

No testing of equipment or material in independent laboratories may be requested at races where a FIS Technical Expert has performed the controls, unless it can be demonstrated that the controls have not been carried out according to the rules.

222.6.1 At all FIS events where official FIS measurement experts using the official FIS measurement tools are appointed, the result of measurements carried out at the time are valid and final, irrespective of previous measurements.

222.7 Prohibited of scientific and medical Equipment at FIS Events

It is prohibited for any National Ski Association, its representative or team members to bring and/or use any of

222.6 **核查**

在赛季之前和赛季期间，或者在有关比赛中向技术代表提出抗议后，竞赛器材委员会的委员或国际雪联的官方竞赛器材核查员可以采取多种核查措施。对于有充分理由怀疑存在违反规定的行为，核查人员或技术代表必须在证人见证下立即没收相关竞赛器材并加封发送国际雪联，由其提交官方认可的机构对竞赛器材进行最终核查。对竞赛器材提出抗议的，败诉方承担调查费用。

在由国际雪联技术专家实施核查的比赛中，除非能够证明核查没有按照规则进行，否则不得要求在独立实验室中对竞赛器材或相关材料进行测试。

222.6.1 在所有指派了使用国际雪联官方测量工具的国际雪联官方测量专家的国际雪联比赛中，无论之前的测量结果如何，由这些测量工具当场实测的结果都是有效的最终结果。

222.7 **国际雪联禁用的科技及医疗器械**

在国际雪联世界锦标赛、世界杯以及纳入《国际雪联竞赛日历》的其他任何比赛中，任何国家滑雪协

the following scientific or medical equipment ("Equipment") into/at any Event Venue during FIS World Championships, World Cups and other competitions registered in the FIS Calendar:

- Oxygen tanks, cylinders and related devices;
- Hypoxic or hyperoxic tents, chambers and related devices;
- Cryogenic chambers for whole body cryotherapy and related devices.

It is the responsibility of the National Ski Association to ensure compliance with this Article 222.7 by all its representatives or team members. Failure to respect this Article 222.7 will be subject to Penalties provided by Article 223.3. In case of recurrence, disqualification of an athlete shall be imposed irrespectively of whether the violation of this provision would result in an advantage for the Athlete(s) with regard to the end result of the competition. In addition to the sanctions listed above, the FIS may order the immediate removal of the Equipment from the Event Venue at the costs of the responsible NSA.

222.8 **Fluorinated ski wax prohibition**

Use of fluorinated wax or tuning products containing fluorine is prohibited for all FIS disciplines and levels.

Fluorinated wax can be a competitive advantage and its use in competition will result in disqualification (see competition rules and equipment specifications).

会或其代表、队员都不得携带以下任何科技及医疗器械（作为“竞赛器材”）进入任何比赛场地或者在其中使用：

- 氧气瓶、氧气筒或者相关设备；
- 低压或者高压氧舱或者相关设备；

- 用于全身降温的超低温温室及相关设备。

国家滑雪协会有义务确保其代表或者队员遵守本 222.7 条的规定。未遵守本 222.7 条规定将受到本规则第 223.3 条规定的处罚。对于累犯的运动员将取消其参赛资格，而无论该违规行为是否使该运动员在比赛成绩方面受益。除受到上列惩罚外，国际雪联可以责令立即从比赛场地移除违规设备，费用由需要对此负责的国家滑雪协会承担。

222.8 **禁用氟化滑雪蜡**

国际雪联所有竞赛分项和级别的比赛都禁止使用氟化滑雪蜡或者类似的含氟产品。

氟化滑雪蜡具有显著竞赛优势，在比赛中使用将被取消资格(另见相关比赛规则及竞赛器材具体规定)。

223 Sanctions

223.1 General Conditions

223.1.1 An offence for which a sanction may apply and a penalty be imposed is defined as conduct that:
- Is in violation or non-observance of competition rules, or
- Constitutes non-compliance with directives of the jury; or individual members of the jury in accordance with art. 224.2;
- Constitutes unsportsmanlike behaviour.

223.1.2 The following conduct shall also be considered an offence:
- Attempting to commit an offence;
- Causing or facilitating others to commit an offence;
- Counselling others to commit an offence.

223.1.3 In determining whether conduct constitutes an offence consideration should be given to:
- Whether the conduct was intentional or unintentional;
- Whether the conduct arose from circumstances of an emergency.

223.1.4 All FIS affiliated associations, including their members registered for accreditation, shall accept and acknowledge these rules and sanctions imposed, subject only to the right to appeal pursuant to the FIS Statutes and ICR.

223 制裁

223.1 一般条件

223.1.1 可适用制裁和处罚的犯规行为是指：

- 违反或不遵守竞赛规则；
- 依据本规则第 224.2 条之规定，构成不服从仲裁委员会或其成员指令的行为；
- 构成缺乏运动员风范的行为。

223.1.2 下列行为也应视为犯规行为：
- 企图实施犯规行为；
- 导致或促使他人犯规；
- 教唆他人犯规。

223.1.3 在认定行为是否构成犯规行为时，应考虑：

- 犯规行为是故意的还是非故意的；
- 犯规行为是否是因紧急情势。

223.1.4 所有国际雪联所属国家滑雪协会，包括其注册会员，均应接受并承认本规则和据此实施的制裁，但可以依据《国际雪联章程》和《国际雪联滑雪竞赛规则》行使申诉的权利。

223.2 Applicability

223.2.1 Persons

These sanctions apply to:

- All persons who are registered with or accredited by the FIS or the organiser of an event published in the FIS calendar (an event) both within and without the confines of the competition area and any location connected with the competition;
- All persons who are not accredited, within the confines of the competition area.

223.3 Penalties

223.3.1 The commission of an offence may subject a person to the following penalties:

- Reprimand - written or verbal;
- Withdrawal of accreditation;
- Denial of accreditation;
- Monetary fine not more than CHF 100’000.--;
- A time penalty.

223.3.1.1 FIS-affiliated associations are liable to the FIS for the payment of any fines and incurred administrative expenses imposed on persons whose registration or accreditation they arranged.

223.3.1.2 Persons not subject to art. 223.3.1.1 are also liable to the FIS for fines and incurred administrative expenses. If

223.2 适用范围

223.2.1 人员

本规则设定的制裁适用于：

- 在国际雪联登记或者经国际雪联注册的所有人员，或《国际雪联竞赛日历》中公布的某一比赛的组织者，不管是在比赛场地内外还是在任何与比赛有关的地方。

- 所有没有受到国际雪联注册但在比赛场地内的工作人员。

223.3 处罚

223.3.1 对违规人员可施以如下处罚：

- 书面或口头警告；
- 撤销注册资格；
- 拒绝予以注册；
- 不超过 10 万瑞士法郎的罚款；
- 罚时。

223.3.1.1 国际雪联所属国家滑雪协会对由其安排登记或者注册的人员所处的罚款和由此产生的管理费用，向国际雪联承担连带支付义务。

223.3.1.2 不受本规则第 223.3.1.1 条约束的人员也有义务向国际雪联缴纳罚款和支付行政费用。如果此类人员不

such persons do not pay these fines, they shall be subject to a withdrawal of any permission to apply for accreditation to FIS events for a period of one year.

223.3.1.3 Payment of fines is due within 8 (eight) days following their imposition.

223.3.2 All competing competitors may be subject to the following additional penalties:
- Disqualification;
- Impairment of their starting position;
- Forfeiture of prizes and benefits in favour of the organiser;
- Suspension from FIS events.

223.3.3 Competitors shall only be disqualified if their mistake would result in an advantage for them with regard to the end result, unless the Rules state otherwise in an individual case.

223.4 A jury may impose the penalties provided in art. 223.3.1 and 223.3.2, however they may not impose a monetary fine of more than CHF 5’000.--or suspend a competitor beyond the series of FIS event at which the offence occurred.

223.5 The following Penalty decisions may be given verbally:
- Reprimands;
- The withdrawal of accreditation for the current event from persons who had not been registered with the organiser through their National Associations;

肯支付罚款，则应取消其所有参加国际雪联比赛的注册，为期一年。

223.3.1.3 罚款应在决定生效后 8 天内支付。

223.3.2 所有运动员都有可能会受到以下额外处罚：

- 取消资格；
- 调整其出发位置；
- 没收奖品并交还组织者；
- 暂停参加国际雪联比赛。

223.3.3 除非《国际雪联滑雪竞赛规则》在个别情况下另有规定，否则运动员只有在其所犯错误会为其最终成绩带来优势的情况下才会被取消资格。

223.4 仲裁委员会可依据本规则第 223.3.1 条和第 223.3.2 条规定实施处罚，但不得处以超过 5000 瑞士法郎的罚款，或在发生违规行为的国际雪联系列赛事以外暂停运动员的参赛资格。

223.5 下列处罚决定可以口头作出：
- 警告；
- 撤销未通过其国家滑雪协会在组织方注册的人员本次比赛的注册；

- The withdrawal of the accreditation for the current event from FIS accredited persons.
- The denial of accreditation to the current event from persons who are within the confines of the competition area or any other location connected with the competition.

223.6 The following Penalty decisions shall be in writing:
- Monetary fines;
- Disqualification;
- Impaired starting position;
- Competition suspensions;
- Withdrawal of accreditation from persons who had been registered through their National Association;
- Withdrawal of accreditation of FIS accredited persons.

223.7 Written Penalty decisions must be sent to the offender (if it is not a competitor), the offender's National Association and the Secretary General of FIS.

223.8 Any disqualification shall be recorded in the Referee's and/or the TD's Report.

223.9 All penalties shall be recorded in the TD's Report.

224 Procedural Guidelines

224.1 Competence of Jury

The Jury at the event has the right to impose sanctions according to the above rules by majority vote. In the case of a

- 撤销国际雪联认证的人员本次比赛的认证；

- 对在比赛场地或与比赛有关的任何其他地点范围内的人员，拒绝给予其本次比赛认证。

223.6 **下列处罚决定应书面作出：**

- 罚款；
- 取消资格；
- 调整出发位置；
- 停赛；
- 撤销通过所属国家滑雪协会获得注册人员的注册；

- 撤销国际雪联认证人员的认证。

223.7 书面处罚决定必须分送违规者（如果不是运动员）、违规者所属国家滑雪协会和国际雪联秘书长。

223.8 取消参赛资格必须记录在裁判长或者技术代表的报告中。

223.9 所有处罚都必须记录在技术代表的报告中。

224 程序指南

224.1 **仲裁委员会的权限**

仲裁委员会在比赛期间有权根据上述规则按简单多数制通过投票实施制裁。如果投票出现平局，仲裁

tie, the Chair of the Jury has the deciding vote.

224.2 Within the location, especially during the training and the competition period, each voting Jury member is authorised to issue oral reprimands and withdraw the accreditation which is issued for the current event.

224.3 **Collective Offences**

If several persons commit the same offence at the same time and under the same circumstances, the Jury's decision as to one offender may be considered binding upon all offenders. The written decision shall include the names of all offenders concerned, and the scope of the penalty to be assessed upon each of them. The decision will be delivered to each offender.

224.4 **Limitation**

A person shall not be sanctioned if proceedings to invoke such sanction have not been commenced against that person within 72 hours following the offence.

224.5 Each person who is a witness to an alleged offence is required to testify at any hearing called by the Jury, and the Jury is required to consider all relevant evidence.

224.6 The Jury may confiscate objects that are suspected of being used in violation of equipment guidelines.

224.7 Prior to the imposition of a penalty (except in cases of

委员会主任拥有最终决定权。

224.2 在比赛场地内，尤其是训练和比赛期间，每一位有投票权的仲裁委员会成员都有权给予违规运动员口头警告并取消其当前比赛的参赛资格。

224.3 **集体犯规**

多人同时在同样情况下违反同样规定的，仲裁委员会对某一违规者作出的决定同样适用于所有违规者。书面处罚决定应包括所有相关违规者的姓名并对每位违规者确定处罚的幅度。决定应分送每位违规者。

224.4 **限制**

如果在违规行为发生后 72 小时内未启动对违规者实施制裁的程序，则不应再对其实施制裁。

224.5 违规行为的目击者应在仲裁委员会召集的听证会上作证。仲裁委员会应该考虑所有相关证据。

224.6 仲裁委员会可以没收涉嫌违反竞赛器材使用规范的器材。

224.7 制裁决定作出前（依据本规则第 223.5 条和第 224.2

reprimands and withdrawal of accreditation according to art. 223.5 and 224.2), the person accused of an offence shall be given the opportunity to present a defence at a hearing, orally or in writing.

224.8 All Jury decisions shall be recorded in writing and shall include:

224.8.1 The offence alleged to have been committed.

224.8.2 The evidence of the offence.

224.8.3 The rule (s) or Jury directives that have been violated.

224.8.4 The penalty imposed.

224.9 The penalty shall be appropriate to the offence. The scope of any penalty imposed by the Jury must consider any mitigating and aggravating circumstances.

224.10 Remedies

224.10.1 Except as provided for in art. 224.11, a penalty decision of the Jury may be appealed in accordance with the provisions in the ICR.

224.10.2 If an appeal is not filed within the deadline established in the ICR, the penalty decision of the Jury becomes final.

条予以警告和撤销注册资格的除外），被指控违规人员有机会通过向听证会提交口头或书面材料为自己辩护。

224.8 仲裁委员会的所有决定均应有书面记录，并应包含以下内容：

224.8.1 所犯违规行为。

224.8.2 违规证据。

224.8.3 违反的规则或仲裁委员会的指令。

224.8.4 实施的制裁。

224.9 处罚应与违规情节相对应。由仲裁委员会实施的制裁的幅度均应考虑所有减轻和加重情形。

224.10 救济

224.10.1 除本规则第 224.11 条规定的以外，对仲裁委员会的处罚决定，可按照《国际雪联滑雪竞赛规则》中的规定申诉。

224.10.2 未在《国际雪联滑雪竞赛规则》规定的最后期限内提起申诉的，仲裁委员会的处罚决定即成为最终决定。

224.11 The following decisions of the Jury are not subject to appeal:

224.11.1 Oral penalties imposed under art. 223.5 and 224.2.

224.11.2 Monetary fines less than CHF 1'000.-- (One Thousand Swiss Francs) for single offence and a further CHF 2'500.-- for repeated offences by the same person.

224.12 In all remaining cases, appeals are to be directed to the Appeals Commission, as per the ICR.

224.13 The Jury shall have the right to submit to the Appeals Commission recommendations for penalties in excess of monetary fines of CHF 5'000.-and suspensions beyond the event in which the offence occurred (art.223.4).

224.14 FIS Council shall have the right to submit to the Appeals Commission comments with respect to any written penalty decisions by the Jury.

224.15 Costs of Proceedings

Fees and cash expenses, including travel expenses (costs of the proceedings) are to be calculated comparable to costs paid to TD's and are to be paid by the offender. In the case of a reversal of Jury decisions, in whole or in part, the FIS covers all costs.

224.11 不得对仲裁委员会的下列决定提出申诉：

224.11.1 按照本规则第 223.5 和第 224.2 条实施的口头处罚。

224.11.2 对单次违规人员处以罚金金额低于 1000 瑞士法郎，对同一人员重复违规加处罚款金额低于 2500 瑞士法郎。

224.12 其他所有案件，可按照《国际雪联滑雪竞赛规则》的规定直接向申诉委员会申诉。

224.13 仲裁委员会有权向申诉委员会提出建议：处以 5000 瑞士法郎以上的罚款以及超出发生违规行为的比赛的禁赛（本规则第 223.4 条）。

224.14 国际雪联理事会有权就由仲裁委员会提出的任何书面处罚决定向申诉委员会提出意见。

224.15 **申诉费用**

包括旅行费用在内的费用和现金花销的审理费用，按照付给技术代表的费用标准计算，由违规者支付。仲裁委员会的决定被完全或部分推翻的案件，由国际雪联承担所有的费用。

224.16 Enforcement of Monetary Fines

224.16.1 The FIS oversees the enforcement of monetary fines and the costs of proceedings. Enforcement costs are considered costs of the proceedings.

224.16.2 Any outstanding monetary fines imposed on an offender is considered a debt of the National Association to which the offender is a member.

224.17 Benefit Fund

All monetary fines are paid into the FIS Youth Promotion Fund.

224.18 These rules are not applicable to any violation of FIS Doping rules.

225 Appeals Commission

225.1 Appointments

225.1.1 The FIS Council shall appoint from the Discipline Sub-Committee for Rules (or Discipline Committee if there is no Rules Sub-Committee) a Chair and a Vice Chair of the Appeals Commission. The Vice Chair shall preside when the Chair is either unavailable or is disqualified for bias and prejudice.

225.1.2 The Chair shall appoint 3 members, to the Appeals

224.16 **罚款的强制执行**

224.16.1 国际雪联监督罚款和审理费用的执行情况。执行费用视为审理费用的一部分。

224.16.2 对违规者处罚但未缴之罚款均视为违规者所属国家滑雪协会之债务。

224.17 **福利基金**

所有罚款都交给国际雪联青少年发展基金。

224.18 以上规则不适用于违反国际雪联反兴奋剂规则的案件。

225 申诉委员会

225.1 **任命**

225.1.1 国际雪联理事会必须从纪律规则分委员会（若无纪律规则分委员会则为纪律委员会）中任命 1 名申诉委员会主任和 1 名副主任。当主任未出席或因偏见回避事由而丧失资格时，由副主任主持。

225.1.2 主任应从纪律规则分委员会或纪律委员会中任命 3 名

Commission from the Discipline Rules Sub-Committee or Discipline Committee for each case appealed or submitted to be heard, which may include the Chair, whose decisions shall be by majority vote.

225.1.3 To avoid either actual bias and prejudice or the appearance of bias and prejudice, members appointed to an Appeals Commission shall not be members of the same National Association as the offender whose case is under appeal. In addition, members appointed to an Appeals Commission must report voluntarily to the Chair any bias and prejudice they may hold for or against the offender. Persons who are biased and prejudiced shall be disqualified from serving on the Appeals Commission by the Chair or, in the event the Chair is disqualified, by the Vice Chair.

225.2 Responsibility

225.2.1 The Appeals Commission shall only hold hearings with respect to appeals by offenders or by the FIS Council from decisions of competition juries, or matters referred to it by competition juries recommending penalties in excess of those provided for in the Sanction rules.

225.3 Procedures

225.3.1 The Appeal must be decided within 72 hours of receipt of the Appeal by the Chair, unless all parties involved in

委员组成申诉委员会（任命人员中可包括主任本人），负责每宗申诉或呈交听证的案件。其决定按简单多数制通过。

225.1.3 为避免偏袒嫌疑或真正的偏袒行为，被指派的申诉委员会成员与在审申诉案件所涉违规者不能同属一个国家滑雪协会。此外，被指派的申诉委员会成员，如果发现自己对违规者可能持有正面或者反面的先入之见，必须主动向主任报告。对于任何持有偏见者，主任（如果主任的资格也被取消，则为副主任）应取消该委员在该案的申诉委员会工作的资格。

225.2 职责

225.2.1 申诉委员会仅在下列情况举行听证会：违规者提起申诉的；国际雪联理事会对比赛仲裁委员会的决定提起申诉的；比赛仲裁委员会建议的处罚超出制裁规则的。

225.3 程序

225.3.1 申请应在申诉委员会主任收到申诉材料后 72 小时内作出决定，除非申诉各方均书面同意为举行听证会

the Appeal agree in writing to an extension of time for the hearing.

225.3.2 All appeals and responses must be submitted in writing, including any evidence the parties intend to offer in support of or in response to the Appeal.

225.3.3 The Appeals Commission shall decide on the location and format for the Appeal (phone conference, in person, e-mail exchanges).

The Appeals Commission members are required to respect the confidentiality of the appeal until the decision is made public and to consult only with the other members of the panel during the deliberations.

The Chair of the Appeals Commission may request additional evidence from any of the parties involved, providing this does not require disproportionate means.

225.3.4 The Appeals Commission shall allocate costs of the appeal pursuant to art. 224.15.

225.3.5 Decisions of the Appeals Commission may be announced orally at the conclusion of the deliberations or hearing should one take place. The decision, together with its reasoning, shall be submitted in writing to the FIS, which shall deliver them to the parties involved, their National Associations and all members of the Jury whose decision was appealed.

In addition, the written decision shall be available at the

而延期。

225.3.2 所有申诉和答复都必须书面形式提交，包括各方为支持申诉或者对申诉答辩而提交的证据。

225.3.3 申诉委员会应决定申诉的地点和形式（电话会议、当面、电子邮件交流）。

申诉委员会成员要在决定公布之前尊重申诉的保密性，并且在审议过程中只可与委员会其他成员商讨。

申诉委员会主任可要求任何当事方提交补充证据，前提是举证方手段必须得当。

225.3.4 申诉委员会应当根据本规则第 224.15 条分配各方应当承担的申诉费用。

225.3.5 申诉委员会的决定在审议或听证会结束时可以口头宣布。决定及其理由应以书面形式提交国际雪联，国际雪联再将上述材料分送各当事方、各方所属国家滑雪协会以及其决定被申诉的仲裁委员会的所有成员。

此外，决定的书面材料可在国际雪联办公室获取。

FIS Office.

225.4 Further Appeals

225.4.1 Decisions of the Appeals Commission may be appealed to the FIS Court in accordance with Article 52,52.1 and 52.2 of the Statutes.

225.4.2 Appeals to the FIS Court shall be in writing and submitted to the FIS Secretary-General in accordance with the time limits prescribed in Article 52, 52.1 and 52.2 of the Statutes from the date of the publication of the Appeals Commission decision.

225.4.3 An Appeal to the Appeals Commission or to the FIS Court will not delay the implementation of any penalty decision of the Competition Jury, Appeals Commission or Council.

226 Violation of Sanctions

Where there is a violation of a sanction that has been imposed (according to ICR art. 223 or the FIS Anti-Doping Rules), the Council may impose such further and other sanctions that it considers appropriate.
In such cases, some or all of the following sanctions may apply:

226.1 Sanctions against individuals involved

- A written reprimand;

225.4 **再申诉**

225.4.1 根据《国际雪联章程》第 52、第 52.1 和第 52.2 条，对申诉委员会的决定还可向国际雪联法庭申诉。

225.4.2 自申诉委员会的决定公布之日起，申诉方应以书面形式，在《国际雪联章程》第 52、第 52.1 和第 52.2 条规定的时限内，将向国际雪联法院提出的再申诉提请国际雪联秘书长转交。

225.4.3 向申诉委员会或者国际雪联法院提出申诉，不影响比赛仲裁委员会、申诉委员会或者国际雪联理事会的处罚决定的执行。

226 违规行为

对于违规行为（依据本规则第 223 条或《国际雪联反兴奋剂规则》），国际雪联理事会可以采取进一步和其认为合理的其他制裁措施。

在这种情况下，可以采取如下部分或全部制裁措施：

226.1 **对个人的制裁包括**

- 书面警告；

- A monetary fine not to exceed the sum of CHF 100’000;
- Competition suspension at the next level of sanction- for example if a three month suspension for a doping offence was imposed, a violation of the suspension will cause a two year suspension; if a two year suspension for a doping offence was imposed, a violation of the suspension will cause a lifetime suspension;
- Withdrawal of accreditation from individuals involved.

226.2 Sanctions against a National Ski Association

- Withdrawal of FIS funding to the National Ski Association;
- Cancellation of future FIS events in the country involved;
- Withdrawal of some or all FIS membership rights, including participation in all FIS calendar competitions, voting rights at the FIS Congress, membership of FIS Committees.

- 不超过 10 万瑞士法郎的罚款；

- 禁赛期限升级一档。例如，某运动员因违反反兴奋剂规则而被禁赛 3 个月，如果违反该禁赛的制裁则会导致禁赛 2 年；某运动员因违反反兴奋剂规则而被禁赛 2 年,违反该禁赛的制裁则会导致终身禁赛；

- 取消其个人参赛资格。

226.2 **对国家滑雪协会的制裁包括**

- 收回国际雪联对该国家滑雪协会的资助；

- 取消涉事国家今后举办国际雪联比赛的资格；

- 撤销其作为国际雪联成员的部分或者全部权利，包括参加《国际雪联竞赛日历》中的所有比赛的权利、在国际雪联代表大会上的表决权以及国际雪联各委员会的会员资格。

2nd Section

Rules Common to Alpine Events

第二部分

高山滑雪竞赛通则

The rules of the FIS Alpine World Cup apply to the technical organisation of the Olympic Winter Games and FIS World Ski Championships (Alpine Events) unless further specific rules have been detailed in the ICR.

600 Organisation

Reference is made to art. 211.

601 Organising Committee and Jury

601.1 Composition

The Organising Committee consists of those members (physical or legal) who are delegated by the organiser and by the International Ski Federation. It carries the rights, duties and obligations of the organiser.

601.2 Appointments by the International Ski Federation

The International Ski Federation appoints the Technical Delegate for all competitions and:

601.2.1 In World Cup Races:

- The Referee (Chief-Race-Director) and the Assistant Referee (Race-Director).

601.2.2 For the Olympic Winter Games and FIS World Ski Championships:

- All Jury members (see art. 601.4.1).

国际雪联《高山滑雪世界杯规则》适用于冬季奥林匹克运动会和国际雪联世界锦标赛（高山滑雪赛事）的技术组织，《国际雪联滑雪竞赛规则》另有进一步的详细规定的除外。

600 组织

参见本规则第 211 条。

601 组委会和仲裁委员会

601.1 机构组成

组委会由组织方和国际雪联委派的成员（自然人或法人的代表）组成，享有组织方的权利、承担组织方的义务和履行组织方的职责。

601.2 国际雪联任命

国际雪联为所有比赛任命技术代表并任命下列比赛官员：

601.2.1 世界杯比赛：

裁判长（竞赛总主任）和副裁判长（竞赛主任）。

601.2.2 冬季奥林匹克运动会和国际雪联世界锦标赛：

仲裁委员会全体成员（参见本规则第 601.4.1 条）。

601.2.3 In all other races the Technical Delegate appoints:
- The Referee ;
- For Downhill and Super-G the Assistant Referee.

601.2.4 By these appointments the above persons become members of the Organising Committee.

601.3 Appointments by the organiser

The Organiser appoints all other members of the Organising Committee(OC). The Chair or a representative represents the Committee in public, leads the meetings and makes decisions concerning all matters that arenot made by other persons or groups. Before, during and after the competition(s) they work closely with the International Ski Federation and its appointed officials and takes on all other duties that are necessary for carrying out the competition.
The following officials must be appointed:

601.3.1 The Chief of Race

The Chief of Race directs all preparation of the competition and supervises the activities in the technical area. The Chief of Race summons meetings for consideration of technical questions and leads the team captains' meetings after consultation with the Technical Delegate.

601.3.2 The Chief of Course

The Chief of Course is responsible for the preparation of the courses in accordance with the directives and

601.2.3 在其他所有比赛中，技术代表任命：
- 裁判长；
- 滑降和超级大回转比赛副裁判长。

601.2.4 获得上述任命者为组委会成员。

601.3 组织方任命

组织方任命组委会其他成员。组委会主任或组委会的代表在公开场合代表组委会、主持组委会会议、决定其他人员或团组未决事宜。组委会及其成员在赛前、赛中和赛后，与国际雪联及其任命的官员在工作中密切合作,承担办好比赛必需的其他所有职责。

下列官员应当由组织方任命：

601.3.1 竞赛长

竞赛长指导比赛的所有准备工作，并监督技术领域的活动，召集会议研究讨论技术问题，经商技术代表后主持领队会议。

601.3.2 赛道长

赛道长根据仲裁委员会的指令和决定负责做好赛道的准备工作，必须熟悉比赛当地与雪道相关的地形

decisions of the Jury. The Chief of Course must be familiar with local snow conditions on the terrain concerned.

601.3.3 The Start Referee

The Start Referee must remain at the start from the beginning of the official inspection time and until the end of a training/event to:

- Make sure that the regulations for the start and the start organisation are properly observed;
- Determine late and false starts;
- Be a point of contact for the Jury at all times and immediately (see art.705.5);
- Report the names of the competitors who did not start to the Referee, and informs the Jury of all infringements against the rules, such as false or delayed starts or violations against the rules for equipment;
- Ensure that reserve bibs are available at the start.

601.3.4 The Finish Referee

The Finish Referee must remain at the finish from the beginning of the official inspection time until the end of a training/event to:

- Make sure that all the regulations for the organisation of the finish and the finish in-run and out-run are properly observed;
- Supervise the finish controller, the timing and the crowd control in the finish area;
- Be a point of contact for the Jury at all times and immediately;

及其雪况。

601.3.3 起点裁判长

从官方视察线路开始直至训练或比赛全部结束，起点裁判长都必须始终坚守在起点，以便履行下列职责：

- 确保有关出发和组织出发方面的规定切实得到遵守；
- 决定延迟出发和出发犯规；
- 作为仲裁委员会可以随时并能即时联系的联系点（参见本规则第 705.5 条）；
- 向裁判长报告未出发运动员的姓名，向仲裁委员会通报所有犯规行为，如出发犯规或延迟出发以及违反竞赛器材规则的行为；
- 确保起点处有备用号码布。

601.3.4 终点裁判长

从官方视察线路开始直至训练和比赛全部结束，终点裁判长必须始终坚守在终点，以便履行下列职责：

- 确保终点区、终点冲刺区和终点停止区的组织规定切实得到遵守；
- 监督终点监督员、计时工作以及终点区观众管理；
- 作为仲裁委员会可以随时并能即时联系的联系点；

- Report the names of the competitors who did not finish to the Referee and informs the Jury of all infringements against the rules.

601.3.5 **The Chief Gate Judge**

The Chief Gate Judge organises and supervises the work of the gate judges. The Chief Gate Judge designates the gates each will supervise and places them in position. At the end of the first run and the end of the race, the Chief Gate Judge collects the gate judges' control cards and delivers them to the Referee.

The Chief Gate Judge distributes, in good time, the material that is needed (control card, pencil, start list, etc.) to each gate judge and is prepared to offer assistance either to help keep the spectators off the competition course or to help maintain the course, etc. The Chief Gate Judge make sure that the numbering and the marking of the gates is completed within the required time.

601.3.6 **The Chief of Timing and Calculations**

The Chief of Timing and Calculations is responsible for the coordination of officials at the start and finish, including timing and calculations. In Slalom, the Chief of Timing and Calculations or a special assistant will decide the interval between starts. The following officials are under The Chief of Timing and Calculations direction:

- Starter;
- Assistant starter;
- Start recorder;

- 向裁判长通报未通过终点的运动员的姓名，向仲裁委员会通报所有犯规行为。

601.3.5 旗门裁判长

旗门裁判长组织和监督旗门裁判员的工作。旗门裁判长指定每一位旗门裁判员所负责监控的旗门并把各旗门裁判员安排到适当的位置；第 1 轮滑行和比赛结束后，负责收集旗门裁判员的监督卡并交裁判长。

旗门裁判长适时向各旗门裁判员分发所需用品（监督卡、铅笔、出发顺序表等），随时准备协助把观众清出赛道或帮助维护赛道等。旗门裁判长确保在规定时间内完成旗门的编号和标记工作。

601.3.6 计时计算长

计时计算长负责协调起、终点的官员以及计时与计算。在回转比赛中，计时计算长或一位特别助理决定出发的间隔时间。计时计算长指挥下列官员：

- 发令员；
- 助理发令员；
- 起点记录员；

- Chief timekeeper;
- Assistant timekeepers;
- Finish controller;
- Chief of calculations and the assistants.

The Chief of Timing and Calculations oversees the preparation of the Timing and Data Technical Report (TDTR) and XML file for the electronic transmittal to FIS following the competition. A copy of the report may also be printed (only if the TD has no access to the TD report) for review prior to the transmission of the XML file. The TDTR Software can be found on the FIS website.

601.3.7 The Race Secretary

The Race Secretary is responsible for all secretarial work for the technical aspects of the competition and amongst others for the preparation of the draw. The Race Secretary ensures that the official results contain the information required by art. 617.3.4. and is responsible for the minutes of the technical officials, the Jury and team captains' meetings.

The Race Secretary ensures that all forms for start, finish, timing,calculations, and gate-judging are well prepared, and handed over to the officials concerned in good order at the proper time.

The Race Secretary facilitates the calculation of results by appropriate preparation and ensures that the result XML file is available for transmission to FIS.

The Race Secretary also ensures the duplication and publication of the official results after the Results are

- 计时长；
- 助理计时员；
- 终点监督员；
- 计算长及其助理。

计时及计算长负责监督比赛后以电子文件方式传输给国际雪联的《计时与数据技术报告（TDTR）》和可扩展标记语言文件（XML）的编制工作。在传输可扩展标记语言文件（XML）之前，可以打印一份《计时与数据技术报告》的副本（仅当技术代表无法查阅该报告时）以供审查。《计时与数据技术报告》的填报软件可在国际雪联官网上找到。

601.3.7 竞赛秘书

竞赛秘书负责整个比赛的竞赛技术方面的所有秘书工作，如做好抽签准备等；确保比赛正式结果包含本规则第 617.3.4 条要求的信息；负责技术官员、仲裁委员会和领队会议的会议记录。

竞赛秘书负责精心准备确保将起点、终点、计时、计算及旗门裁判员需要的所有表格，并按照正确顺序在恰当的时间送交有关官员。

竞赛秘书通过适当的准备促进比赛成绩的计算，确保包含比赛成绩的可扩展标记语言文件（XML）准备就绪以便传输给国际雪联。

竞赛秘书确保在比赛成绩被认定为“对国际雪联积分系统有效”后，复制并公布正式成绩。可扩展标

considered "Valid for FIS points" . In the case that the transmission of the electronic XML result file is delayed, results may be duplicated and published with the permission of the TD.

601.3.8 **The Chief of Medical and Rescue Services**

The Chief of Medical and Rescue Services is responsible for organising adequate first aid and medical coverage during the official training periods and the actual competition.

The Chief of Medical and Rescue Services must arrange an appropriate facility to which injured competitors should be taken and treated.

The Chief of Medical and Rescue Services coordinates plans with the team doctors before the start of the official training or the start of any competition.

During training and the races The Chief of Medical and Rescue Services must be in telephone or radio communication with the assistants and must co-ordinate plans with the Chief of Race before the start of the official training, or start of any competition.

A doctor, who should be a good skier, should be ready at the start to deal with any eventuality and must stay in contact with the Jury and the members of the rescue service. This task can be delegated to a team doctor. Details of the Medical Support Requirements are given in chapter 1 of the FIS Medical Guide.

601.3.9 **Other officials within the Organising Committee (OC)**

The following officials may also be appointed:

记语言文件（XML）的传输延迟的，经技术代表允许，可以复制并公布成绩。

601.3.8 医疗与救援主管

医疗与救援主管负责：

在场地适应训练和正式比赛期间组织充分的现场急救和医疗服务工作；

安排好适当的设备以接纳并救治受伤运动员。

在场地适应训练或任何比赛开始前与随队医生协调工作计划。

在训练和比赛期间，必须与助手保持电话或无线电对讲通信；

在场地适应训练或任何比赛开始前与竞赛长协调工作计划。

在起点处安排一位滑雪技术过硬的医生负责随时准备处理任何意外，该医生必须与仲裁委员会及救护人员持续保持联系。此项任务可指派给一位随队医生。详细的医疗支持服务要求见《国际雪联医疗指南》第一章。

601.3.9 组委会（OC）的其他官员

下列官员也可由任命产生：

601.3.9.1 The Chief of Finish Area

The Finish Area Coordinator is responsible for coordinating the various requirements in the finish area to deal with any request the demanding, pre, during and post-competition activities. Responsibilities include construction and coordination of the mixed-zone, television and press interviews, winner ceremonies, doping control facility and the coordination with security for these areas. The collaboration is between the LOC's Finish Area Coordinator and persons managing the above areas, together with the FIS personnel handling equipment control, teams, accreditation and access, media, ceremonies and doping controls, from the planning stages through to implementation during the event.

601.3.9.2 The Chief of Course Equipment and Technical Equipment

The Chief of Course Equipment is responsible for the provision of equipment and tools needed for the preparation and maintenance of the competition courses and the conduct of the race, where these duties have not been assigned to another official.

601.3.9.3 The Chief of Press

The Chief of Press is responsible for all briefing and information provided to journalists, photographers, television and radio reporters, in accordance with the instructions of the Organising Committee.

601.3.9.1 终点区域主管

终点区域协调员负责整合对终点区域提出的各种要求，以处理在赛前、赛中及赛后终点区域的活动产生的任何需要。终点区域主管的职责为：创建和协调混合区域、电视和媒体采访、颁奖仪式、兴奋剂控制设施，并协调该区域的安全。

终点区域管理合作是建立在组委会委派的终点区域协调员和管理该区域的工作人员之间的，与国际雪联工作人员协同完成。他们在赛事计划阶段直至赛事执行过程中要处理竞赛器材检查、运动队管理、注册与准入、媒体、颁奖仪式和兴奋剂控制等各方面的工作。

601.3.9.2 赛道设备和技术设备主管（设备长）

设备长负责提供赛道准备和维护以及维持比赛的运行所需的设备和工具。上述职责中未指派给其他官员的，均应由设备长负责。

601.3.9.3 新闻媒体主管

新闻媒体主管根据组委会的指令，负责向新闻记者、摄影记者、电视和电台记者通报情况并为其提供信息。

601.3.9.4 The following additional officials are recommended:
- Chief of finance (treasurer);
- Chief of accommodation and meals;
- Chief of protocol.

The Organiser is authorised to include other officials within the Organising Committee.

601.4 The Jury

The following members of the Jury, who are members of the Organising Committee are responsible for technical matters within the closed competition areas (see job description World Cup Rules of the Race Directors and TD's for Olympic Winter Games, FIS World Ski Championships and World Cup):
- The Technical Delegate;
- The Referee;
- The Chief of Race;
- The Assistant Referee for Downhill and Super-G (and also for Slalom and Giant Slalom for Olympic Winter Games, FIS World Ski Championships and World Cup);
- The Start Referee (Olympic Winter Games and FIS World Ski Championships);
- The Finish Referee (Olympic Winter Games and FIS World Ski Championships).

601.4.1 Appointment of the Jury for Olympic Winter Games and FIS World Ski Championships

601.3.9.4 建议增设以下官员 ：
- 财务主管（司库）;
- 食宿主管 ;
- 礼宾主管。
组织方有权将其他官员纳入组委会。

601.4 仲裁委员会

组委会成员兼任的仲裁委员会以下成员，负责封闭的比赛场地内的技术性事务（参见《世界杯赛事总监规则》《冬季奥林匹克运动会、国际雪联世界滑雪锦标赛和国际雪联世界杯赛技术代表规则》中的职位说明）:

- 技术代表 ;
- 裁判长 ;
- 竞赛长 ;
- 滑降和超级大回转比赛项目的副裁判长（以及冬季奥林匹克运动会、国际雪联世界滑雪锦标赛和世界杯赛回转和大回转比赛项目的副裁判长）;
- 起点裁判长（冬季奥林匹克运动会和国际雪联世界锦标赛）;
- 终点裁判长（冬季奥林匹克运动会和国际雪联世界锦标赛）。

601.4.1 冬季奥林匹克运动会和国际雪联世界锦标赛仲裁委员会的任命

601.4.1.1 The FIS Council appoints:
- The Technical Delegate;
- The Referee;
- The Assistant Referee;
- The Start Referee;
- The Finish Referee.

601.4.1.2 The Sub-Committee for Alpine Technical Delegates proposes qualified TD's as Jury members to the Alpine Committee, who in turn submit the names to the FIS Council for approval.
In order to qualify, a proposed member must hold a valid licence as a Technical Delegate of the FIS.

601.4.1.3 The organising National Ski Association submits its proposals for the Chief of Race in the Organising Committee to the FIS Council for approval.

601.4.1.4 The Jury of a women race must include at least one woman.

601.4.1.5 All members of the Jury must be able to understand each other in one and the same FIS language.

601.4.1.6 Persons who work for a National Ski Association with responsibility for a ski team must not be members of the Jury.

601.4.1.7 For Olympic Winter Games and FIS World Ski Championships a visiting nation can be represented on the Jury

601.4.1.1 国际雪联理事会任命：
- 技术代表；
- 裁判长；
- 副裁判长；
- 起点裁判长；
- 终点裁判长。

601.4.1.2 高山滑雪技术代表分委员会向高山滑雪委员会推荐符合资格的技术代表为仲裁委员会成员，高山滑雪委员会将名单提请国际雪联理事会批准。

为取得资格，获得推荐的成员必须持有效的国际雪联技术代表证书。

601.4.1.3 组织比赛的国家滑雪协会向国际雪联理事会提交组委会竞赛长人选建议以待批准。

601.4.1.4 女子比赛的仲裁委员会必须包含至少一位女性成员。

601.4.1.5 仲裁委员会所有成员均须能够使用同一种国际雪联官方语言交流，以便相互理解。

601.4.1.6 在国家滑雪协会任职且对本国滑雪队负有职责者不得成为仲裁委员会成员。

601.4.1.7 对于冬季奥林匹克运动会和国际雪联世界滑雪锦标赛，观察员国只能由一名国际雪联理事会指定的成

by only one FIS Council appointed member (not including the TD).

601.4.2 Appointment of the Jury for International Races (World Cup: see World Cup Rules).

601.4.2.1 The Sub-Committee for Alpine Technical Delegates appoints the Technical Delegate.

601.4.2.2 The TD appoints

- the Referee, and for Downhill and Super-G, the Assistant Referee and substitutes Jury members in case of force majeure.

601.4.2.3 For international races for women the Jury should where possible include a woman.

601.4.2.4 The Chief of Race must belong to the organising National Ski Association.

601.4.3 Exclusions

601.4.3.1 A competitor cannot be a member of the Jury.

601.4.4 Tenure of the Jury

601.4.4.1 The appointed Jury members gather for their first meeting prior to the first Team Captain's meeting.

601.4.4.2 The active duty of the Jury begins with its first meeting

员（不包括技术代表）担任代表该国的仲裁委员会成员。

601.4.2 国际比赛仲裁委员会的任命（世界杯赛：参见《国际雪联世界杯规则》）。

601.4.2.1 高山滑雪技术代表分委员会任命技术代表。

601.4.2.2 技术代表任命

技术代表任命裁判长、滑降和超级大回转比赛项目的副裁判长，以及遇有不可抗力情势时仲裁委员会成员的替换人选。

601.4.2.3 如有可能，女子国际比赛的仲裁委员会中应包含一位女性成员。

601.4.2.4 竞赛长必须是组织方的国家滑雪协会成员。

601.4.3 例外事项

601.4.3.1 运动员不得担任仲裁委员会成员。

601.4.4 仲裁委员会的任期

601.4.4.1 获任仲裁委员会成员必须在第一次领队会议前举行第一次会议。

601.4.4.2 仲裁委员会自第一次会议开始履行职责，并在无人

and ends, if no protest is submitted, at the expiration of the protest deadline, otherwise after settlement of all submitted protests.

601.4.5 Franchise and Voting (World Cup: See also World Cup Rules)

The TD is Chair of the Jury and conducts the meetings. Each of the following has one vote in the Jury:

601.4.5.1 For Olympic Winter Games and FIS World Ski Championships, all Jury members.

601.4.5.2 For International races
The TD, Chief of Race, Referee and in the case of Downhill and Super-G, the Assistant Referee.

601.4.5.3 Decisions are made by simple majority vote of members present and voting (exception art. 646.3).

601.4.5.4 In the case of a tie, the TD has the casting vote (also see World Cup Rules).

601.4.5.5 Minutes must be kept of all meetings and decisions of the Jury and signed by each individual member of the Jury, with each individual vote on decisions recorded, as per art. 601.3.7.

601.4.5.6 The Minutes must be written in at least one of the FIS languages (English, French or German).

提出抗议时，于抗议期限届满时职责结束；否则，其职责需在处理完全部抗议后结束。

601.4.5 特权和表决权（世界杯：另参见《国际雪联世界杯规则》）
技术代表是仲裁委员会主任并主持会议。下列人员在仲裁委员会中各有 1 票表决权：

601.4.5.1 冬季奥林匹克运动会和国际雪联世界滑雪锦标赛的全体仲裁委员会成员。

601.4.5.2 国际比赛
国际比赛的技术代表、竞赛长、裁判长以及滑降和超级大回转比赛中的副裁判长。

601.4.5.3 由出席会议的成员按简单多数制投票形成决定（本规则第 646.3 条规定的除外）。

601.4.5.4 表决出现平局时，技术代表拥有最终决定权（另参见《国际雪联世界杯规则》）。

601.4.5.5 依照本规则第 601.3.7 条，必须保存由每位仲裁委员会成员签名的所有会议记录和仲裁委员会决定，并记录每位成员对决定的投票情况。

601.4.5.6 会议记录必须至少使用 1 种国际雪联官方语言（英语、法语或德语）。

601.4.5.7 In cases where an immediate decision must be made and it is not possible to convene the entire Jury, each member of the Jury has the right, prior to or during the race, to make decisions which according to the rules are reserved to the Jury as a whole; but only provisionally with the obligation to have the decision confirmed by the Jury as soon as possible.

601.4.6 Duties of the Jury

The Jury monitors the adherence to the rules throughout the entire race, including the official training.

601.4.6.1 From a technical standpoint particularly by:

- Checking the competition course and the set courses;
- Checking the snow conditions;
- Checking the preparation of the course;
- Approving the use of snow compactors and other chemicals;
- Checking the crowd control systems;
- Checking the start, the finish and the run-out from the finish;
- Checking the first aid service;
- Appointing the course setters;
- Fixing the time of course setting;
- Overseeing the work of the course setters;
- Spot-checking of the gate panels;
- Opening or closing competition courses for training after consideration of the technical preparations and the prevailing weather conditions;

601.4.5.7 必须立即作出决定但不可能召集仲裁委员会全体成员开会的，仲裁委员会每一位成员均有权在比赛前或比赛中行使根据规则本应由仲裁委员会作为一个整体保留的决定权；但只能作出临时性决定，仲裁委员会必须尽快追认。

601.4.6 仲裁委员会的职责

整个比赛过程中，包括场地适应训练期间，仲裁委员会始终负责监督比赛规则的遵守情况。

601.4.6.1 在技术方面，仲裁委员会主要负责：

- 检查赛道和旗门设计；
- 检查雪况；
- 检查赛道的准备工作；
- 批准使用压雪机及融雪剂等化学品；

- 检查观众管理系统；
- 检查出发区、终点区域和终点坡道延伸部分；

- 检查急救服务体系；
- 任命旗门设计员；
- 确定旗门设计时间；
- 监督旗门设计员的工作；
- 对旗门布进行抽检；
- 根据技术准备状况和当前天气情况，决定开放或关闭用于训练的赛道；

- Determining the method of the competitor's course inspection;
- Inspection of the course before the race;
- Determining the number of forerunners for each run and setting the start order of the forerunners;
- Debriefing the forerunners as necessary;
- Changing the start order after consideration of course conditions and in extraordinary conditions;
- Changing the start intervals;
- Giving instructions to and obtaining information from the gate judges.

For Downhill:

- Arrangement of an additional competitor's inspection in unusual weather conditions;
- Shortening the official training;
- Positioning of yellow flag;
- Checking on the setting of gates;
- Changing the position and distance of the gates or adding extra gates as indicated by the experience gained in the training runs. Following significant changes, the competitors must be allowed at least one more training run on the course.

601.4.6.2 From an organisational viewpoint particularly by:

- Ranking of the competitors for the draw;
- Division of the competitors without points into groups according to some determined basis;
- Granting of re-runs;
- Cancellation of the race (beforehand);

- 决定运动员视察线路的方式；

- 赛前视察线路；
- 决定每轮滑行的试滑员人数及出发顺序；

- 必要时要求试滑员汇报试滑情况；
- 根据赛道情况及特殊情况，改变出发顺序；

- 改变出发时间间隔；
- 指挥并听取旗门裁判员的汇报。

对于滑降比赛：
- 天气条件异常的，额外安排一次运动员视察线路；

- 缩短场地适应训练的时间；
- 确定黄旗的位置；
- 检查旗门设置情况；
- 根据在场地适应训练中获得的体验，调整旗门位置和间距，或者增加旗门数量。如调整较大，必须允许运动员再进行 1 次场地适应训练。

601.4.6.2 在组织方面，仲裁委员会主要负责：
- 安排运动员抽签顺序；
- 根据某些客观标准，对没有积分的运动员进行分组；
- 批准重滑；
- （基于如下情况，事先决定）取消比赛；

- if snow conditions are unsuitable;
- the recommendations of the Technical Advisor's report have not been carried out;
- the first aid and medical service are inadequate or missing;
- the crowd control is insufficient;
- Shortening the course, if snow or weather conditions make this appear necessary;
- Interruption of the race if the prerequisites of art. 624 are present;
- Termination of the race if the prerequisites of art. 625 are present.

601.4.6.3 From a disciplinary viewpoint particularly by:

- Decision on a proposal of the Technical Delegate or a Jury member to exclude a competitor for lack of physical and technical ability;
- Enforcement of the checks on regulations concerning advertising on equipment and clothing in the competition area;
- Decisions on limitation of quotas for officials, technicians and medical personnel for admission to the racecourse;
- Imposition of sanctions;
- Decisions on protests;
- Issue of particular directives throughout the entire event.

601.4.7 Questions not Covered by Rules

In general, the Jury makes decisions on all questions not clarified by the Rules.

- 雪况不适宜比赛；
- 未落实技术顾问报告中的建议；

- 急救和医疗服务不足或缺失；
- 观众管理工作不到位；
- 缩短赛道，如果雪况或天气条件表明这样做明显必要时；
- 暂停比赛，如果出现本规则第 624 条中的情况；

- 终止比赛，如果出现本规则第 625 条中的情况。

601.4.6.3 在纪律方面，仲裁委员会主要负责：

- 根据技术代表或仲裁委员会成员的建议，勒令身体条件和技能不足的运动员退出比赛；

- 在比赛场地实施对器材和服装上的广告是否合规的检查；
- 决定压缩进入赛道的官员、技术人员和医务人员的配额；

- 实施制裁；
- 裁断抗议；
- 在整个比赛期间发布特别指令。

601.4.7 《国际雪联滑雪竞赛规则》未涉及的问题

一般情况下，对于《国际雪联滑雪竞赛规则》未明确的问题，仲裁委员会有权作出决定。

601.4.8 **Radios**

At all competitions published in the FIS Calendar, the Jury members plus Start and Finish Referee must be equipped with radios. These must function on a single reserved frequency and be free of interference.

601.4.9 **Duties of the TD for all Events**

For FIS World Cup, FIS World Ski Championships and Olympic Winter Games the duties of the TDs are defined in the World Cup rules.

601.4.9.1 Before the race

The TD

- Reviews the homologation file and consults the organiser regarding the existence of a special authorisation;
- If it is established that no homologation exists, the Jury must cancel the race (see art. 650);
- Reads the TD reports concerning previous events at the site and checks whether any improvements proposed in these reports have been carried out;
- Inspects the liability insurance certificate as required by art. 212.2 and reports where necessary to the FIS;
- Inspects the competition courses;
- Supervises the compliance with art. 704 concerning the official training;
- Spot checks the gate panels;
- Collaborates in the administrative and technical preparations;
- Checks the official entry lists, including FIS points;

601.4.8 对讲机

在《国际雪联竞赛日历》中公布的所有比赛中，仲裁委员会成员以及起点和终点裁判长均需配备使用专属频率且不受干扰的对讲机。

601.4.9 技术代表在所有比赛中的职责

技术代表在国际雪联世界杯、国际雪联世界锦标赛和冬季奥林匹克运动会的职责，参见世界杯规则。

601.4.9.1 赛前职责

技术代表负责：

- 复审赛道认证文件，询问组织方赛道是否获得专门授权；
- 如果技术代表认为赛道未经认证，仲裁委员会必须取消该比赛（见本规则第 650 条）；
- 查阅该赛场以往赛事的技术代表报告，检查报告中提出的改进建议是否已经落实；

- 检查已经投保本规则第 212.2 条要求的责任保险的确认证明，必要时报告国际雪联；
- 视察赛道；
- 监督对本规则第 704 条关于场地适应训练之规定的遵守情况；
- 抽检旗门布；
- 协调赛事组织和技术准备工作；

- 检查正式报名表，特别是其中填报的国际雪联积分；

- Checks on the presence of sufficient radios for all members of the Jury (with separate frequencies);
- Takes note of the accreditation and the authorisation for entry to the competition course;
- Checks over the competition courses with regard to preparation, marking, crowd control, as well as the layout of start and finish areas;
- Supervises the course setting together with the Jury;
- Checks on the location of the television towers and sees that they are adequately protected if necessary;
- Checks the locations of the first aid service along the course as well as the organisation of the medical care;
- Checks on all technical installations such as timekeeping, hand timing, communications, transport of people, etc;
- Is present in the race area during all official trainings;
- Takes part in all meetings of the Jury and of the team captains;
- Works closely together with the officials of the Organising Committee and the FIS technical advisor;
- Is Chair of the Jury with a casting vote in case of a tie;
- If necessary, appoints members to the Jury;
- Has the right, if a Slalom or Giant Slalom cannot be carried out on the homologated competition course owing "force majeure" , to move the race to a "substitute competition course" proposed by the organiser.

This is on the explicit condition that the necessary homologation measures can be fulfilled. For Downhill and Super-G there is only the possibility of shortening the

- 检查是否为仲裁委员会所有成员准备了足够的对讲机（具备不同的频率）；
- 记录进入赛道的注册与授权情况；

- 检查赛道的准备、标识、观众管理以及起点、终点区的布置等情况；

- 会同仲裁委员会一起监督旗门的设计；
- 检查电视塔的位置，确保其在必要时得到妥善保护；
- 检查赛道沿线各急救站的位置和医疗服务的组织情况；
- 检查所有技术装置，如计时、手动计时、通讯、人员转运等；
- 所有场地适应训练期间应亲临比赛区域；
- 参加所有仲裁委员会会议和领队会议；

- 与组委会官员和国际雪联技术顾问在工作中密切合作；
- 担任仲裁委员会主任，并在表决出现平局时拥有最终决定权；
- 如有必要，任命仲裁委员会成员；
- 因“不可抗力”因素导致回转和大回转比赛不能在获得认证的赛道上进行时，有权根据组织者的建议，把比赛移到替补赛道上举行。这样做必须满足的明确条件是，替补赛道满足必要的认证措施。
  在滑降和超级大回转比赛中，只可以在批准的赛道上缩短比赛距离。但在任何情况下，均需确保达到规定的最小的垂直落差。

run on a homologated competition course.The minimum prescribed vertical drops must, however, be observed in every case.

601.4.9.2 During the race

The TD

- Must be present in the competition area;
- Works closely with the Jury, the team captains and the coaches;
- Observes that the valid rules and directives with regard to advertising, on clothing and race equipment are obeyed;
- Supervises the technical and organisational conduct of the event;
- Advises the organisation concerning the observance of the FIS Rules and regulations, and directives of the Jury.

601.4.9.3 After the race

The TD

- Helps with the compilation of the Referee' s report;
- Calculates the race and penalty points for the individual races. If these points are calculated by computer, it is the TD' s duty to re-check the points and to confirm their accuracy with a personal signature. Above all, it is important to check the correct use of the corresponding F value for each event;
- Presents properly submitted protests to the Jury for decision;
- Signs the official result lists provided by the race secretary and give the authorisation for the award ceremony;

601.4.9.2 比赛期间职责

在比赛期间，技术代表：

- 必须亲临比赛场地；
- 与仲裁委员会、领队和教练员在工作中密切合作；
- 确保关于比赛服装和竞赛器材上广告标识的有效规则和指令得到遵守；
- 监督比赛的技术与组织实施工作；
- 就遵守《国际雪联滑雪竞赛规则》及相关规定与仲裁委员会的指令向组织方建言献策。

601.4.9.3 赛后职责

比赛结束后，技术代表应当：

- 协助撰写裁判长报告；
- 计算比赛积分和判罚分。如果积分由电脑计算，技术代表的职责是复核积分，并在确认其准确性后签名。最重要的是检查本次比赛对应的 F 值是否运用正确；
- 将适当提出的抗议转交仲裁委员会裁决；
- 在竞赛秘书提供的正式成绩列表上签名，批准举行颁奖仪式；

- Oversees the electronic transmission of the Timing Report (TDTR) xml files and completes the TD Report online immediately after the event and must also check that the results are correct on the FIS website. For more information see Rules of the FIS points;
- Presents to the FIS proposals for changes in the competition rules on the basis of practical experience at the event in question.

601.4.9.4 In general

The TD

- Decides on questions which are not covered or are insufficiently covered by the FIS Rules, in so far as these have not already been decided by the Jury and do not fall within the scope of other authorities;
- Works very closely with the Referee and Assistant Referee;
- Has the right to propose to the Jury the exclusion of competitors from participating in the race;
- Has the right to obtain support from the Organising Committee and all officials under its jurisdiction in all matters necessary for the fulfilment of the TD'S duties.

601.4.9.5 Olympic Winter Games, FIS World Ski Championships and FIS Junior World Ski Championships

The TD prepares a detailed final report to be sent to the FIS and the Organising Committee.

601.4.10 Duties and Rights of the Referee

- The Referee supervises the draw;

- 监督《计时报告》（TDTR）及可扩展标记语言文件（XML）的电子传输工作，在赛事结束后立即在线完成《技术代表报告》，检查国际雪联网站上的成绩是否正确。详见《国际雪联积分规则》；

- 以本次比赛的实际经验为基础，向国际雪联提出修改比赛规则的建议。

601.4.9.4 一般职责

技术代表负责：

- 对于《国际雪联滑雪竞赛规则》没有涉及或涵盖不足的问题，若尚未由仲裁委员会作出决定，也不属于其他部门的职权范围，由技术代表作出决定；

- 与裁判长和副裁判长在工作中密切合作；
- 有权向仲裁委员会提议勒令运动员退出比赛；

- 在履行职责时，有权获得组委会和所有在组委会管辖权限范围内的官员就履行技术代表的职责所必需的支持。

601.4.9.5 冬季奥林匹克运动会、国际雪联世界滑雪锦标赛和国际雪联世界青少年锦标赛

技术代表准备详细的最终报告，提交国际雪联和组委会。

601.4.10 裁判长的职责与权利

- 裁判长监督抽签；

- At the end of the first run, and again at the end of the race, the Referee will receive the Start and Finish Referees' reports, and any other official reports regarding breach of rules and disqualifications;
- Checks, signs and posts the Referee's Report on the official notice board at the end of each run, and at the end of the race, including a list of disqualified competitors, the gate numbers where the faults occurred, the name of the relevant gate judge or judges, and the exact time of the posting;
- Sends a report to the FIS should unusual circumstances arise or in the event of a serious difference of opinion among the Jury members or in the case of severe injury to a competitor.

601.4.10.1 Collaboration with the TD

The Referee and the Assistant Referee work very closely with the TD.

601.4.11 The Technical Adviser

To support the Jury, the Alpine Committee can appoint technical advisers for all categories of races.

The technical adviser has the right to express an opinion within the Jury without the right to vote.

601.5 The FIS can impose sanctions against a Jury or individual Jury members

- 在第一轮滑行结束后和比赛结束后，裁判长负责接收起点、终点裁判长的报告及其他关于违反规则和取消资格的官方报告；

- 在每一轮滑行结束后和比赛结束后，裁判长要检查、签署裁判长报告单并张贴在官方公告板上。丧失资格运动员名单、发生失误的旗门号码、相关旗门裁判员的姓名及张贴的准确时间，均应在该报告单中体现出来；

- 出现特殊情况、仲裁委员会成员意见严重分歧或运动员受重伤时，应向国际雪联递交报告。

601.4.10.1 与技术代表合作

裁判长和副裁判长应与技术代表在工作中保持非常密切的合作。

601.4.11 技术顾问

为支持仲裁委员会的工作，高山滑雪委员会可以为各种比赛任命技术顾问。

技术顾问在仲裁委员会中有权发表意见，但无权表决。

601.5 国际雪联可以对仲裁委员会或其成员进行处罚

602 The Technical Delegate (TD)

602.1 Definition

602.1.1 The primary duties of the TD

- To make sure that the rules and directions of the FIS are followed;
- To see that the event runs smoothly;
- To advise the organisers about the scope of their duties;
- To be the official representative of the FIS.

602.1.2 Responsibility

The TD structure comes under the responsibility of the Alpine Committee.The Sub-Committee for Alpine Technical Delegates exercises this authority.

602.1.3 Prerequisites

The TD must hold a valid TD licence (exception see art. 602.3).

602.1.4 Development

602.1.4.1 The development of a TD is:

- Applicant;
- Observer at National Level FIS races;
- Oral entrance examination;
- Written entrance examination;
- Candidate;
- Practical examination (Downhill Event acting as the

602 技术代表（TD）

602.1 定义

602.1.1 技术代表的主要职责
- 确保国际雪联的规则和指示得到遵守；

- 确保比赛顺利进行；
- 就组织方的职责范围向其提出建议；
- 担任国际雪联的正式代表。

602.1.2 责任
技术代表的组织结构由高山滑雪委员会负责。高山滑雪技术代表分委员会行使该权力。

602.1.3 前提条件
技术代表须持有效的技术代表许可（例外情况参见本规则第602.3条）。

602.1.4 选拔

602.1.4.1 技术代表选拔过程如下：
- 申请；
- 成为国家级国际雪联比赛观察员；
- 口试；
- 笔试；
- 成为候选人；
- 实践考核（在滑降比赛中担任副裁判长）；

Assistant Referee);
- Practical examination (Giant Slalom or Slalom acting as TD);
- TD

The FIS recommends that the National Ski Associations apply a maximum age limit of 40 for applicants and 65 years for TD's (qualifying date: 1st July).

602.1.4.2 Each National Ski Association should nominate capable persons to train as a TD. The Sub-Committee for Alpine Technical Delegates has the final decision as to their acceptance.

602.1.5 Training

602.1.5.1 The basic training of the applicant is the responsibility of each National Ski Association.

602.1.5.2 Applicants must be nominated by their respective NSA.

First Year

- The applicants must attend the annual TD update course held by the NSA (June-July Southern Hemisphere, October-November Northern Hemisphere);
- Attend two FIS races held in their country in order to gain experience under the supervision of the TD Commissioner or an appointed representative;
- Complete official reports for these assignments and send them to their TD Commissioner, with copies to the FIS (in an official language);

- 实践考核（在大回转或回转比赛中担任技术代表）；

- 成为技术代表
国际雪联建议，国家滑雪协会对申请人的最高年龄限制为40岁,对技术代表的最高年龄限制为65岁(有效日期：7月1日)。

602.1.4.2　各国家滑雪协会应选拔本协会有能力的人员作为技术代表培养对象，高山滑雪技术代表分委员会有权最终决定是否接纳他们。

602.1.5　培训

602.1.5.1　申请人的基本培训由各国家滑雪协会负责。

602.1.5.2　申请人必须由其各自所属的国家滑雪协会提名。

第一年

- 申请人必须参加每年由国家滑雪协会举办的技术代表进修课程（南半球6月至7月，北半球10月至11月）；
- 参加两次在申请者本国举办的国际雪联比赛，以便在技术代表专员或指定的代表的监督下积累经验；

- 完成有关上述任务的正式报告，并将报告原件送交其所属的技术代表专员，同时将复印件送交国际雪联（使用一种国际雪联的官方语言）；

- At the end of the season the NSA applies to the FIS for official acceptance of the applicant, copy to the TD Commissioner.

Second Year

- The applicant must attend the annual national TD update;
- Must pass the written and oral entrance examination conducted in an official FIS language.

As a Candidate

Is assigned under the supervision of a TD Examiner (from another country) to a:

- Practical examination (Downhill event acting as the Assistant Referee);
- Practical examination (Giant Slalom or Slalom and acting as the TD);
- If an event consists of more than one competition the examination starts with the arrival according to 602.4.3 and has to be executed on the first competition day;
- Complete official reports for these assignments and send them to the TD Commissioner, with copies to the FIS (in an official language);
- The FIS Office will verify all the information from the different reports from the candidate and examiners and provide such details as necessary to the Sub-Committee for TDs;
- The Sub-Committee may decide not to issue a TD licence if the candidate has not completed all requirements or is deemed to be unsuitable. In this event the Sub-Committee may decide as to whether the candidate may continue to train as a FIS TD and which parts of the procedure have to be repeated;

- 在赛季末，国家滑雪协会向国际雪联申请正式接纳申请人，并将复印件发送技术代表专员。

第二年

- 申请人必须参加年度国家技术代表进修培训；
- 必须通过以国际雪联官方语言之一进行的笔试和口试。

作为候选人

被指派在技术代表审查员（来自另一国家）的监督下参加：

- 实践考核（滑降比赛中担任副裁判长）；

- 实践考核（在大回转或回转比赛中担任技术代表）；

- 如果一项赛事由多场比赛组成，则考核将从 602.4.3 规定的到达开始，且必须在第一个比赛日进行；

- 完成有关上述任务的正式报告，将报告原件送交其技术代表专员，同时将复印件送交国际雪联（使用一种官方语言）；
- 国际雪联办公室将对来自候选人和审查员的不同报告中的全部信息进行审查，并将必要的详细信息送交技术代表分委员会；
- 候选人未符合所有要求或被判定不符合资格的，分委员会有权决定不颁发技术代表许可。随后，分委员会有权决定候选人是否可以继续作为国际雪联技术代表的培养对象，以及哪些程序应该重来；

- If the candidates are considered to be suitable they will become official FIS Alpine Technical Delegates after the next TD update course.

602.1.5.3 At any event only one TD candidate may serve with a TD. Exceptions can be authorised by the FIS.

602.1.5.4 The assignment of the TD candidates is conducted, on proposal of the national responsible officials for TD questions, by the FIS, which also checks the performances of the individual candidates.

602.1.5.5 The TD candidate has no right to reimbursement of costs.

602.1.5.6 TDs are responsible for training the candidate assigned to them.

602.1.6 Licence

The licence is a numbered identification document valid for 12 months. It must be renewed each year and is obligatory for every TD.

602.1.7 Further Training and Expiration of Licence

Every licensed TD must take part annually in a further training course supervised by FIS. TDs will lose their licence if they miss two consecutive TD updates or miss two years' assignments and can show no good reason for their absence. To regain their licence they must once again undergo the TD Candidate procedures.

- 被认定合格的候选人参加完下一次技术代表进修课程后，成为正式的国际雪联高山滑雪技术代表。

602.1.5.3 每项赛事只能有 1 名技术代表候选人与 1 名技术代表一起工作。但国际雪联有权准予例外。

602.1.5.4 根据成员国家滑雪协会负责技术代表事务官员的建议，国际雪联实施技术代表候选人的配置工作，并检查各候选人的实际表现。

602.1.5.5 技术代表候选人无权要求报销费用。

602.1.5.6 技术代表负责培训分配给他的技术代表候选人。

602.1.6 **证书**

技术代表许可证书是一份编号的身份证明文件，有效期 12 个月。每位技术代表有义务每年更新其许可。

602.1.7 **继续培训与证书有效期**

每位持证的技术代表必须参加每年由国际雪联督办的培训课程。如果连续 2 次未参加培训或 2 年未被委任工作，且无缺席的正当理由，技术代表将失去其许可。若想重新获得许可，须按技术代表候选人的选拔程序重新申请。

602.2 Appointment

602.2.1 For Olympic Winter Games, FIS World Ski Championships and FIS Junior World Ski Championships the appointment is made by the FIS Council on recommendation of the Alpine Committee.

602.2.2 For all other competitions, the appointment is made by the Sub-Committee for Alpine Technical Delegates.

602.2.3 An exception is made for Youth, CIT, Masters, World Cup DAR, DAR, CISM, Customs and UNI races, for which the TD's are proposed by the Sub-Committee in question and confirmed by the Sub-Committee for Alpine Technical Delegates.

602.2.4 A TD cannot be member of the organising association. In exceptional cases the Sub-Committee for Alpine Technical Delegates may appoint a TD from the same country. The TD must, however, not be a member of the organising club or of the regional association.

602.3 TD Replacement

602.3.1 If the TD for Olympic Winter Games, FIS World Ski Championships or FIS Junior World Ski Championships is unable to serve, the FIS Council as well as the National Ski Association to which the TD belongs must be notified. The FIS Council must appoint another TD immediately.

602.2 技术代表的任命

602.2.1 冬季奥林匹克运动会、国际雪联世界锦标赛和国际雪联世界青少年锦标赛的技术代表由高山滑雪委员会推荐，国际雪联理事会任命。

602.2.2 所有其他比赛的技术代表由高山滑雪技术代表分委员会任命。

602.2.3 作为例外，青少年赛、公民赛、大师赛、残疾人世界杯赛、残疾人赛、国际军人运动理事会的赛事和大学生赛等比赛的技术代表，由上述有关分委员会提名，由高山滑雪技术代表分委员会确认。

602.2.4 技术代表不能是赛事组织方国家滑雪协会会员。
特殊情况下，高山滑雪技术代表分委员会可以从赛事组织方国家滑雪协会会员中任命 1 名技术代表。但该技术代表不得是作为赛事组织方的俱乐部或地区滑雪协会的会员。

602.3 技术代表的更换

602.3.1 冬季奥林匹克运动会、国际雪联世界锦标赛或国际雪联世界青少年滑雪锦标赛的技术代表不能履职的，应通知国际雪联理事会以及该技术代表所属国家滑雪协会。国际雪联理事会须立即另任命一名技术代表。

602.3.2 For all other races the National Ski Association to which the TD belongs is responsible for the immediate appointment of a replacement. The Organising Committee in question and the FIS are to be informed immediately.

602.3.3 If for unforeseen reasons, a TD for the Olympic Winter Games or FIS World Ski Championships does not arrive or arrives too late at a competition and is thereby partly or completely unable to fulfil his/her function at the competition, a deputy is to be named by the FIS Council from amongst the members of the Jury present at the competition site.

602.3.4 At all other international races, a deputy for the absent TD is to be named on the spot by the Jury. The replacement must likewise meet the requirements of art. 602.1.6.

In an emergency, a TD can also be named who does not meet these requirements, but is competent to ensure the conduct (or continuation) of the race. Stringent criteria must be applied when choosing this person.

602.3.5 The replacement TD has the same rights and duties as the TD originally appointed.

602.4 Organisation of the Assignments

602.4.1 The TD must establish early contact with the Organiser.

602.3.2 在所有其他比赛中，不能履职的技术代表所属国家滑雪协会负责立即指派一名接替者，并应立即通知相关组委会和国际雪联。

602.3.3 因无法预料的原因，冬季奥林匹克运动会和国际雪联世界锦标赛的技术代表未能或很晚抵达比赛赛场，以致不能完成其在比赛中的部分或全部工作任务的，国际雪联理事会可以从已抵达比赛现场的仲裁委员会成员中指派一位代理技术代表。

602.3.4 在所有其他国际比赛中技术代表缺席的，仲裁委员会可以当场任命代理技术代表。代理技术代表须符合本规则第 602.1.6 条要求。

在紧急情况下，也可以任命一位不符合上述条件但有能力保证比赛进行（或继续）的技术代表。选择这样的人选时应采用严格的标准。

602.3.5 代理技术代表具有与原技术代表同样的权利与义务。

602.4 赛事组织工作的安排

602.4.1 技术代表必须尽早与组织方建立联系。

602.4.2 Cancellations or postponements of events must be announced to the TD and to the FIS immediately, taking into account any applicable deadlines.

602.4.3 For Downhill and Super-G, the TD must arrive at the competition site at least 48 hours before the draw for the first training. In all other events this must be at least 24 hours before the draw for the event concerned.

602.5 Expense Accounts

The TD[2] has a right to reimbursement for travel expenses up to a maximum of CHF 600.--[1] (highway taxes included), as well as free accommodation and meals during the assignment. This rule also applies to agreed inspections as well as the trip to the competition (train, first class; for longer distances air fare, tourist class; or payment of a per kilometre fee of CHF 0.70 or equivalent).

In addition a fixed daily rate of CHF 100. -- is added for the travel days to and from, as well as each day of the assignment, which includes postage charges for mailing reports, etc. Double charges (e.g. travelling home on the same day as the last race) are not permitted. If overnight accommodation during the journey to and from the assignment is necessary, this must be justified and reimbursed separately.

[1] The maximum payment of CHF 600. -- is valid for all races except Olympic Winter Games, World Cup and Continental Cup.

602.4.2 如需取消或延期比赛，必须立即通报技术代表和国际雪联，同时要考虑可适用的期限。

602.4.3 在滑降和超级大回转比赛中，技术代表必须至少在第一次训练的抽签前 48 小时到达比赛场地。在所有其他比赛项目中，必须至少在相关比赛抽签前 24 小时到达比赛场地。

602.5 费用账目

技术代表[2)]有权报销交通费,最高为 600 瑞士法郎[1)]（含高速公路费），履职期间的食宿免费。这项规则也适用于经双方同意的视察及相应的到比赛场地的旅行（火车头等车厢；长途飞行经济舱；或付给每公里 0.70 瑞士法郎或等值货币）。

另外还须支付固定的每日（包括履职的每一天以及往返旅行日）100 瑞士法郎的履职补助费，其中包括邮寄工作报告的邮费等。不得重复支付费用（如在比赛最后一天就回到了家）。往返旅途中的过夜住宿费必须正当合理，并单独报销。

[1)] 最高支付 600 瑞士法郎。适用于除冬季奥林匹克运动会、世界杯和洲际杯外的所有比赛。

2) This rule applies to all jury members at the Olympic Winter Games and FIS World Championships.

603 Course Setter

603.1 Prerequisites

603.1.1 For Olympic Winter Games, FIS World Ski Championships and World Cup:
- nomination by the National Ski Association team captain to the Coaches Working Group and;
- proof of appropriate experience in the setting of courses for World Cup events, Olympic Winter Games or FIS World Ski Championships.

603.1.2 For all other competitions entered in the FIS Calendar:
- Continental Cup: Nomination from National Ski Associations to Cup Coordinators or Working Group;
- All other events in the FIS Calendar: Nomination through the Jury or Organising Committee.

603.1.3 For Downhill's, the course setter must be familiar with the particular competition course.

603.2 Appointment

603.2.1 For Olympic Winter Games, FIS World Ski Championships and World Cups, the appointment is made after examination by the Chief Race Director.

2) 本条适用于冬季奥林匹克运动会和国际雪联世界锦标赛的所有仲裁委员会成员。

603 旗门设计员

603.1 先决条件

603.1.1 对于冬季奥林匹克运动会、国际雪联世界锦标赛和世界杯：
- 由国家滑雪协会领队向赛会竞赛组提名；
- 证明有在世界杯、冬季奥林匹克运动会和国际雪联世界锦标赛旗门设计的实践经验。

603.1.2 对于纳入《国际雪联竞赛日历》中的所有其他比赛：
- 洲际杯：由国家滑雪协会向赛会竞赛组提名；
-《国际雪联竞赛日历》所有其他比赛：通过仲裁委员会或组委会提名。

603.1.3 滑降比赛中，旗门设计员须熟悉具体赛道。

603.2 任命

603.2.1 冬季奥林匹克运动会、国际雪联世界锦标赛和国际雪联世界杯，由单项竞赛总主任考核后任命。

603.2.2 For European Cup, the EC Coordinator appoints the course setters.

603.2.3 For all other competitions included in the FIS Calendar, the appointment is made by the Jury. For competitions consisting of two runs, each run is to be set by a different course setter. One of the two course setters may be named by the organiser.

603.3 Supervision of the Course Setters

603.3.1 The work of the course setters is supervised by the Jury.

603.4 Organisation of the Assignment

For Olympic Winter Games, FIS World Ski Championships and World Cup races the course setter assignment is managed by the Chief Race Director. For European Cup races the course setter assignment is managed by the EC Coordinator. For all remaining races the assignment is managed by the Jury.

603.5 Replacement of Course Setters

603.5.1 For Olympic Winter Games and FIS World Ski Championships, the Chief Race Director names a replacement course setter immediately, details of which are published by the FIS Office.

603.5.2 For all other competitions entered in the FIS Calendar,

603.2.2　欧洲杯，由其杯赛协调员任命。

603.2.3　《国际雪联竞赛日历》其他所有国际比赛，由仲裁委员会任命。比赛包括两轮滑行的，每轮滑行的线路应由不同的旗门设计员设计，其中的一名可由组织方任命。

603.3　对旗门设计员的监督

603.3.1　旗门设计员的工作由仲裁委员会监督。

603.4　责任分工的安排

冬季奥林匹克运动会、国际雪联世界滑雪锦标赛和世界杯的旗门设计员的职责分工由竞赛总主任负责。欧洲杯的旗门设计员的职责分工由欧洲杯协调员负责，其余所有比赛由仲裁委员会负责。

603.5　旗门设计员的递补

603.5.1　在冬季奥林匹克运动会和国际雪联世界锦标赛中，递补旗门设计员由竞赛总主任立即任命，具体内容由国际雪联办公室发布。

603.5.2　对于其他纳入《国际雪联竞赛日历》中的所有比赛，

the Jury names a replacement course setter.

603.5.3 The replacement course setter should have the same qualifications as the original course setter.

603.6 Rights of the Course Setter

603.6.1 To recommend the introduction of changes in the competition terrain and in the safety measures.

603.6.2 Availability of a sufficient number of helpers for the setting of the course, so that the course setter can concentrate solely on the course setting.

603.6.3 Provision of all necessary materials by the chief of course equipment.

603.6.4 Immediate completion of the finishing touches to the race course.

603.7 Duties of the Course Setter

603.7.1 In order to set the course appropriately, respecting the terrain, the snow cover and the ability of the participating competitors, the course setter conducts a pre-inspection of the race terrain in the presence of the TD, the Referee, the Chief of Race, and the Chief of Course.

603.7.2 The course setter sets the course respecting the existing safety measures and course preparation. The course setter

由仲裁委员会任命递补旗门设计员。

603.5.3　递补旗门设计员应具备与原旗门设计员相同的资质。

603.6　旗门设计员的权利

603.6.1　有权建议对旗门的地形和安全设施进行调整。

603.6.2　为使旗门设计员集中精力只进行旗门设计，必须为其提供足够多的助手来具体落实旗门设计。

603.6.3　设备长应提供所有必需品。

603.6.4　及时完成旗门设计的收尾工作。

603.7　旗门设计员的职责

603.7.1　为合理设计比赛线路，要考虑地形、积雪、参赛运动员的滑雪技能等情况，旗门设计员应和技术代表、裁判长、竞赛长、赛道长一起预视察赛道的地形。

603.7.2　旗门设计员设计比赛线路应考虑现有的安全措施和赛道的前期准备工作，必须考虑速度的控制。

must take speed control into consideration.

603.7.3 All courses must be set according to the ICR.

603.7.4 The courses must be set and ready in time, so that the competitors are not disturbed during course inspection.

603.7.5 The course setters should take care that the difference between the winning times of each run of Slalom and Giant Slalom will not be too great.

603.7.6 The course setting is a task of the course setter alone, who is responsible for adhering to the rules of the ICR and may be advised by members of the Jury, and by the technical advisor in Downhill and Super-G, if present.

603.7.7 The course setters must participate in all team captains' meetings at which a report is to be made about the course.

603.8 Arrival at the Race Site

603.8.1 For Downhill and Super-G races, this should be no later than the morning of the day of the first team captains' meeting, so that if required any additional course preparation or safety measures can be implemented.

603.8.2 For Slalom and Giant Slalom races if possible this should be the day before, but always before the first team captains' meeting.

603.7.3 所有比赛线路的设计必须按照《国际雪联滑雪竞赛规则》进行设计。

603.7.4 比赛线路要按时完成设计并准备就绪，以免干扰运动员视察线路。

603.7.5 旗门设计员应该注意，回转和大回转每一轮滑行中获胜者用时的差别不宜太大。

603.7.6 旗门设计是旗门设计员本人的任务，必须遵守《国际雪联滑雪竞赛规则》，仲裁委员会成员、滑降和超级大回转技术顾问如果在场，可以向旗门设计员提出建议。

603.7.7 旗门设计员须参加每次领队会议，并在会上报告比赛线路的设计情况。

603.8 到达比赛场所

603.8.1 对于滑降和超级大回转比赛，旗门设计员应不迟于召开第一次领队会议的当天早晨到达比赛场地，以便在需要时进行额外的赛道准备或安全措施调整等工作。

603.8.2 对于回转和大回转比赛，如有可能，旗门设计员应再提前一天到达比赛场地，但必须早于第一次领队会议。

604 Accreditation / Rights and Duties of Team Officials

604.1 Officials, Medical* and Technical Personnel

Quotas for the right of access to the closed race course:

- Up to 3 competitors: 3 trainers 2 doctors* 2 technicians;

- 4 or 5 competitors: 4 trainers 2 doctors* 3 technicians;

- 6 to 10 competitors: 5 trainers 2 doctors* 4 technicians

As well as representatives of the FIS in an official capacity. These quotas include the national team officials (team captains, etc.).

These persons must be identified by armband or another clearly visible accreditation. If necessary, the Jury can reduce these quotas, Cup Rules can determine special quotas. The persons accredited according to art. 220.3 and 220.5, as well as the official technicians and medical personnel must comply with the directions of the officials charged by the organisers with responsibility for overall security (e.g.: stewards, police, etc.).

The instructions given by the Jury to accredited journalists, coaches and team captains have priority in all cases.

*) Medical personnel includes doctors, physiotherapists, first aid people etc.

604.2 Team Captains and Trainers

The team captains and trainers must be accredited by the organisers according to quota. The accreditation gives

604 随队官员的注册及其权利与职责

604.1 官员、医务人员*和技术人员

有权进入封闭赛道的人员配额：
- 不足 3 名参赛运动员的：3 名教练员、2 名医生*、2 名技术人员；
- 4 到 5 名参赛运动员：4 名教练员、2 名医生*、3 名技术人员；
- 6 到 10 名参赛运动员：5 名教练员、2 名医生*、4 名技术人员。

以及具备官方身份的国际雪联代表。
上述配额包括国家队官员（领队等）。
所有获得配额的人员须佩戴袖章或其他显著的用于识别的注册证件。如有必要，仲裁委员会可以减少上述配额，国际雪联的杯赛规则可设定特别配额。
依照本规则第 220.3 条和第 220.5 条注册的人员以及官方技术人员和医务人员，须服从组织方委任的负责整体安全的官员（管理人员、警察等）的指挥。

仲裁委员会给注册记者、教练员及领队下达的指令在任何情况下都应当优先遵守。
* 医务人员包括医生、理疗师、急救人员等。

604.2 领队和教练员

领队和教练员必须根据配额由组织方注册，注册后赋予如下权利和义务：

the following rights and duties:

- To be a member of the Jury;
- To be nominated as a competition official if these have not been appointed by the FIS or if the appointed person is not present;
- To be issued with a lift pass or armband during the training or competition (or reimbursement for costs if a lift pass has not been provided);
- To be issued with a pass or armband stating the function or written "Competition Course".

604.2.1 Team captains and trainers must obey the ICR and the decisions of the Jury, and must behave in a proper and sportsmanlike manner.

604.2.2 Team captains or trainers must fulfil the duties they have accepted as a member of the Jury, or as a course setter.

604.3 Team Captains Meetings and Draw

In accordance with ICR 213.4 and 216 the time and location of the first team captain's meeting and of the draw must be shown in the program.

An actual meeting, attended in person or held online, by team captains, jury, and race officials is an inseparable part of the competition and is important for communication of jury instructions, support of the OC, OC requests and information as well as a critical element for risk management and liability related matters. Art. 216 and 217 apply in all cases.

- 成为仲裁委员会成员；
- 本人尚未获得国际雪联任命或获得任命之人不在场的，可被提名为竞赛官员；

- 在训练或比赛期间获得缆车通行证或臂章（未提供缆车通行证的，报销缆车费）；

- 获颁通行证或臂章，注明其职能或写上“赛道”字样。

604.2.1 领队及教练员必须遵守《国际雪联滑雪竞赛规则》和仲裁委员会的决定;必须举止得体，具有运动员风范。

604.2.2 领队或教练员被接纳为仲裁委员会成员或旗门设计员的，必须履行其应尽的义务。

604.3 领队会议和抽签

依照本规则第 213.4 条和第 216 条，第一次领队会议及抽签的时间和地点必须在秩序册上写明。

由领队、仲裁委员会委员和竞赛官员本人实际参加或在线参加的会议，是比赛不可分割的一部分，对传达仲裁委员会的指令、支持组委会、通报组委会的要求和信息等都具有重要的意义，也是风险管理和有关责任事项的关键因素。本规则第 216 条和第 217 条规定适用于所有情况。

604.4 Entries and Draw

604.4.1 The Organiser must determine the final date of entry (art. 213.8) between 24 h and 48 h (art. 215.1) before the first Team Captains'Meeting.

604.4.2 A Team Captain may only make substitutions before the Draw.

604.4.3 The event programme as determined in art. 213 must be published on the FIS website alpine competition calendar.

605 Forerunners

605.1 The organiser is obliged to provide at least three forerunners who have signed the FIS Athletes Declaration. The forerunner is a member of the Organising Committee. In Downhill, the forerunners should participate in all training runs. In extraordinary conditions, the Jury may increase the number of forerunners.
The Jury may designate different forerunners for each run.

605.2 The forerunners must wear forerunners' start numbers (bibs).

605.3 The nominated forerunners should have the skiing ability to ski the course in a racing manner.

605.4 Forerunners are not permitted to start in the competition.

605.5 The Jury determines the forerunners and their start order. After an interruption of the race additional forerunners

604.4 **报名与抽签**

604.4.1 组织方必须在首次领队会议前 24 至 48 小时（本规则第 215.1 条）确定报名截止日期（本规则第 213.8 条）。

604.4.2 替换领队只能在抽签前进行。

604.4.3 本规则第 213 条确定的比赛项目秩序册必须在国际雪联官网高山滑雪竞赛日历中公布。

605 试滑员

605.1 组织者有义务提供至少 3 名已签署国际雪联《运动员宣言》的试滑员，试滑员是组委会的成员。在滑降比赛中，试滑员须参加所有轮次的滑行训练。在特殊情况下，仲裁委员会可以增加试滑员的人数。

仲裁委员会可以为每轮滑行指定不同的试滑员。

605.2 试滑员必须佩戴试滑员出发号码（号码布）。

605.3 被任命的试滑员应具备以比赛方式滑完全程的滑雪能力。

605.4 试滑员不得再参加相应比赛。

605.5 仲裁委员会确定每轮滑行的试滑员及其出发顺序。比赛暂停后，如果需要可额外增加试滑员。

may be authorised as necessary.

605.6 The times of the forerunners should not be published.

605.7 Upon request the forerunners must report to members of the Jury regarding the snow conditions, the visibility and the race line, as the case requires

606 Competitors' Equipment (see also Specifications for Alpine Competition Equipment)

606.1 Equipment Rules

For more details, see ICR, art. 222 and following and the FIS Specifications Commercial Markings on Equipment and Advertising Rules.

606.2 Competition Suits

606.2.1 For all Alpine Events (except Slalom) at all FIS levels, competition suits must conform to the specifications for competition equipment.

606.2.2 At all Alpine Events (except Slalom), the competition suit for Olympic Winter Games, FIS World Ski Championships, FIS World Cup (level 0), FIS Continental Cups, Universiade and FIS World Junior Championships (level 1) must have a label attesting conformity with FIS specifications for competition suits.

605.6 试滑员的滑行时间不应公布。

605.7 试滑员必须根据要求向仲裁委员会成员报告雪况、能见度和赛道线路等情况。

606 运动员竞赛器材

另见《高山滑雪竞赛器材具体规定》

606.1 竞赛器材规则

详见本规则第 222 条及其后内容以及《国际雪联竞赛器材上的商业标识具体规定》《国际雪联广告规则》。

606.2 比赛服装

606.2.1 国际雪联所有级别的高山滑雪比赛（回转比赛除外）中，比赛服装必须符合有关竞赛器材的具体规定。

606.2.2 所有高山滑雪比赛（回转比赛除外）中，参加冬季奥林匹克运动会、国际雪联世界锦标赛、国际雪联世界杯（0 级）、国际雪联洲际杯、世界大学生运动会以及国际雪联世界青少年锦标赛（1 级）的比赛服装必须带有证明符合国际雪联比赛服装具体规定的标签。

For level 0 and 1, athletes with competition suits without label will not be permitted to start (art. 627.2).

606.2.3 In this case or when a doubt exists concerning subsequent modification of a racing suit or if there is a protest, and if there is no official FIS Equipment Controller appointed, the following procedure must be followed:
Following recognition of one of the above circumstances the racing suit is immediately marked. At the end of the race the TD must confiscate this competition suit and send it to the FIS for control.

606.2.4 Official FIS Equipment Controller present at competitions and appointed for suit controls by the Committee for Competition Equipment has the right to make re-examinations on site.

606.3 Ski Brakes

For competitions and official training only skis with ski brakes must be used. Competitors without ski brakes are not allowed to start.

606.4 Helmets

In all events all competitors and forerunners are obliged to wear crash helmets that conform to the Specifications for Alpine Competition Equipment.

606.5 Start Numbers (Bibs)

All competitors must wear the official start numbers

参加 0 级及 1 级比赛的运动员的比赛服装没有上述标签的不得出发（参见本规则第 627.2 条。）

606.2.3 对比赛服装的后续改动存在疑问、有人提出抗议或者不是指定的正式国际雪联竞赛器材检查员的，必须遵循以下程序：

确认发生以上任一情况后，应立即在该件比赛服装上做标记。比赛结束后，技术代表应没收这件比赛服装，并交国际雪联核查。

606.2.4 竞赛器材检查员是竞赛器材委员会任命的负责服装检查的正式官员，在其莅临比赛现场时有权当场对比赛服装进行复查。

606.3 滑雪板制动器

在比赛和场地适应训练中，必须使用带有制动器的滑雪板，否则禁止出发。

606.4 头盔

所有比赛项目的全体运动员和试滑员都必须穿戴符合《高山滑雪竞赛器材具体规定》的防护头盔。

606.5 出发号码（号码布）

所有参赛运动员比赛时必须佩戴正式出发号码（号

(Bibs) during the race. For the design of bibs and the commercial imprints see specifications in the FIS Advertising Rules. All bibs used during a single competition must have the same shape and size lettering and attachment method must not be altered.

606.6 Advertising

Advertising on material and equipment which is worn during races and training must conform to the FIS Specifications for Competition Equipment and Commercial Markings.

607 Age Limits

607.1 The FIS competition year is July 1st - June 30th of the following year.

In order to compete in international competitions (except U16 - U14 competitions) a competitor must be no younger than age group U18.

607.2 International junior competitions are restricted to U18 and U21 age group. (Exception National Junior Championship).

607.3 Classification at International Competitions

Admitted years of birth

码布）。出发号码布的设计和其上商业广告的印制，参见《国际雪联广告规则》。每一赛事所用出发号码布必须统一形状和字体尺寸，佩戴方式不得改动。

606.6 **广告**

训练和比赛期间使用的材料和竞赛器材上的广告，必须符合《国际雪联竞赛器材与商业标识具体规定》。

607 年龄限制

607.1 国际雪联比赛年度为 7 月 1 日至次年 6 月 30 日。

参加国际比赛的运动员的年龄不得低于 U18 年龄组（U16—U14 比赛除外）。

607.2 国际青少年比赛仅限于 U18 和 U21 年龄组（国家级青少年锦标赛除外）。

607.3 **国际比赛中的年龄分组**

准许参赛的出生年份

FIS Competition Year	21/22	22/23
U14	2009	2010
	2008	2009
U16	2007	2008
	2006	2007
U18	2005	2006
	2004	2005
U21	2003	2004
	2002	2003
	2001	2002
Licensed	2005 and earlier	2006 and earlier
Masters A (Men)	1991 to 1967	1992 to 1968
Masters B (Men)	1966 and earlier	1967 and earlier
Masters C (Women)	1991 and earlier	1992 and earlier

608 Youth International Alpine Competitions

608.1 Approval by the FIS

International U16 - U14 competitions are to be approved by the FIS and published in the FIS Calendar.

608.2 TD Assignment

TD's are proposed by the Youth Sub-Committee and are to be confirmed by the Sub-Committee for Alpine Technical Delegates. (art. 602.2.3)

608.3 Age Limits

International U16 - U14 competitions are restricted to U14 and U16 age group. Each competitor at U16 - U14

比赛年度	2021/2022 年度	2022/2023 年度
U14	2009 年 2008 年	2010 年 2009 年
U16	2007 年 2006 年	2008 年 2007 年
U18	2005 年 2004 年	2006 年 2005 年
U21	2003 年 2002 年 2001 年	2004 年 2003 年 2002 年
持证运动员	2005 年及以前	2006 年及以前
大师 A（男子）	1991 年至 1967 年	1992 年至 1968 年
大师 B（男子）	1966 年及以前	1967 年及以前
大师 C（女子）	1991 年及以前	1992 年及以前

608 国际青少年高山滑雪比赛

608.1 经国际雪联批准

国际 U16—U14 比赛由国际雪联批准并在《国际雪联竞赛日历》中公布。

608.2 技术代表的任命

青少年比赛的技术代表由青少年分委员会提名、高山滑雪技术代表分委员会确认（本规则第 602.2.3 条）。

608.3 年龄限制

国际 U16—U14 比赛仅限 U14 和 U16 年龄组运动员参赛。U16—U14 赛事每位参赛者都要出具官方文件

events has to prove their year of birth with an official document (Identity card, passport). The year of birth has to be mentioned on the race entry. Admitted years of birth, see art. 607.3.

608.4 Quota regulations

608.4.1 The quota per nation is max. 4 (four) U14 and 6 (six) U16 resulting in the total number of max. 10 competing athletes per nation. No more than 4 (four) athletes of the same gender may be registered within each category. The organising nation is entitled to a double quota that is maximum 20 competing athletes. In case of events within multiple races the quota is for the event and not for the race.

608.4.2 Under normal circumstances, the max. number of competing athletes must not exceed 140 per category and gender.

608.4.3 Pursuant to Rules of the FIS Alpine Points, the organising nation may register more than the double quota of participants other nations may also register more than the double quota, by invitation.

608.4.4 If the organising nation is unable to fill their legitimate quota other nations may be invited to participate with a double quota, at the invitation of the organising nation.

（身份证、护照）证明其出生年份。报名参赛时必须注明出生年份。准许参赛年份参见本规则第607.3条。

608.4 配额规定

608.4.1 各国配额最多4名U14和6名U16，即每个国家最多10名运动员参赛。每一组别的注册人数中，性别相同的运动员不得超过4名。主办国有权获得最多20名参赛运动员的双倍配额。如果赛事包括多个比赛项目（小项），配额是针对比赛项目（小项），而不是针对该赛事。

608.4.2 通常情况下，参加每个比赛项目的每个组别和性别的运动员不能超过140人。

608.4.3 根据《国际雪联高山滑雪积分规则》，比赛组织国可以注册多于2倍配额的参赛运动员；通过邀请，其他国家也可以注册多于2倍配额的参赛运动员。

608.4.4 比赛组织国参赛运动员未能凑满配额的，其他国家应比赛组织国的邀请，可以2倍配额的运动员参赛。

608.5 Allotment into groups and start order

608.5.1 In each group each participating nation is allotted one starting place max.

608.5.2 If more than 15 nations have registered, the following principles apply:

> Group 1: The first group will contain one athlete from each nation registered. Each nation is allotted one start place only.

> Group 2 - 3 - 4: Same as group 1.

> Last group: The last group consists of athletes from the organising nation, with its double quota. If the total number of competing athletes is thereby exceeded, a separate last group will be formed, using the same procedure as in Group 1.

608.5.3 In U16 - U14 races with few participants (see art. 608.5.4), the draw follows the principles described for the double quota of organising nations.

608.5.4 The team leaders are responsible for the identification of participants in each group.

608.5.5 Each group is drawn separately.

608.5.6 Start order 2nd runs - The best 30 of the 1st run start in the reversed order.

608.5.7 Specific starting orders approved by the Youth and

608.5 分组和出发顺序

608.5.1 每组每个参赛国最多分得 1 个出发位置。

608.5.2 注册参赛国家超过 15 个的，适用如下原则：

>第 1 组：包含每个注册参赛国家的 1 名运动员。每个国家只能分得 1 个出发位置。

>第 2—3—4 组：同第 1 组。

>最后 1 组：由拥有 2 倍配额的组织方国家的运动员组成。参赛运动员的总数因此超额的，采用与第 1 组相同的程序另外建立一个最后 1 组。

608.5.3 在参赛人数较少的 U16—U14 比赛中（参见本规则第 608.5.4 条），抽签遵循组织方国家拥有双倍配额的原则。

608.5.4 队伍管理者负责每一组别运动员的身份确认工作。

608.5.5 各组单独抽签。

608.5.6 第 2 轮滑行出发顺序：第 1 轮滑行成绩前 30 名选手倒序出发。

608.5.7 经青少年和儿童分委员会批准的特别出发顺序，可

Children's Sub-Committee can be used and sent with the invitation by each Organising Committee.

608.6 U16 – U14 Events

608.6.1 U16 - U14 events may include Slalom, Giant Slalom, Super-G, Parallel, Kombi events, team competition (e.g. Mixed Team Parallel).

608.6.2 Except where noted in ICR 608 for Youth the Alpine Rules in ICR are to be followed.

608.6.3 Team competitions may be conducted for U14 and U16. Such team competitions should be described as "Specifications for Youth Team Competitions".

608.6.3.1 For the team evaluation, only the team declared at the first team captains meeting as "A" will be considered.

608.7 Equipment

608.7.1 All equipment used by Youth is governed by the FIS Specifications for Competition Equipment.

608.7.2 Youth are required to wear a crash helmet that conforms to the FIS Specifications for Competition Equipment.

608.8 Parallel Events

The FIS ICR for the running of Parallel (art. 1220) applies.

由各组委会使用并在发出邀请时随附。

608.6 U16—U14 赛事

608.6.1 U16—U14 比赛项目可包括回转、大回转、超级大回转、平行式比赛、组合赛、团体赛（如混合队式平行式比赛）。

608.6.2 应当遵守《国际雪联竞赛规则》第 608 条有关青少年高山滑雪的例外规定。

608.6.3 U14 和 U16 可以组织团体比赛。这种团体赛应称为“青年团体特别赛”。

608.6.3.1 团队评估只考虑在第一次团队领队会议上宣布为“A”的团队。

608.7 竞赛器材

608.7.1 青少年比赛使用的所有竞赛器材均受《国际雪联竞赛器材具体规定》的约束。

608.7.2 青少年运动员必须穿戴符合《国际雪联竞赛器材具体规定》防护头盔。

608.8 平行式比赛

适用《国际雪联竞赛规则有关举办平行式比赛的规则（本规则第 1220 条）。

608.9 Kombi

The U16 - U14 Kombi is an internationally recognized event that consists of a mixture of standard turns and gates. The event meets developmental needs for this age group, creating a tactical awareness by blending sections of different gates in a flowing, rhythmical, constantly changing pattern. Results may be determined by combined times of each run, or each run may be classified separately. The OC must indicate the method in advance.

608.9.1 Course Setting

608.9.1.2 The Course Setter and Jury are to provide an interesting and controlled course.

608.9.1.3 The competitor' s speed must be controlled when transitioning from one section to a different section and the course setting should allow skiers a smooth transition from jumps or waves back into the course.

608.9.2 Kombi Design

There can be 2 different forms of the Kombi:

SL / GS Format (technical orientation) Setting with stubbies, SL gates and GS gates or coloured ground indicators and GS / SG Format (speed orientation) Setting with GS and SG gates or coloured ground indicators.

The selected race style must be announced on the race notice prior to the race and again at the first team captains meeting.

608.9 **组合赛**

U16—U14 组合赛是一项国际承认的比赛，由一系列不同标准弯道和旗门组合而成。这项比赛满足了这一年龄段的发展需要，通过将包括多个旗门的不同旗门组以一种流畅的、有节奏的、不断变化的模式混合在一起，创造一种战术意识。比赛成绩可以根据各轮滑行的总时间确定，或者每轮滑行单独决胜负。组委会必须提前说明竞赛模式。

608.9.1 旗门设计

608.9.1.2 旗门设计员和仲裁委员会应提供一条有趣且安全的线路。

608.9.1.3 当选手从一个旗门组切换到另一个旗门组时必须能够控制速度，且比赛线路的设计必须能让选手从跳跃或波浪部分流畅地切换回比赛线路。

608.9.2 组合赛设计

组合赛可以有两种不同的模式：

回转 / 大回转组合模式（技术偏好）：旗门设计用短杆，回转和大回转旗门或彩色地面指示标。大回转 / 超级大回转模式（速度偏好）：旗门设计用大回转和超级大回转旗门或彩色地面指示标。

必须在赛前的竞赛公告中公布拟采用的竞赛组合模式，第一次领队会议时应再次通告。

608.9.3 **SL / GS Kombi: Technical Data**

Slalom Skis are recommended to be used for SL/GS Kombi and the OC must announce in advance the type of Kombi in order to enable correct ski selection.

608.9.3.1 Terrain and Vertical drop

Use U16 - U14 GS slope, vertical drop between 140 - 200 meters.

608.9.3.2 Gates

Gates consist of two poles. The outside gate must be the same type as the turning gate (stubby gate with stubby gate, SL gate with SL gate, GS panel with GS panel).

- Consecutive gates must alternate in red and blue;
- SL gates must have a minimum distance of 4m and max. 6m;
- GS gates must have a minimum distance of 4m and a max. 8m;
- SL Minimum distance between turning gate to turning gate 0.75m;
- SL Maximum distance turning gate to turning gate 12m;
- GS Minimum distance turning gate to turning gate. No minimum restriction;
- GS Maximum distance turning gate to turning gate 20m.

608.9.3.3 Course characteristics and recommendations:

- Minimum of 30 turns;

608.9.3 **回转/大回转组合赛：技术数据**

回转/大回转组合赛建议使用回转滑雪板，组委会必须提前宣布组合赛的模式，以便选择正确的滑雪板。

608.9.3.1 地形和垂直落差

采用 U16—U14 大回转坡道，垂直落差在 140 米至 200 米。

608.9.3.2 旗门

旗门由 2 根旗杆组成。外侧旗门和转弯旗门必须规格相同（短杆旗门布搭配短杆旗门，回转旗门布搭配回转旗门，大回转旗门布搭配大回转旗门）。

- 连续的旗门必须红蓝交替；
- 回转旗门间距最小 4 米，最大 6 米；
- 大回转旗门间距最小 4 米，最大 8 米；
- 回转转弯旗门之间最小间距为 0.75 米；
- 回转转弯旗门之间最大间距为 12 米；
- 大回转转弯旗门之间没有最小距离限制；
- 大回转转弯旗门之间最大间距为 20 米。

608.9.3.3 比赛线路特点与建议：

- 最少 30 个转弯；

- Recommended to have a minimum of 5 different sections;
- Slalom skis recommended;
- The course should test the skier's ability to react and adapt to an ever changing rhythm and radius, but allow the competitors smooth transition between the various sections of gates;
- Building terrain is optional but not necessary as the course itself should apply enough demand. Use creativity with available terrain;
- Include a minimum of one jump;
- Avoid gates that cause sudden braking and deceleration;
- Use the entire slope and natural terrain and skiing across the fall line as often as possible;
- It is recommended to use only a single pole for vertical combinations;
- The first and last gates should give the competitor the general direction;
- There should be at least one section of stubby gates;
- Forerunners or course testers should be available for course setting.

608.9.4 GS / SG Kombi: Technical Data

Giant Slalom Skis are recommended to be used for GS/SG Kombi and the OC must announce in advance the type of Kombi in order to enable correct ski selection.

608.9.4.1 Terrain and Vertical drop.

Use homologated GS course, 250 meters maximum vertical drop.

- 建议最少设 5 个不同的旗门组；
- 建议使用回转滑雪板；
- 比赛线路应该检测滑雪者对不断变化的节奏和转弯半径的反应和适应能力，但要能让选手在不同旗门组的旗门之间流畅转换；

- 可以改造赛道地形，但不是必需的，赛道本身应充分满足需要。要创造性地利用现有的可用地形；

- 至少包含一处跳跃；
- 应避免造成急停和减速的旗门；
- 利用整个坡道和自然地形，引导运动员尽可能连续地穿越滚落线；
- 在设计垂直组合时建议仅使用单旗门杆；

- 第一组旗门和最后一组旗门应给参赛运动员指明基本的方向；
- 应至少有一个旗门组用短杆旗门；
- 试滑员或线路检验员应随时待命、保障旗门设计。

608.9.4　大回转 / 超级大回转组合赛：技术数据

大回转 / 超级大回转组合赛建议选用大回转滑雪板，组委会必须提前宣布组合赛的模式，以便准备适宜的滑雪板。

608.9.4.1　地形和垂直落差

使用经认证的大回转赛道，垂直落差最大 250 米。

608.9.4.2 Gates

- Gates consist of two poles. Outside gate must be the same as turning gate;
- Consecutive gates must alternate in red and blue.
- GS gates must have a minimum distance of 4m and a max. 8m;
- SG gates must have a minimum distance of 6m and a max 8m;
- GS turning gate to turning gate minimum 10m maximum 20m;
- SG turning gate to turning gate minimum 15m maximum 28m.

608.9.4.3 Course characteristics and recommendations:

- Number of Direction changes 10% to 12% of Vertical drop;
- Recommended to have 3-5 different sections;
- Giant Slalom skis recommended;
- The course should test the skier's ability to react and adapt to an ever changing rhythm and radius, but allow the competitors smooth transition between the various sections of gates;
- Building terrain is optional but must allow course to flow smoothly;
- Include a minimum of one jump;
- Avoid gates that cause sudden braking and deceleration;
- The first and last gates should give the competitor the general direction;
- Forerunners or course testers should be available for course setting.

608.9.4.2 旗门
- 旗门由 2 根旗杆组成。外侧旗门和转弯旗门必须相同；
- 连续的旗门必须红蓝交替；
- 大回转旗门间距须最小 4 米，最大 8 米；

- 超级大回转旗门间距须最小 6 米，最大 8 米；

- 大回转转弯旗门之间距离为最小 10 米,最大 20 米;

- 超级大回转转弯旗门之间距离为最小 15 米，最大 28 米。

608.9.4.3 比赛线路特点与建议：
- 换向次数在垂直落差的 10% 到 12%；
- 建议设 3 到 5 个不同旗门组；
- 建议使用大回转滑雪板；
- 比赛线路应该检验滑雪者对不断变化的节奏和转弯半径的反应和适应能力，但要能让选手在不同旗门组的旗门之间流畅转换；

- 可以改造地形，但必须使线路保持流畅；

- 至少包含一处跳跃；
- 应避免造成急停和减速的旗门；
- 第一组旗门和最后一组旗门应给参赛运动员指明基本的方向；
- 试滑员或线路检验员应随时待命、保障旗门设计。

608.9.5 **Kombi Inspection**

A normal competitor's inspection and with a time limit established by the Jury is suggested. The concept is to test reaction and adaptability from the normal amount of inspection time.

608.9.6 **Number of runs**

The OC and Jury should decide on the number of runs by the first team captains meeting. Depending on weather and course conditions it is recommended that entries up to 140 competitors should be 2 runs and entries over 140 competitors should be one run.

608.9.7 **Rules**

The ICR Slalom and Giant Slalom rules apply for running of the Kombi race except as modified in art. 608.

608.9.8 **Starting order**

By team seeding.

608.9.9 **Gate judging**

A sufficient number of gate judges should be present. For the Stubby sections it is recommended to have one gate judge for every two gates. It is also recommended to spray a blue line on the inside of the gate to help to identify straddles.

608.9.5　组合赛线路视察

建议安排常规的运动员视察线路活动，时限由仲裁委员会确定。目的是检测运动员在常规视察线路时限内所作的反应和适应能力。

608.9.6　滑行轮次数

组委会和仲裁委员会应在第一次领队会议前决定滑行轮次数。根据天气情况和赛道条件，建议在报名参赛运动员不到 140 名时采取 2 轮滑行，超过 140 名时采取 1 轮滑行。

608.9.7　规则

本规则有关回转和大回转的规则可用于组合赛，但本规则第 608 条特别调整的内容除外。

608.9.8　出发顺序

依据代表队排名确定。

608.9.9　旗门裁判

应当配备足够数量的旗门裁判员。建议在短杆旗门组每 2 个旗门设置 1 个旗门裁判员，在旗门内侧喷涂蓝线以便选手确认是否正确越过旗门。

610 Start, Finish, Timing and Calculations

611 Technical Installations

611.1 Communications & Cabling

In all international competitions, it is highly recommended that there is multiple communications (telephone or radios, etc.) between the Start and Finish. Voice communication between Start and Finish must be assured by fixed wire connection or radio. In case of radio, this must be on a separate channel from that used by any other function of the OC.

In Olympic Winter Games and FIS World Championships all communications and timing connections between Start and Finish must be assured by fixed wiring.

611.2 Timing Equipment

For all events in the FIS Calendar, electronic timers, start gates and photocells homologated by the FIS must be used. A list of these approved devices will be published. Races using timing equipment other than those on the homologated FIS list will not be considered for FIS points.

Specifications and procedures for timing are more fully described in a separate FIS Timing Booklet.

611.2.1 Electric Timing

For all international competitions, FIS World Cup, FIS Continental Cups and FIS competitions, two synchronised

610　起点、终点、计时与计算

611　技术设备

611.1　通讯联系与布线

在所有的国际比赛中，起点与终点之间须有多种通讯联系（电话或对讲机等）。起点和终点的语音联系须使用固定的有线连接或对讲机。若使用对讲机，必须使用单独的频率，以免被组委会其他通讯内容干扰。

在冬季奥林匹克运动会和国际雪联世界锦标赛中，起点和终点之间所有通讯和计时连接都必须使用固定电缆。

611.2　计时设备

所有《国际雪联竞赛日历》中的比赛，均须使用经国际雪联认证的电子计时器、出发门及切光器。应公布被认证的计时设备名单。参加未使用列入国际雪联认证清单的此类计时设备比赛没有国际雪联积分。

《国际雪联计时手册》专门对计时具体要求和程序有更全面的说明。

611.2.1　电子计时

包括国际雪联世界杯赛、国际雪联洲际杯赛、国际雪联比赛的所有国际比赛，应使用两套彼此独立运

electronically isolated timing systems operating in time-of-day must be used. One system will be designated system A (main system), the other system B (back-up system) prior to the beginning of the race. Only exception for Parallel competitions, on Level 2, 3 and 4 where no system B is required.

Time of day times must be immediately and automatically sequentially recorded on printed strips at the maximum precision of the timing device according to the requirements for homologation. The final result is calculated by subtracting the start time from the finish time for each skier' s run and is then expressed to 1/100th (0.01) precision by truncating the calculated net time on course.

All times used for the final result must be from system A. If there is a failure of system A, a calculated net time from system B must be used following the same procedure as set out in art. 611.3.2.1. It is not permitted to substitute time-of-day times from system B for use with system A for the purpose of net time calculations.

For all events, system A must be connected to its respective start gate contact. System B must be separately connected to another electronically isolated start gate contact.

Refer to the FIS Timing Booklet for more details regarding cabling and complete wiring descriptions, diagrams and start gate installations.

All timing equipment and technical installation should be set up or protected in such a way that danger to the

行且电控同步的电子计时系统。赛前确定其中一套系统为 A 系统（主系统），另一套为 B 系统（备份系统）。仅平行式比赛为例外，第 2、3、4 级比赛不要求有备份系统。

比赛中需要记录的时间信息，必须按照计时装置认证所要求的最高精度、立即自动地按顺序记录并打印。每名运动员的最终成绩是通过其结束时间减去出发时间计算出每次滑行的赛道净用时，再四舍五入以 1/100（0.01）秒的精度表示。

用于计算最终成绩的所有基础时间数据都必须来自 A 系统。如果 A 系统出现故障，则必须按照本规则第 611.3.2.1 条规定的同一程序使用 B 系统计算得出的净时间。不允许不按本规则第 611.3.2.1 条规定的程序、简单地用 B 系统的时间数据代替 A 系统的时间数据来计算净用时。
对于所有赛事，A 系统必须与各出发门相连接，B 系统也必须同样地与各出发门相连接，但必须与 A 系统电子隔离。

有关布线和完整接线说明、图表和出发门安装更详细的信息，参见《国际雪联计时手册》。

所有计时设备和技术装置都应妥善安装并做好绝缘等保护，避免对运动员构成危险。

competitors is avoided where possible.

Synchronisation of the timing systems must occur as close as possible to the scheduled start for the first run of the day. Synchronisation of all systems must be maintained throughout each run. Timers must not be resynchronised during any run.

611.2.1.1 Start Gate

The start gate must have separate electronically isolated switch contacts for triggering the start inputs of both system A & B.

If a start gate or start wand requires replacement during a run, it must be replaced with identical equipment in the same position.

611.2.1.2 Photocells

For all events, there must be two photocell system(s) homologated by the FIS installed at the finish line. One is connected to system A. The other is connected to system B. Procedures and regulations for start gates and photocells are found in the FIS Timing Booklet.

611.2.1.3 Start Clock

For DH, SG and GS, the use of a start clock that provides at least an acoustic countdown signal on the fixed start interval as prescribed by the Jury should be used as an aid to race management. This is mandatory for all Level 0,1 and 2 races.

计时系统的时间同步操作，必须尽可能邻近秩序册中每天第一轮滑行的出发时间。在每一轮滑行过程中都必须保持所有系统自始至终时间同步。计时器在任何一轮滑行期间均不得重新同步。

611.2.1.1 出发门

出发门必须具有两套相互电子隔离的电子开关触点，以触发 A 系统和 B 系统的出发时间信号输入。

如果在某轮滑行中要更换出发门或起滑杆，必须确保在同一位置的 AB 系统更换完全相同的设备。

611.2.1.2 切光器

所有比赛的终点线上都必须安装两套经国际雪联认证的切光系统。其中一套连接到 A 系统，另一套连接到 B 系统。
出发门和切光器的程序和规定参见《国际雪联计时手册》。

611.2.1.3 出发钟

在滑降、超级大回转和大回转比赛中，应至少装备一套按仲裁委员会确定的固定出发时间间隔自动发出倒计时信号的出发钟，用作比赛管理的辅助工具。这是所有 0 级、1 级和 2 级比赛的强制性要求。

611.2.2 **Hand Timing**

Manual (hand) timing, completely separate and independent of the electronic timing, must be used for all competitions listed in the FIS Calendar. Stopwatches or hand operated battery powered timers that are installed at both the Start and the Finish and capable of expressing the time of day to at least 1/100th (0.01) precision qualify as proper hand timing devices. They must be synchronised prior to the start of the first run, with the same time-of-day as system A and system B (see art. 611.2.1). Printed records, either automatic or hand-written, of recorded hand times must be immediately available at the start and at the finish.

611.2.3 **Presentation of times**

Organisers should provide appropriate facilities for continuous presentation of all registered times of all competitors.

611.2.4 **Timing without Cable**

For FIS Level 3 events only, it is permitted to use homologated timing equipment in such a way that hill cable connection between start and finish is not required. Refer to the FIS Timing Booklet for a detailed discussion of how this is possible.

611.3 Timing

611.3.1 With electronic timing, the time is taken when a competitor

611.2.2 手动计时

手动计时完全独立于电子计时，必须用于《国际雪联竞赛日历》中的所有比赛。起点、终点处安装的秒表或手动操作电池驱动的计时器，必须同适格的手动计时工具一样，计时精度能够达到 1/100（0.01）秒。手动计时器必须在第一轮滑行开始前进行同步，与 A 系统和 B 系统运行在同一当前时间（见本规则第 611.2.1）。自动或手写的手动计时的打印记录，必须能够在出发区和终点区立即提供。

611.2.3 时间显示

组织者应提供适当的设施，可连续显示所有运动员已记录的滑行时间。

611.2.4 无线计时

允许在起点终点间无高山电缆连接的情况下使用经认证的计时设备，这一规定仅适用于第 3 级别的比赛。具体操作的详细说明见《国际雪联计时手册》。

611.3 计时

611.3.1 使用电子计时设备时，当运动员通过终点线并因切

crosses the finish line and triggers the beam between the photo cells.
In case of a fall at the finish where the competitor does not come to a full stop, the time can be taken without both of the competitor's feet having crossed the finish line.
For the registered time to become valid, the competitor must immediately completely cross the finish line with or without skis. With hand timing the time will be taken when any part of the competitor crosses the finish line.
The finish controller determines the correctness of passage across the finish line.

611.3.2 In the case of a failure of the main electronic timing system (system A), the results of the electronic back-up system (system B) will be valid as per art. 611.2.1. For the Olympic Winter Games, FIS World Ski Championships and FIS World Cup, a synchronised electronic timing system with printers, connected to the starting gate and to the photocells at the finish is obligatory.
In case of a failure in the lines of the timing system between start and finish, this back-up system will allow the calculation of the times to 1/100ths of a second.
In the case that time of day from either system A or system B are not available for a competitor, the calculated time of day as per art. 611.3.2.1 will be considered valid.

611.3.2.1 Utilisation of times taken by hand
Hand times may be used in the official results after a

入切光器间的光束而触发切光器时，该时间即被记录。
运动员在终点摔倒（没有完全抵达终点）的，即使其双腿还未完全越过终点线，其触线时间也应被记录。
为使记录时间生效，运动员必须立即完全越过终点线，无论有没有穿滑雪板。采用手动计时时，应记录运动员身体的任何一部分越过终点线的时间。
终点监督员判定运动员是否正确越过终点线。

611.3.2 电子计时主系统A系统失灵的，根据本规则第611.2.1条，备份电子计时系统B系统的成绩将有效。冬季奥林匹克运动会、国际雪联世界锦标赛和国际雪联世界杯上，必须配备一套带打印机的同步电子计时系统与起点门和终点的切光器相连是强制性义务。

计时系统连接起点、终点的导线失灵的，上述备份系统可用于计算时间，精确到1/100秒。

计时系统中的A系统和B系统中记录的时间数据对某个运动员而言，均无法用于计算其比赛净用时的，则根据本规则第611.3.2.1条利用手动计时系统的时间数据的计算结果视为有效。

611.3.2.1 手动计时的使用
在算出时间修正值后，正式成绩可采用手动计时时间。

correction has been calculated.
Calculation of the correction:
Subtract the electronic time from the time taken by hand for the 10 competitors starting before the missing time. If there are not 10 times before, complete the calculation with the remaining times after the missed time.
The sum of the 10 time differences is divided by 10 and rounded up or down (0.044 -> 0.04, 0.045 -> 0.05) to give the correction which must be applied to the hand time of the competitor without an electronic time.

611.3.2.2 Photo Finish
A Photo Finish System may be used to determine a competitor's finish time. In case of a failure of system "A" and "B", and where the competition has been recorded by the Photo Finish System, this time must be used in place of hand-timing without any correction.
The photo finish time is taken when any part of the competitor's body first crosses the Finish line. The photo finish result is to be provided to the Jury only.

611.3.3 The official timing strips from the printer will be given to the Technical Delegate for review. They will be kept by the OC until the official approval of the race or after any appeal dealing with timing or race results.
A technical timing report form as prescribed by the FIS must accompany the race results and must be reviewed and sent by the chief of timing and reviewed and confirmed by the TD as approval of the race.

修正值的计算方法如下：
计算缺失时间的运动员之前出发的 10 名运动员手动计时时间减去电子计时时间的差。如果在缺失时间的运动员之前出发的运动员不足 10 名，则用其后出发的运动员的记录时间数据完成上述计算。
10 个时间差之和除以 10，四舍五入（0.044- > 0.04，0.045- > 0.05）后得出的即为修正值，该修正值必须从缺失电子计时时间的运动员的手动计时中减去，以得到其最终成绩。

611.3.2.2　终点录像
终点录像系统用来确定运动员的完赛时间。A 系统和 B 系统同时故障，并且比赛已由终点录像系统记录下来的，必须使用终点录像系统记录的时间代替手动计时，不需要任何修正。
运动员身体的任何部位首先切入终点线的时间，即为终点录像计时时间。终点录像成绩只提供给仲裁委员会。

611.3.3　打印的正式时间列表应交给技术代表检查，并由组委会一直保存到比赛成绩获正式核准，或任何有关计时或比赛成绩的申诉终结后。

国际雪联规定的计时技术报告表必须与比赛成绩一并提交，并由计时长审查并发送，再由技术代表审查并确认，作为对比赛成绩的核准。

All printed records from system A, system B and hand timing must be retained by the OC for a period of three (3) months after the competition or after any appeal dealing with timing or race results.

611.3.4 When the official printing timer allows manual input or correction of a time, some type of indication (star, asterisk or other) concerning any effected change must be printed on all timing documentation.

611.3.5 Computer software calculating net times must use the precision of the time of the day as used in the timing device.

611.4 Private timing and speed measurement equipment of the Teams

Any request to install such equipment has to be made to the Jury by the team captain concerned, and the Jury decides concerning approval of the installation. At Olympic Winter Games, FIS World Ski Championships and FIS World Cup only the organisers timing equipment is permitted.

612 Start and Finish Officials

612.1 The Starter

The starter must synchronise a watch with those of the assistant starter and by telephone or radio with the chief timekeeper within ten minutes of the start. The starter is responsible for the warning signal and the start commandas well as for the accuracy of the intervals between these

所有 A 系统和 B 系统的打印记录和手动计时记录要由组委会保留，直到比赛结束后或任何关于计时和比赛结果的申诉终结后 3 个月。

611.3.4　正式打印计时器允许手工输入或修正其计时的，要在所有的时间记录文件中的任何有效改变处打印某种标记（星号等）。

611.3.5　用计算机软件计算净用时的，必须使用与计时设备一样精度的时间。

611.4　各队自用计时和测速设备

任何安装计时设备的请求均须由有关领队向仲裁委员会提出，由仲裁委员会裁定是否同意安装。在冬季奥林匹克运动会、国际雪联世界锦标赛和国际雪联世界杯上，仅可使用组织方的计时设备。

612　起点与终点官员

612.1　发令员

出发时间前 10 分钟内，发令员须用某一计时表与其助理发令员的计时表同步，并用电话或对讲机与计时长进行时间同步。发令员负责发出准备信号和出发命令，并准确控制这些信号之间的间隔。发令员向助理发令员指派监督运动员的任务。

signals and assigns the supervision of the competitors to the assistant starter.

612.2 **The Assistant Starter**

The assistant starter is responsible for calling the competitors to the start in their correct order.

612.3 **The Start Recorder**

The start recorder is responsible for recording the actual start times of all competitors.

612.4 **The Chief Timekeeper**

The chief timekeeper is responsible for the accuracy of the timing and synchronises the watches with the starter as shortly before and after the race as is possible. The chief timekeeper must publish unofficial times as quickly as possible (on the score-board, etc.). If the electric timing fails, the chief timekeeper must communicate immediately with the start referee and the TD.

612.5 **The Assistant Timekeeper**

Two assistant timekeepers operate stop watches according to art. 611.2.2. One assistant timekeeper maintains a complete record with the registered times of all competitors.

612.6 **The Finish Controller**

The finish controller has the following duties:

- Supervision of the section between the last gate and the finish;

612.2 **助理发令员**

助理发令员负责严格按出发顺序召集运动员到起点区。

612.3 **出发记录员**

出发记录员负责记录运动员的实际出发时间。

612.4 **计时长**

计时长负责计时的准确性。在比赛前后，要与发令员在尽可能接近比赛开始的时间内对计时表进行时间同步，尽快公布非正式成绩（在成绩板上）。如果电子计时装置失灵，计时长须立即与起点裁判员和技术代表联系。

612.5 **助理计时员**

2 名助理计时员按本规则第 611.2.2 条操作秒表。1 名助理计时员保留所有运动员登记时间的完整记录。

612.6 **终点监督员**

终点监督员负有以下职责：

- 监督最后 1 道旗门至终点的区域；

- Supervision of the proper crossing of the finish line;
- Recording of the order of finishing of all competitors who complete the course.

612.7 The Chief of Calculations

The chief of calculations is responsible for quick and accurate calculation of results and supervises the immediate duplication of unofficial results and the publication of official results after expiration of the protest interval, or after any protests have been dealt with.

613 The Start

613.1 The Start Area

The start area must be closed off to everyone except the starting competitor, accompanied by only one trainer and the start officials.

The start area must be protected appropriately against inclement weather.

A special roped off area must be provided for trainers, team captains, service personnel etc., in which they may take care of the waiting competitors without being interrupted by the public. An adequate shelter must be prepared for the competitors waiting for the call to start.

The competitor enters the defined start hut with both skis attached without any covers on them.

613.2 The Start Ramp

The start ramp should be prepared in such a way that the

- 监督运动员是否正确越过终点线；
- 记录所有完赛运动员到达终点的顺序。

612.7 **计算长**

计算长负责迅速准确地计算比赛成绩，监督非正式成绩的立即备份，在抗议期限届满或所有抗议处理完毕后公布正式成绩。

613 出发

613.1 **出发区**

出发区必须清空所有人，但将要出发的运动员及陪同的 1 名教练和起点官员除外。

出发区必须加以适当防护以抵御恶劣天气。

必须用安全网为教练、领队、服务人员等围出一块特别隔离区（紧邻出发区），以便他们在此照顾等待出场的运动员而免受观众的打扰。必须为等待叫号出发的运动员准备适用的遮蔽棚。

运动员进入指定的出发棚，携带滑雪板，滑雪板上没有任何覆盖物。

613.2 **出发台**

出发台应准备得使运动员能够放松地站立在起点线

competitors can stand relaxed on the starting line and can quickly reach full speed after leaving the start.

613.3 Start Procedure

No official or attendant who could possibly give an advantage to or disturb the starting competitors can be behind them. All outside help is forbidden.

By order of the starter, competitors must plant their poles in front of the start line, or where indicated. The Starter must not touch the competitor at the start. Pushing off from the start posts or other aids is forbidden and competitors must start only with the help of their ski poles.

613.4 Start Signals

10 seconds before the start, the starter will tell each competitor "10 seconds" . Five seconds before the start, the starter should count "5, 4, 3, 2, 1" and then give the start command "Go - Partez - Los" .(For Slalom see art. 805.3).

If possible, an automatic audible signal is to be used (art. 611.2.1.3). The starter will let the competitor see the start clock.

613.5 Start Timing

The start timing must measure the exact time when the competitors cross the start line with their leg below the knee.

上，且出发后能很快达到全速。

613.3 **出发程序**

出发运动员身后不得有任何可能帮助或妨碍的官员或陪同人员。任何外部帮助均在禁止之列。

按发令员的命令，运动员必须把雪杖插在出发线前或指定位置。出发时，发令员不能接触运动员，运动员出发时仅可凭借其雪杖，不得借助蹬推出发杆或其他辅助。

613.4 **出发信号**

出发前 10 秒，发令员提示即将出发的运动员："10 秒"。出发前 5 秒时，发令员开始倒计数"5、4、3、2、1"，然后发出出发命令："出发（发音为：Go-Partez-Los）"（回转赛参见本规则第 805.3 条）。

如果可能，可使用自动语音信号（本规则第 611.2.1.3 条）。发令员应指引运动员注意出发钟。

613.5 **出发计时**

出发时间必须测量到运动员膝盖以下的腿部切入出发线的准确时间。

613.6 **Delayed Start**

A competitor who is not ready to start on time will be sanctioned. The Start Referee may however excuse such a delay if, in the start referee's opinion the delay is due to "force majeure".

For example, breakdown of a competitor's personal equipment or minor sickness of a competitor does not constitute "force majeure".

In case of doubt, the Jury may allow the start provisionally.

613.6.1 The start referee makes the decisions after consultation with the Jury (according to art. 613.6.2 and 613.6.3) and must record the start numbers and names of competitors who were not allowed to start because of late appearance, or who were allowed to start in spite of late appearance, or who were allowed to start provisionally.

613.6.2 In the case of fixed start intervals, delayed competitors may start at the fixed interval after they have reported to the start referee, in accordance with the decision of the Jury. The Start Referee informs the Jury as to when (after which start number) a delayed competitor is starting.

613.6.3 In the case of irregular start intervals, the delayed competitor will start according to art. 805.3. The start referee informs the Jury as to when (after which start number) a delayed competitor is starting.

613.6 **出发延迟**

不能按时出发的运动员要受到制裁。起点裁判长认定因“不可抗力”耽搁出发的，可以放行。

但是，运动员的轻微病症或者自用竞赛器材故障，不构成“不可抗力”因素。

如有疑问，仲裁委员会可允许运动员临时出发。

613.6.1 起点裁判长在同仲裁委员会协商后作出决定（根据本规则第 613.6.2 条和 613.6.3 条）并相应记录以下内容：因迟到而决定禁止出发、尽管迟到仍允许出发或获准临时出发的运动员的出发号码和姓名。

613.6.2 采用固定出发间隔的比赛，迟到运动员向起点裁判长报告后，根据仲裁委员会的决定，可以在该固定间隔时间出发。迟到运动员出发前，起点裁判长通知仲裁委员会（在哪个出发号码运动员后出发）。

613.6.3 采用非固定出发间隔出发的比赛，迟到运动员可按本规则第 805.3 条规定出发。迟到运动员出发前，起点裁判长通知仲裁委员会（在哪个出发号码运动员后出发）。

613.7 Valid and False Starts

In competitions with a fixed start interval, the competitor must start on the start signal. The start time is valid if it occurs within the following limits: 5 seconds before and 5 seconds after the official start time. A competitor who does not start within that space of time will be disqualified.

The start referee must inform the Referee of the start numbers and names of the competitors who made a false start or have contravened the starting rules.

614 Competition Course, Competition and Inspection

614.1 Competition Course

614.1.1 Competition Course and Technical Parts

A competition course is a designated area on a specific ski-slope, described by the respective FIS homologation. Start and Finish installations, television towers, measuring equipment, sponsor advertising equipment etc. are necessary items for a competition and are part of the competition course.

614.1.2 Course Setting

614.1.2.1 Assistance

Assistance must be provided at a time to be fixed by the Jury, so that the course setter can concentrate on the actual course setting and not be distracted by fetching poles, etc.

613.7 **有效出发和错误出发**

在固定出发间隔的比赛中，运动员须按出发信号出发。运动员的实际出发时间在以下时限内的，为有效出发：出发信号指示的正式出发时间前后 5 秒。运动员未在此时限内出发的，取消资格。

起点裁判长须将错误出发或违反出发规则的运动员姓名和出发号码通知裁判长。

614 赛道、比赛和视察线路

614.1 赛道

614.1.1 赛道及技术部分

赛道是从某一特定雪道中围出的区域，并（其技术参数等）由各自的国际雪联认定证书具体描述。起点和终点设备、电视塔、测量器材、赞助者广告器材等，是比赛必需的物品，并成为赛道的组成部分。

614.1.2 旗门设计

614.1.2.1 协助

在仲裁委员会指定的时间内，必须为旗门设计员提供协助，以便其全神贯注于旗门设计事务，不致因取旗门杆等事务分神。

The Chief of Course Equipment must provide enough of the following:

- Enough blue and red slalom poles;
- A corresponding number of gate panels, divided by colours;
- Hammers, drills, gate-keys, wedges etc;
- Enough gate numbers;
- Colouring substance for marking the position of the poles.

614.1.2.2 Marking of the gates

The positions of the gate poles may be marked with an easily recognisable colouring substance which remains visible throughout the entire race.

614.1.2.3 Numbering the gates

The gates must be numbered from top to bottom of the course. Start and Finish are not counted.

614.1.2.4 Marking of the course and terrain

In Downhill and in Super-G the course should be marked using:

- On the inside and/or outside of the racing line before and after the gate;
- Small pine needles or similar material spread on the course;
- Coloured dye used vertically from gate to gate as well as horizontally across the course or the inside and/or outside of the racing line before and after the

设备长必须足量提供下列设备：

- 足够的蓝色和红色回转旗杆；
- 有相应数量以颜色区分的旗门布；

- 大锤、电钻、旗门扳子、楔子等；
- 足够的旗门号码；
- 标记旗门杆位置的彩色涂料。

614.1.2.2　标示旗门

旗门杆的位置可以用易于辨认的彩色涂料标明，并在整个比赛期间都清晰可见。

614.1.2.3　对旗门进行编号

旗门必须自线路起点至终点用数字编号。起点和终点不计在内。

614.1.2.4　标示比赛线路和地形

在滑降和超级大回转项目中，比赛线路应进行如下标示：

- 在进入旗门前和出旗门后的比赛线路内侧或外侧；
- 将小松针或类似材料撒在赛道上；

- 用染料明显标示下列区域：旗门间沿赛道的垂直或者水平方向，在进入旗门前和出旗门后的线路内

gate notably on the approaches indicating changes in terrain, jumps, etc.

614.1.2.5 Spare Poles

The Chief of Course Equipment is responsible for the availability and correct placing of enough spare poles. The poles are to be placed so that the competitors are not mislead by them.

614.1.3 Training on Competition Courses and Warm up Slopes

Official training in Downhill is part of the competition and governed in art. 704.

For other types of Alpine events, the Jury may approve special training with or without gates (free ski) which can take place on the competition courses. In that case, the training has to be controlled by the Jury and the Race Organisation.

Warm up slopes outside the competition courses should be made available to the participating teams under specific guidelines by the Organiser.

Warm up slopes are not under the control of the Jury and are not governed by the ICR.

614.1.4 Closing and Modification of the Course

A competition course is closed from the time the course setting begins. Nobody except for the Jury is permitted to change gates, gate panels, markings, etc. or modify the course structure (jumps, bumps, etc.) on a closed course.

侧或外侧雪道上，尤其要明显标示通往地形变化及跳跃赛段的路段。

614.1.2.5 备用旗门杆

设备长负责准备随时可用并便于准确布置的数量充足的备用旗门杆并妥善存放以免误导运动员。

614.1.3 在赛道和热身雪道上训练

场地适应训练是滑降比赛项目的组成部分并受本规则 704 条规制。

对于滑降以外的其他高山滑雪比赛项目，仲裁委员会可以批准在赛道上进行带旗门或者不带旗门（即自由滑）的专门训练。此时，这类训练必须在仲裁委员会及竞赛组织机构的监督下进行。

赛道之外的热身雪道应提前备妥以供各参赛队在组织方的特别指引下使用。

热身雪道不受仲裁委员会管控，也不受《国际雪联滑雪竞赛规则》规制。

614.1.4 赛道的关闭与修整

从旗门设计开始封闭赛道。除仲裁委员会外，任何人不得在关闭赛道内改动旗门、旗门布、旗门标志等，或修改旗门组合结构（跳跃、起伏处等）。

Competitors are not permitted to enter a closed competition course.

Trainers, servicemen etc., who are allowed on a closed competition course are to be decided by the Jury.

Photographers and camera teams are allowed into a closed course area for the necessary documentation of the competition. Their total number can be limited by the Jury. They will be located by the Jury where possible and must remain only in this area.

The Jury or the Organising Committee may close a competition course or sections of a course to competitors, trainers, media and service personnel outside of the actual competition or training times for preparation and maintenance purposes.

614.1.5 Course changes

In case of necessary changes on the course, such as small relocation of gates, an additional inspection or training run is not necessary.

Details must be communicated to all team captains and competitors must be informed by the Start Referee at the Start.

614.1.6 Downhill and Super-G at FIS World Ski Championships and Olympic Winter Games

Alpine men's and women's Downhill and Super-G competitions should be carried out on independent competition courses, but start and finish installations and short sections of the courses can be used for both events.

运动员不得进入关闭赛道。

可以进入关闭赛道的教练员、服务人员由仲裁委员会决定。
为留存必要的比赛音像资料的摄影师与摄制组可以进入封闭的赛道区域，其总人数由仲裁委员会限定，其活动区域也由仲裁委员会限定且只能在指定区域活动。

为了准备或维护赛场的需要，仲裁委员会或者组委会可以在实际比赛或训练时间以外对运动员、教练员、媒体及服务人员关闭赛道或其部分赛段。

614.1.5 线路调整
如需要对线路进行必要调整，例如略微移动旗门位置等，则无须额外的线路视察或试滑训练。

所有变更细节必须通报领队并由起点裁判长在起点处告知参赛运动员。

614.1.6 国际雪联世界锦标赛和冬季奥林匹克运动会中的滑降和超级大回转
高山滑雪男女滑降和超级大回转比赛应在彼此独立的赛道上进行，但是赛道起点和终点的装置和赛道中的部分赛段可以共享。

614.2 Competition

614.2.1 Passage of the Gates

A gate must be passed according to art. 661.4.1.

614.2.2 Interdiction to Continue after a Gate Fault

If competitors miss a gate, they must no longer continue through further gates.

614.2.3 Interdiction to Continue after a competitor stops

If competitors come to a complete stop (e.g. after a fall), they must no longer continue through previous or further gates. This interdiction is valid in all events with a fixed start interval (Downhill, Super-G, Giant Slalom, Parallel). Only exception is for Slalom (art. 661.4.1), as long as the competitor:

- does not interfere with the run of the next competitor;
- have not been passed by the next competitor.

614.2.4 Loss of one ski

If competitors lose a ski without having committed a gate fault or without coming to a complete stop, they may continue, as long as they:

- does not interfere with the run of the next competitor;
- have not been passed by the next competitor.

See also details in art. 615.3, 661.4.1, 804.3, 904.3.

614.2 比赛

614.2.1 通过旗门

运动员必须按照本规则第 661.4.1 条的规定通过旗门。

614.2.2 旗门失误后禁止继续比赛

运动员漏过 1 个旗门，不得继续通过后续旗门。

614.2.3 运动员停止后禁止继续比赛

运动员完全停止（如摔倒之后）后，不能继续通过之前或后续旗门。此项规定适用于所有固定出发间隔的比赛（滑降、超级大回转、大回转、平行式比赛）。只有回转比赛有例外(见本规则第 661.4.1 条)，即只要运动员尚未出现下列情形仍可继续比赛：

- 没有干扰下一名运动员的滑行；
- 未被下一名运动员超越。

614.2.4 一只滑雪板脱落

运动员一只滑雪板脱落但没有出现旗门犯规也没有完全停止的，可以继续比赛，但是必须：

- 没有干扰下一名运动员的滑行
- 未被下一名运动员超越。

另详见本规则第 615.3 条、第 661.4.1 条、第 804.3 条、第 904.3 条。

614.3 Inspection

614.3.1 Jury inspection

On race day, the Jury inspects the course and has to confirm the FIS programme for the day. Team Captains may accompany the Jury.

614.3.2 Competitor inspection

The competitor inspection is held after Jury inspection and after the Jury has opened the competition course and is normally inspected, from top to bottom of the course. The course must be in racing condition from the time the competitor's inspection starts and the competitors must not be disturbed during the inspection by workers on the course or similar. The competitors are authorised to study the final setting of the course by either skiing down at the side of the course at low speed, or side slipping through the gates (inspection). Skiing through gates or making practice turns parallel to those required by gates on the course is not allowed.

Competitors must carry their start numbers. Fenced, roped or blocked off sections of the course or gates must be respected. By the end of the inspection time, Competitors have to be outside the competition course.

Competitors are not permitted to enter the competition course on foot without skis.

614.3.3 Jury decisions

The time and duration of the competitors inspection is

614.3 视察线路

614.3.1 仲裁委员会视察赛道

仲裁委员会在每个比赛当日视察线路，同时还要确认当天的国际雪联竞赛秩序册。领队可陪同仲裁委员会视察。

614.3.2 运动员视察线路

仲裁委员会视察线路完毕并决定开放线路后，运动员可从线路的起点到终点对线路进行常规视察。从运动员开始视察线路时起，赛道必须进入竞赛状态，在赛道上或者其他区域的工作人员不得打扰视察线路的运动员。允许运动员研究完成最后设计的线路，他们有权从旗门一侧低速滑行或以横板滑降（平整赛道滑行）通过旗门的方式来视察旗门。禁止滑行穿过旗门或在旗门旁的平行赛段上模拟练习如何按要求转弯通过该旗门。

运动员必须携带其出发号码布。运动员必须远离赛道上用防护网、安全绳隔离或封闭的赛段或者旗门。视察线路时间结束后，运动员必须退出赛道。

禁止运动员不穿滑雪板徒步进入赛道。

614.3.3 仲裁委员会决定

运动员视察赛道的开始和持续时间由仲裁委员会决

determined by the Jury and scheduled at the team captains meeting. If necessary (e.g. because of special weather conditions), the Jury may decide on special-methods of competitors inspection.

615 The Finish

615.1 The Finish Area

615.1.1 The finish area should be plainly visible to competitors approaching the finish. It must be wide with a gently sloped smooth run-out.

615.1.2 In setting the course with gates particular attention should be paid to directing competitors across the finish on a natural line adapted to the terrain.

615.1.3 The finish area is to be fenced in. Any unauthorised entry is not allowed.

615.1.4 Finish installations and closures should be set up or secured through suitable protection measures.

615.1.5 For competitors who have finished their runs, a special area separated from the actual finish, is to be provided. In this area or corridor, it should be possible to make contact with the press (print, radio, TV and film) located in the media corridors.

定并在领队会议上发出通知。必要时（如特殊天气原因），仲裁委员会可决定采用特殊方式让运动员视察线路。

615 终点

615.1 终点区

615.1.1 终点区应让接近终点的运动员清晰可见。终点区要开阔，终点线后须有一段逆坡缓冲区。

615.1.2 在用旗门设计比赛线路时，尤其要注意引导运动员按地形的自然线形通过终点。

615.1.3 整个终点区须完全用防护网围起，任何人未经授权不得入内。

615.1.4 终点区应建终点设施和关闭装置或通过适当的措施予以保护。

615.1.5 应为已经结束其滑行轮次的运动员提供一处与实际终点分离的特别区域，在该区域或者走廊内运动员可与位于媒体走廊的媒体（文字、电台、电视和电影）接触。

615.1.6 The competitor must leave the finish area through the official exit with all the competition equipment used in the race.

615.2 The Finish and its Markings

The Finish is marked by two poles or vertical banners which may be connected by a horizontal banner. In Downhill and Super-G races, the finish must be no less than 15 metres wide and in Slalom and Giant Slalom no less than 10 metres wide. In exceptional cases, the Jury may decrease this distance on the spot for technical reasons or because of the terrain. The width of the finish is considered to be the distance between the two finish poles or banners. The supports used to mount the timing devices must also be at least this far apart.

The timing supports can usually be placed behind the finish poles or banners, on the downhill side. The finish line between the timing cells must be clearly marked horizontally with colouring substance.

615.3 Crossing of the Finish Line and Recording of the Times

The finish line must be crossed:

- on both skis;
- on one ski;
- with both feet in case of a fall between the last gate and the finish line. In this case the time is taken when any part of the competitor's body stops the timekeeping system.

615.1.6 运动员必须携带所有在比赛中使用的竞赛器材，从正式的出口离开终点区。

615.2 **终点及其标识**

终点由 2 个标杆或中间由 1 个横幅连接的 2 根竖直旗标标示。在滑降和超级大回转比赛中，终点宽度不得少于 15 米；在回转和大回转比赛中，终点宽度应不少于 10 米。在特殊情况下，因技术原因或地形原因，仲裁委员会可以在现场缩短终点宽度。终点宽度应视为 2 个标杆或旗标之间的距离。用于安装计时装置的立柱至少也要相隔同等宽度。

计时装置的支柱通常安置在终点标杆或旗标的山下一侧的后面。位于计时切光器之间的终点线须沿水平方向用彩色涂料清楚地标明。

615.3 **越过终点线和记录时间**

必须以如下方式之一通过终点线：
- 穿着两只滑雪板；
- 穿着一只滑雪板；
- 双脚未穿滑雪板通过，限于在终点线与最后一个旗门之间摔倒的情况。在这种情况下，计取运动员身体的任何一部分触发计时系统停止计时的时间。

615.4 Report

The Finish Referee must make a report to the Referee immediately after the race or the official training.

616 Microphones and Special Electronic Devices

616.1 Within the areas of Start and Finish as well as in the area of the closed competition course, the use of microphones installed without the agreement of the organiser and the Jury ("roving" and so-called "gallows" , microphones set into cameras or other technical instruments) is forbidden in training as well as in the race.

616.2 Unmanned and anchorless aerial vehicles (UAV) such as Drones or Quadrocopters etc., are strictly prohibited over the Race Course area during inspection, training or competition, unless approved by the Jury and the organiser in writing subject to any prohibitions imposed by local laws or the property owners. The Race Course area is defined by the Jury.

Violators will be subject to sanctions by the Jury in accordance with ICR art. 223.

617 Calculation and Announcement of Results

617.1 Unofficial Times

Times taken by the timekeepers must be considered

615.4 **报告**

终点裁判长应在比赛或场地适应训练后立即向裁判长报告。

616 话筒和特殊电子设备

616.1 在训练和比赛期间，在终点和起点区域以及封闭的赛道区域，不得使用未经组织方和仲裁委员会允许而安装的各种话筒（包括移动话筒和安装在三脚架上的话筒、照相机及其他技术设备的内置话筒）。

616.2 在视察赛道、训练或比赛期间，严禁在比赛用赛道区域上空使用无人驾驶和无锚定飞行器 (UAV)，如无人机或四轴飞行器等设备，除非在不违反当地法律或者业主设定的禁止性条件的情况下，经仲裁委员会会同组织方以书面形式批准才能够使用。赛道区域的范围由仲裁委员会界定。

违规者由仲裁委员会根据本规则第 223 条进行处罚。

617 计算与公布成绩

617.1 **非正式成绩**

计时员所计的时间应视为非正式成绩。这样的成绩

unofficial times. They should be posted on a score-board which should be readily visible from the area provided for the competitors who have finished, and from the press area. Whenever possible, unofficial times should be announced to the public over loud-speakers.

617.2 Announcement of Unofficial Times and Disqualifications

617.2.1 As soon as possible after completion of the race, unofficial times and disqualifications must be published on the official notice board at the finish.
The time limit for protest is counted from the moment of this announcement. (art. 643.4, 643.5)

617.2.2 Oral announcement of disqualifications may replace the publication on the official notice board.
It can be decided that protests can be delivered verbally to the Referee at the Finish within 15 minutes after the announcement of the disqualification. Protests submitted after this are considered null and void.
The team captains must be informed beforehand of the announcement and protest procedure.

617.3 Official Results

617.3.1 Results are determined from the official times of those competitors who have been officially classified.

应张贴在成绩板上，在专门为到达终点的运动员特设的区域和采访区内都清晰可见。如有可能，非正式成绩应通过扩音器向观众公布。

617.2 非正式成绩和取消资格的公布

617.2.1 比赛结束后，必须尽快在设立于终点区的正式告示板上公布非正式成绩和取消资格情况。

抗议期限自公告之时起计算（另见本规则第 643.4 条、第 643.5 条）。

617.2.2 可以口头宣布取消资格的方式代替正式告示板上的公告。
可以决定在宣布取消比赛资格后 15 分钟内，在终点区口头向终点裁判长提出抗议。在此之后提交的抗议被视为无效。

领队必须在宣布取消资格和抗议程序之前先得到通知。

617.3 正式成绩

617.3.1 比赛成绩取决于正式分组的运动员的正式比赛时间。

617.3.2 Combined results are calculated by adding together the race times obtained in each event of the combined event. (or by adding the race points).

617.3.3 If two or more competitors have the same time or the same number of points, the competitor with the higher start number must be listed first on the official list of results (ex aequo).

617.3.4 The official result list must contain:

- The name of the organising club or association;
- The name of the competition, the site, event, category and gender;
- The date of the race;
- All technical data such as the name of the competition course, altitude at start and finish, vertical drop, FIS homologation number and, for Downhill and Super-G, the length of the course;
- The names and nations of the members of the Jury;
- For each run, the names and nations of the course setter and the forerunners, the number of gates (Slalom, Giant Slalom and Super-G between brackets number of direction changes) and the start time;
- The weather, the snow conditions on the course and the air temperature at race start and finish recorded at time of race start;
- All details concerning the competitors, ranking, start number, code number, name and first name, nation (and possibly club), time and race points;

617.3.2 全能比赛成绩，就是将全能比赛中每项比赛的时间相加（或将比赛积分相加）。

617.3.3 如果有两名或更多的运动员所用的时间相等或积分相同，在正式成绩公告中出发号码大的运动员要排在前面（公平原则）。

617.3.4 正式成绩列表应当包含：

- 作为组织方的俱乐部或协会的名称；
- 比赛名称、地点、比赛项目、组别和性别；

- 比赛日期；
- 所有技术数据，如赛道名称、起点终点的海拔高度、垂直落差、国际雪联的认证号码以及滑降和超级大回转比赛线路长度；

- 仲裁委员会成员的姓名和国籍；
- 每一轮滑行中旗门设计员和试滑员的姓名和国籍、旗门数量（回转、大回转和超级大回转换向次数）和出发时间；

- 比赛开始时在比赛起点和终点记录的天气、赛道上的雪况和气温；

- 有关运动员、排名、出发号码、注册代码、姓名、国家（也可能是俱乐部）、时间和比赛积分等所有详细信息；

- The start number, code number, name, first name and nation of those competitors who were not at the start, did not finish or were disqualified in each run;
- The names of the official service companies, e.g. timing company, computer service etc;
- The codex and F value;
- The penalty calculation sheet;
- The signature of the Technical Delegate.

617.3.5 Nations must be indicated by the designated FIS code of three capital letters (see FIS Bulletin or FIS Website).

618 FIS Points and Participation at FIS competitions

Reference is made to the Rules for the FIS Alpine Points (integral part of the ICR).

619 Award Ceremony

The official award ceremony must not be held before the completion of the race and not before the Technical Delegate has authorised it.

The organiser has the right to present the probable winners before this time. This presentation is unofficial and is organised at a place different from that of the official award ceremony.

620 Start Order

For the Olympic Winter Games, FIS World Ski Championships, FIS World Cup and the FIS Continental Cups

- 每轮未到出发区、没有完成比赛、取消资格的运动员的出发号码、注册代码、姓名和国籍；

- 官方服务公司（如计时公司、计算机服务公司等）的名称；
- 比赛代码和 F 值；
- 判罚计算表；
- 技术代表的签名。

617.3.5 各国均须以指定的 3 个大写字母组成的国际雪联代码指代（参见国际雪联公告或其官网）。

618 国际雪联积分与参加国际雪联比赛

请参考《国际雪联高山滑雪积分规则》(《国际雪联滑雪竞赛规则》的组成部分)。

619 颁奖仪式

比赛结束前以及技术代表尚未授权前，不得举行正式颁奖仪式。

组织方有权在正式颁奖仪式前向准获胜者提前颁奖，但这样的颁奖是非正式的，并且是在不同于正式颁奖仪式的地点进行。

620 出发顺序

对于冬季奥林匹克运动会、国际雪联世界滑雪锦标赛、国际雪联世界杯和国际雪联洲际杯，可以颁布

special regulations may be issued.

621 Group Draw and Start Order

621.1 The classification of competitors who are present is made by the Jury.

621.2 The FIS Points List worked out by FIS must be used for the classification of competitors. If competitors do not appear in the last valid FIS points list, they will be assigned to that group of competitors without FIS points.

621.3 The starting order of the competitors in all alpine competitions is determined by their FIS points (Downhill, Slalom, Giant Slalom, Super-G and Alpine Combined). A first group of a maximum of the 15 best competitors present regardless of nationality will be drawn.The group may be increased if two or more competitors share the 15th rank.

All remaining competitors start in order of their FIS points. All competitors without FIS points will be drawn in the last group.

If in the first 15 competitors present, the points difference between one and the next competitor is too great; the Jury will decide the number of competitors in the first group. The rest will start in the order of their FIS points.

特别规定。

621 分组抽签和出发顺序

621.1 仲裁委员会负责参赛运动员的分组。

621.2 运动员分组时应使用由国际雪联制定的国际雪联积分榜。如果某运动员未被纳入最新的国际雪联积分榜，应被分入无国际雪联积分的运动员组。

621.3 所有高山滑雪比赛中参赛运动员的出发顺序由其国际雪联积分（滑降、回转、大回转、超级大回转和全能赛）决定。第一组运动员最多 15 名，从参赛的积分最高的运动员中抽出，不分国籍。如果有两名或以上的参赛运动员并列第 15 名，则该组人数可以增加。

其余运动员将按其国际雪联积分顺序出发。没有国际雪联积分的所有参赛运动员都会被抽到最后一组。

如果参赛的前 15 名运动员中，紧挨着的两人积分相差太大，由仲裁委员会决定第一组的人数。其余运动员按其国际雪联积分排名出发。

621.3.1 Youth Competition (see art. 608.6).

621.3.2 **Starting Order at National Championships (NC)**

As an alternative to art. 621.3 for National Championships the Jury may permit the draw/choice of start numbers to be as follows:

For Slalom and Giant Slalom the first 15 ranked competitors according to current FIS points will be divided into two groups (1 to 7 and 8 to 15) Start numbers will then be drawn within the groups by double draw.

For Downhill, Super-G and Alpine Combined the first 15 ranked competitors according to current FIS points, in ranked order, may choose a start number between 1 and 30. The remaining start numbers between 1 and 30 will then be drawn amongst the competitors ranked 16 to 30 according to current FIS points. All other competitors start in the order of their FIS points.

621.3.3 **Starting order Alpine Combined**

If the Slalom run takes place before the Downhill or Super-G, competitors who are shown as DNS, NPS, DNF or DSQ will start in the Downhill or Super-G with their original bib after the last qualified competitor in the Slalom Run, with the exception of Olympic Winter Games, FIS World Ski Championships, World Cup and European Cup competitions. The starting order of AC competitions is determined by AC FIS points. Exception: AC competitions at NC and NJC may be seeded by DH or SG FIS points.

621.3.1 青少年比赛（参见本规则第 608.6 条）。

621.3.2 国内锦标赛（NC）中的出发顺序
作为国内锦标赛针对本规则第 621.3 条的替代方案，仲裁委员会可允许采取如下方式抽签或选择出发号码：
在回转和大回转比赛中，第一组的 15 名运动员根据国际雪联的积分分成 2 组（1~7 号及 8~15 号）。然后在组内通过双重抽签抽取出发号码。

在滑降、超级大回转和全能赛比赛中，根据现有国际雪联积分排名前 15 的运动员，可以按排名顺序选择 1~30 的出发号码。1~30 号中剩余的号码将根据现有国际雪联积分，在排名 16~30 名的运动员中抽签决定。所有其他运动员按照其国际雪联积分排名出发。

621.3.3 高山全能出发顺序
如果回转项目在滑降和超级大回转之前举行，被判罚未出发（DNS）、禁止出发（NPS）、未完成（DNF）或取消资格（DSQ）的运动员在参加滑降和超级大回转比赛时仍佩戴最初的出发号码布，其顺序应安排在有资格参加回转比赛的最后 1 名运动员之后。以上规定不适用于冬季奥林匹克运动会、国际雪联世界锦标赛、世界杯和欧洲杯的比赛。高山全能比赛的出发顺序由高山全能国际雪联积分决定。例外情况：国内锦标赛和国内青少年锦标赛中的高山全能比赛可由滑降或超级大回转国际雪联积分确定种子选手。

621.4 If the number without FIS points is too great, the Jury must divide them into several groups. In this case, each nation announces the groups to which it wishes its competitors to belong. Each group is then drawn separately. The Jury should whenever possible, take into account the observations made during the official downhill training and must divide the competitors from several nations fairly between the groups without FIS points. As a rule, each nation who has entered competitors without FIS points puts one competitor into the first group of competitors without FIS points.

621.5 The Jury has the right to change the starting order if they consider the condition of the course warrants it.

621.6 The draw must take place on the day before the race. For night races, the draw must take place at the latest before noon on the race day.

621.7 The first group and the groups without FIS Points in downhill training must be drawn every day.

621.8 The draw (first group and groups without FIS points) must be held in a team captains' meeting.
A double draw is recommended with a simultaneous draw of the start number and the name of the competitor.

621.9 The Jury may allow a computer-assisted draw. A representative of each nation is required to sign the team entry

621.4 无国际雪联积分的人数过多的，仲裁委员会必须将其分成若干组。此时，每个国家都宣布希望其运动员归属的分组，然后每组单独抽签。如有可能，仲裁委员会应在考虑滑降适应场地训练期间观察到的运动员表现的基础上，将来自不同国家的运动员公平分配到没有国际雪联积分的各组中。原则上，每个派出无国际雪联积分选手参赛的国家都要有一名选手放入由没有国际雪联积分选手组成的第一组中。

621.5 仲裁委员会有权根据赛道条件需要更改出发顺序。

621.6 抽签须在比赛的前一天进行。如果比赛在夜间进行，抽签最迟在比赛日的午前进行。

621.7 第一组和滑降训练中无国际雪联积分的各训练组，每天都必须抽签。

621.8 抽签（第一组和无国际雪联积分各组）必须在领队会议上进行。
建议采用双重抽签法，即同时抽出出发顺序号码和运动员的姓名。

621.9 仲裁委员会可以允许计算机辅助抽签。在采用计算机抽签之前，每个国家的代表都必须在领队会议上

at the team captains' meeting before the draw is conducted by computer.

621.10 **Starting Order in Extraordinary Conditions (Snow)**

In extraordinary conditions, the Jury may change the starting order of a Downhill race, a Giant Slalom or a Super-G (when snowing, etc.). A group of at least 6 competitors, nominated in advance, start before start number one.

These 6 competitors are drawn from among the last 20% of the start list.They will start in reverse order of their start numbers.

621.11 **Starting Order for the 2nd Run**

621.11.1 In competitions with two runs, the starting order for the second run is determined by the result list of the first run except for the first 30 places.

621.11.2 For the first 30 places the starting order is as follows:

- The 30th in the result list starts 1st;
- The 29th in the result list starts 2nd;
- The 28th in the result list starts 3rd;
- The 27th in the result list starts 4th;

……

- The 1st in the result list starts 30th;
- From the 31st onward according to the result list of the first run.

If more than one competitor is ranked 30th, the competi

的参赛队签到表中签名。

621.10 **特殊情况下的出发顺序（下雪）**

在特殊情况下（如下雪等），仲裁委员会可以改变滑降、大回转和超级大回转的出发顺序。事先提名的由至少 6 名运动员组成的小组，在第一出发顺序之前出发。
这 6 名运动员从出发顺序表最后 20% 的运动员中抽签选出。按他们的出发顺序号倒序出发。

621.11 **第二轮滑行出发顺序**

621.11.1 有两轮滑行的比赛项目，第二轮滑行的出发顺序由第一轮滑行成绩列表决定，前 30 名除外。

621.11.2 成绩列表中位居前 30 名的运动员出发顺序如下：
- 第 30 名第 1 个出发；
- 第 29 名第 2 个出发；
- 第 28 名第 3 个出发；
- 第 27 名第 4 个出发；
……
- 第 1 名第 30 个出发；
- 从第 31 名起，按第一轮滑行成绩列表顺序出发。

如果有不止一名运动员排在第 30 名，出发号码小的

tor with the lowest start number will start first.

621.11.3 **Starting Order for the 2nd Run at FIS Races（All Levels）**
The Jury has the right to decide no later than one hour before the start of the first run; whether the reversed order shall be reduced to the first fifteen placed competitors from the first run.

621.11.4 A start list for the second run must be published in good time and made available to teams and officials at the start for the second run.

621.12 Double Entries

If competitors have started in a competition they cannot appear as DNS 1 in another competition on the same day, except for a DH training. If competitors are entered into and drawn for a DH competition and subsequently leaves this competition in order to participate in another DH competition, they will not be permitted to return to the first DH competition.
The FIS Office will refer all double entries to the FIS Council for appropriate action.

622 Start Intervals

622.1 Regular Intervals

In Downhill, Giant Slalom and Super-G, competitors will normally start at regular intervals of 60 seconds; for Slalom see art. 805.1. The Jury may fix different intervals.

先出发。

621.11.3 国际雪联比赛中第二轮滑行的出发顺序（所有等级）
仲裁委员会有权在第一轮滑行开始 1 个小时前决定，是否将倒序出发的运动员减到第一轮滑行的前 15 名。

621.11.4 必须及时发布第二轮滑行的出发顺序，并在第二轮滑行的出发区提供给代表队和其随队官员。

621.12 **双重报名**
除滑降训练外，已经在比赛中出发的运动员不能以未出发 1（DNS 1）的身份在同一天参加其他比赛。如果运动员报名参加滑降比赛并已抽签，然后为参加另一项滑降比赛而离开了该次比赛，则不能再返回参加该次滑降比赛。

国际雪联办公室将向国际雪联理事会报告所有双重报名的情况以采取适当措施。

622 出发间隔

622.1 **正常出发间隔**
在滑降、大回转和超级大回转比赛中，运动员通常按 60 秒的正常间隔出发；回转比赛参见本规则第 805.1 条。仲裁委员会可以确定不同的间隔时间。

622.2 Special Start Intervals

The start intervals in Downhill, Super-G and if necessary, Giant Slalom may be changed under the following conditions:

622.2.1 The time extension must be used for sensible TV transmission of interesting sections of the entire course.

622.2.2 The start interval is determined by the Jury.

622.2.3 The start interval must not be less than 40 seconds in Downhill and Super-G and 30 seconds in Giant Slalom.

622.2.4 Further exceptions to art. 622.2.2 and 622.2.3 can be made only by the FIS Council (World Cup: According to World Cup Rules).

623 Re-runs

623.1 Prerequisites

623.1.1 Competitors who are obstructed while racing must stop immediately after the incident takes place and report this to the nearest gate judge. They may apply to any member of the Jury for a re-run. This claim can also be made by the team captain of the obstructed competitor. Competitors should make their way to the Finish along the side of the course.

622.2 **特殊出发间隔**

在滑降、超级大回转比赛中，以及必要时在大回转比赛中，如遇下列情况可改变出发间隔。

622.2.1 电视合理转播整个比赛中最精彩的旗门组时，必须延长出发间隔。

622.2.2 出发间隔由仲裁委员会决定。

622.2.3 滑降和超级大回转的出发间隔不得少于40秒，大回转的出发间隔不得少于30秒。

622.2.4 只有国际雪联理事会方可进一步作出本规则第622.2.2条和第622.2.3条以外的规定（世界杯赛：参照《世界杯规则》）。

623 重滑

623.1 先决条件

623.1.1 运动员在比赛中受到阻碍，应在事故发生后立即停下并向距离最近的旗门裁判员报告。受阻运动员或由其领队可以向仲裁委员会的任何成员提出重滑要求。运动员应设法沿着赛道边缘抵达终点。

623.1.2 In special situations (e.g. failure of the timekeeping system or other technical failures), the Jury may grant a re-run.

623.1.3 When competitors are waved down by a yellow flag, they must stop immediately. They have the right to a re-run, provided that the Jury considers this possible from an organisational point of view. The Jury should ensure that the competitor's re-run takes place before the last competitor on the start list of the race, or training run in the case of Downhill (see art. 705.2 and 705.3).

623.2 Grounds for Interference

623.2.1 Blocking of the course by an official, a spectator, an animal or other Obstruction.

623.2.2 Blocking of the course by a fallen competitor who does not clear the course quickly enough.

623.2.3 Objects in the course such as a lost ski pole or the ski of a previous competitor.

623.2.4 Activities of the first aid service which obstruct the competitor.

623.2.5 Absence of a gate that has not been promptly replaced.

623.2.6 Other similar incidents beyond the will and control of the competitor, which cause significant loss of speed or

623.1.2　在特殊情况下(如计时系统失灵或其他技术性故障)，仲裁委员会可下令重滑。

623.1.3　运动员看到挥舞黄旗必须立即停止滑行。若仲裁委员会从赛事组织的角度认为可行，运动员有权重滑。仲裁委员会应确保其在出发顺序表最后 1 名运动员出发前或在滑降中的训练前重滑（参见本规则第 705.2 条、第 705.3 条）。

623.2　干扰的情形

623.2.1　在赛道上受到官员、观众、动物或其他障碍物的阻碍。

623.2.2　在赛道上受到滑倒而又没有及时离开线路的运动员的阻碍。

623.2.3　受到赛道上物品的阻碍，如前面运动员丢落的滑雪杖、滑雪板。

623.2.4　受到急救活动的阻碍。

623.2.5　旗门缺失并且没有及时重新安放好。

623.2.6　其他类似的超出运动员意志力和控制范围的事故，造成其速度明显减慢或比赛线路的实际延长，进而

a lengthening of the racing line and consequently affect the competitor's time.

623.2.7 Interruption by an official with a Yellow Flag (see art. 623.1.3).

623.3 Validity of a Re–run

623.3.1 If the Referee or another Jury member is unable to question the appropriate officials immediately or to judge the justification for the re-run they may grant a provisional re-run, to avoid delay for the competitor. This re-run will be valid only if it is subsequently confirmed by the Jury.

623.3.2 If competitors were already disqualified before the incident entitling them to a re-run, the re-run is not valid.

623.3.3 The provisional or subsequently approved run remains valid even if it proves slower than the obstructed one.

623.4 Start Time of the Re–run

623.4.1 In the case of fixed start intervals, competitors must start at the fixed interval, after they have reported to the start referee, in accordance with the decision of the start referee.

623.4.2 With non-fixed start intervals, the procedure is in accordance with the provisions of art. 805.3.

影响运动员的用时。

623.2.7 受到手持黄旗的官员的干扰而暂停滑行（见本规则第 623.1.3 条）。

623.3 重滑的有效性

623.3.1 如果裁判长或者其他仲裁委员会成员不能马上询问有关官员或无法判定重滑的正当理由，为避免耽误运动员，可批准临时重滑一次。临时重滑只有随后经仲裁委员会确认后方为有效。

623.3.2 运动员在赋予其重滑权利的事故发生前已被取消资格的，重滑无效。

623.3.3 临时获准或随后正式获批的重滑，即便比受到阻碍的第一次滑行还慢，重滑成绩仍然有效。

623.4 重滑的出发时间

623.4.1 在采用固定出发间隔的比赛中，重新出发的运动员向起点裁判长报告后，根据其决定在固定的出发间隔时间出发。

623.4.2 在采用非固定出发间隔的比赛中，出发程序按本规则第 805.3 条执行。

624 Interruption of the Run or Training

If an interrupted run cannot be finished on the same day, it is to be treated as a terminated run.

624.1 By the Jury

624.1.1 to allow course maintenance.

624.1.2 for unfavourable or inconsistent weather and snow conditions.

624.1.2.1 The race is to be restarted as soon as the work on the course has finished and if the weather and snow conditions have changed so that a fair competition can be assured.

624.1.2.2 A repeated interruption of the race ordered for the same reason should lead to a termination. A Downhill, a Super-G, as well as one run of Slalom or Giant Slalom may not last longer than four hours.

624.2 Brief Interruption

Each member of the Jury is entitled to order a brief interruption of the run, including at the request of a gate judge.

625 Termination of a Competition

625.1 By the Jury

- If the competitors are significantly affected by outside

624 比赛或训练的暂停

如果被暂停的比赛不能在当天结束，应视为被终止的比赛。

624.1 由仲裁委员会决定

624.1.1 因需平整赛道。

624.1.2 因恶劣或不稳定的天气及雪况。

624.1.2.1 一旦赛道平整完毕，如果天气和雪况发生变化，比赛继续进行，以确保公平竞争。

624.1.2.2 因相同原因致使比赛赛序反复被打断的，应终止比赛。滑降、超级大回转及回转或大回转任何一轮滑行时间不得超过 4 小时。

624.2 短时暂停比赛

仲裁委员会的每一位成员都有权命令比赛短时暂停，包括应旗门裁判员请求的情形。

625 终止比赛

625.1 由仲裁委员会决定

- 参赛运动员明显受到外界干扰影响；

disturbing influences;
- If conditions arise that interfere with the fairness of the race or if the proper conduct of the race may no longer be guaranteed.

626 Report

For all interrupted or terminated competitions (art. 624 and 625), a full and detailed report is to be made by the TD to the FIS and the organising National Ski Association. The report must contain a well-founded recommendation, as to whether the terminated competition is to be taken into consideration for FIS points or not.

627 Not Permitted to Start (NPS)

A competitor will not be permitted to start (NPS) in any FIS International Ski competition who:

627.1 wears obscene names and/or symbols on clothing and equipment (art. 207.1) or behaves in an unsportsmanlike manner in the start area (art. 205.5, 223.1.1)

627.2 violates the FIS rules in regard to the FIS Specifications for Alpine Competition Equipment and Commercial Markings on Equipment (art. 222 and 207). (Exception art. 606.2 Competition Suits)

627.3 refuses to undertake a FIS required medical examination (art. 221.2)

- 发生妨碍比赛公平或不能保证比赛正常进行的情况。

626 报告

对于所有暂停或终止的比赛（本规则第 624 条和第 625 条），应由技术代表向国际雪联和组织比赛的国家滑雪协会提交一份完整详细的报告。报告必须包含有理有据的建议，内容涉及是否考虑将被终止的比赛算入国际雪联积分。

627 禁止出发（NPS）

有如下违规行为的运动员在任何国际雪联国际比赛中均禁止出发。

627.1 比赛服装或竞赛器材上带有淫秽名称或者标识的（本规则第 207.1 条），或在出发区行为举止缺乏运动员风范（本规则第 205.5 条，第 223.1.1 条）。

627.2 违反《国际雪联高山滑雪竞赛器材与竞赛器材上的商业标识的具体规定》（本规则第 222 条和第 207 条）（本规则第 606.2 条比赛服装除外）。

627.3 拒绝接受国际雪联要求执行的医学检查（本规则第 221.2 条）。

627.4 trains on a course closed for competitors (art. 614.1.4)

627.5 in training for Downhill has not participated in at least one timed training run (art. 704.8.3)

627.6 does not wear a crash helmet that conforms to the Specifications for Alpine Competition Equipment (art. 606.4), or does not have ski brakes on their skis (art. 606.3), does not wear or carry an official start number according to the rules. (art. 606.1)

627.7 was disqualified(DSQ),did not start (DNS), not permitted to start (NPS) or did not finish (DNF) in the first run. Alpine Combined FIS races are exempt from this rule. A competitor who was DSQ, DNS, NPS or DNF in the slalom run can start the speed event. If the speed event precedes the slalom run the exemption does not apply. (art. 621.3.3)

628 Penalties

A penalty will be assessed by the Jury especially where the competitor:

628.1 violate the rules governing advertising on equipment (art. 207.)

628.2 alters the start number (Bib) in a way which is not permitted (art. 606.1)

627.4　在不对运动员开放的赛道上训练（本规则第 614.1.4 条）。

627.5　在滑降训练中，没有参加至少一轮的计时训练（本规则第 704.8.3 条）。

627.6　不穿戴符合《高山滑雪竞赛器材具体规定》的防护头盔（本规则第 606.4 条），或滑雪板上没有制动器（本规则第 606.3 条），不按照规定佩戴或携带正式出发号码（本规则第 606.1 条）。

627.7　在第一轮滑行中被裁定取消资格（DSQ）、未出发（DNS）、禁止出发（NPS）或者未完成（DNF）。国际雪联高山滑雪全能赛不受此规则的限制。在回转比赛中被判取消资格、未出发、禁止出发或没有完成比赛的运动员可以参加竞速项目。如果竞速项目安排在回转比赛之前，则不适用（本规则第 621.3.3 条）。

628　处罚

仲裁委员会将对是否给予处罚进行评估，特别是运动员有如下行为的。

628.1　违反在竞赛器材上作广告的规则(本规则第 207 条）。

628.2　以未经允许手段改变出发号码（号码布）（本规则第 606.1 条）。

628.3 does not wear or carry the official start number according to the rules. (art. 606.1, 614.3)

628.4 skis through set gates or practices turns parallel to the course or violates in any way rules of competitors' inspection (art. 614.3)

628.5 is not ready to start on time or makes a false start (art. 613.6, 613.7, 805.3.1, 805.4, 1226.3)

628.6 violates rules of the start or starts in a manner that is not permitted by the rules (art. 613.3)

628.7 requests a re-run which proves not to be valid (art. 623.3.2)

628.8 continues to race after committing a gate fault or after a complete stop or violates the rule Loss of one Ski (art. 614.2.2, 614.2.3, 614.2.4)

628.9 fails to cross the finish line correctly (art. 615.3)

628.10 does not leave the finish area through the official exit with all the competition equipment used in the race (art. 615.1.6)

628.11 takes skis to the official ceremonies (art. 206.6)

628.12 receives outside help during a competition (art. 661.3)

628.3 未按规则佩戴或携带正式出发号码（本规则第 606.1 条、第 614.3 条）。

628.4 滑行穿过旗门或在旗门旁的平行赛段练习转弯，或违反有关运动员视察线路的规定（本规则第 614.3 条）。

628.5 未能按时出发或违反出发规定（本规则第 613.6 条、第 613.7 条、第 805.3.1 条、第 805.4 条和 1226.3 条）。

628.6 违反了出发规则或以其他规则不允许的方式出发（本规则第 613.3 条）。

628.7 要求重滑但重滑后未获得有效确认（本规则第 623.3.2 条）。

628.8 导致旗门失误、完全停止或者违反失去一只滑雪板的规定（本规则第 614.2.2 条、614.2.3 条、614.2.4 条）继续滑行的。

628.9 未正确通过终点线（本规则第 615.3 条）。

628.10 未携带比赛中使用的所有竞赛器材从正式出口离开终点区（本规则第 615.1.6 条）。

628.11 携带滑雪板参加正式颁奖仪式（本规则第 206.6 条）。

628.12 比赛中得到外界帮助（本规则第 661.3 条）。

628.13 wears obscene names and/or symbols on clothing and equipment (art. 207.1) or behaves in an unsportsmanlike manner in the competition area (art. 205.5, 223.1.1)

628.14 has actually started in a competition and is later determined by the Jury to have been in violation of art. 627 rules

629 Disqualifications

Competitors will be disqualified if they:

629.1 participate in the race under false pretences

629.2 jeopardise the security of persons or property or causes actual injury or damage

629.3 do not pass through a gate correctly (art. 661.4) or does not start within the time limits defined by art. 613.7.

640 Protests

640.1 A Jury must only accept a protest if it is based upon physical evidence.

640.2 A Jury is only permitted to re-evaluate its previous decision where new evidence exists that relates to the original Jury decision.

640.3 All Jury decisions are final except those that may be protested under art. 641. Appeals can be made as per art. 647.1.1.

628.13 比赛服装或竞赛器材上带有淫秽名称或者标识的（本规则第 207.1 条），或在比赛场地的行为举止缺乏运动员风范（本规则第 205.5 条、第 223.1.1 条）。

628.14 实际上已经在比赛中出发，但随后被仲裁委员会认定为违反本规则第 627 条。

629 取消资格

运动员有如下行为将被取消资格。

629.1 弄虚作假参加比赛。

629.2 危及人身、财产安全或者造成实际伤害、损害。

629.3 未正确通过旗门（本规则第 661.4 条），或没有按本规则第 613.7 条在限定时间内出发。

640 抗议

640.1 仲裁委员会仅接受以实质性证据为基础的抗议。

640.2 仲裁委员会只有发现与其原决定有关的新证据时，才可以重审先前的决定。

640.3 除根据本规则第 641 条提出抗议外，仲裁委员会的所有决定均为最终决定。可根据本规则第 647.1.1 条提出申诉。

641 Types of Protests

641.1 Against admittance of competitors or their competition equipment

641.2 Against the course or its condition

641.3 Against a competitor or against an official during the race

641.4 Against disqualifications

641.5 Against timekeeping

641.6 Against instructions of the Jury

642 Place of Submittal

The various protests are to be submitted as follows:

642.1 Protests according to the art. 641.1-641.6 at the location designated on the official notice board or at a place announced at a team captains' meeting.

643 Deadlines for Submittal

643.1 **Against the admittance of a competitor:**
Before the Draw.

643.2 **Against the course or its condition:**
Not later than 60 minutes before the beginning of the race.

641 抗议的类型

641.1 对授予运动员参赛资格或者认可竞赛器材方面的决定的抗议。

641.2 对赛道或其状况的抗议。

641.3 比赛期间对某位运动员或官员的抗议。

641.4 对取消资格的抗议。

641.5 对计时的抗议。

641.6 对仲裁委员会指令的抗议。

642 提交地点

各类抗议应提交至如下地点：

642.1 根据本规则第 641.1 条至第 641.6 条提出的抗议，提交至官方公告牌所标示的地点或领队会议上宣布的地点。

643 提交期限

643.1 **运动员参赛资格方面：**
抽签前。

643.2 **赛道及其状况方面：**
不迟于比赛开始前 60 分钟。

643.3 **Against a competitor or competitor's equipment or against an official because of irregular behaviour during the competition:**
Within 15 minutes after the last competitor has passed the finish.

643.4 **Against disqualification:**
Within 15 minutes after the posting or announcement of the disqualification.

643.5 **Against the timekeeping:**
Within 15 minutes after the posting of the unofficial result list.

643.6 **Against all instructions of the Jury:**
Immediately and no later than the deadlines for submittal of protest according to the art. 643.4.

644 Form of Protests

644.1 Protests are to be submitted in writing.

644.2 As exceptions, protests according to the art. 641.3, 641.4 and 641.5 can be made verbally (art. 617.2.2).

644.3 Protests must be substantiated in detail. Proof must be submitted and any evidence must be included.

644.4 CHF 100. or the equivalent in another valid currency

643.3 **对某运动员、其竞赛器材或某官员比赛期间的不合常规行为：**

最后一位参赛运动员通过终点后 15 分钟内。

643.4 **对取消资格的抗议：**
取消资格公告或宣布后 15 分钟内。

643.5 **对计时的抗议：**
公告非正式成绩列表后 15 分钟内。

643.6 **针对仲裁委员会指令的：**
立即提出，且不晚于本规则第 643.4 条规定的最后提交期限。

644 抗议的形式

644.1 抗议应采用书面形式提交。

644.2 根据本规则第 641.3 条、第 641.4 条和第 641.5 条提交抗议，作为例外，可以口头提出（本规则第 617.2.2 条）。

644.3 抗议必须依据详细事实，并提交证明抗议成立的所有证据。

644.4 提交抗议时，须随附 100 瑞士法郎或其他等值有效

must accompany the protest. This deposit will be returned if the protest is upheld, otherwise it goes to the account of the FIS.

644.5 A protest may be withdrawn by the protesting party before the publication of a decision by the Jury.
In this case, the money deposit must be returned. A withdrawal of the protest is not possible when the Jury or a member of the Jury takes, an intermediate decision for reasons of time, e.g. a decision “with reserve”.

644.6 Protests not submitted on time in the correct manner or submitted without the protest fee will not be considered.

645 Authorisation

The following are authorised to submit protests:
- National Ski Associations;
- Trainers;
- Team Captains.

646 Settlement of Protests by the Jury

646.1 The Jury meets to deal with the protests at a predetermined place and time fixed and announced by it.

646.2 In dealing with a protest against disqualification (art. 661.4), the gate judge and, if needed, the gate judge of the adjacent gate combinations or other involved officials, the competitor in question and the protesting team

货币作为押金。如果抗议成立，该押金退回；否则转入国际雪联账户。

644.5 仲裁委员会的决定公布前，提出抗议方可以撤回抗议。

此时，押金须退回。但仲裁委员会或其成员因时间原因已作出了居中决定（例如“有保留意见”的决定）的，不能再撤回抗议。

644.6 未按正确方式及时提交或未随附押金的抗议不予受理。

645 抗议权

有权提交抗议者包括：
- 国家滑雪协会；
- 教练员；
- 领队。

646 仲裁委员会对抗议的处理

646.1 仲裁委员会在其事先确定和宣布的地点和时间举行会议，处理抗议问题。

646.2 处理针对取消资格（本规则第 661.4 条）提出的抗议时，技术代表或裁判长必须邀请旗门裁判员参加；如果需要的话，还要邀请临近旗门区的旗门裁判员或其他涉及此事的官员、当事运动员及提出抗议的

captain or trainer must be invited to attend by the TD or Referee.

In addition any other requested evidence such as videotape, photos, and films should be checked.

646.3 At the vote on the protest, only the Jury members are to be present. The TD chairs the proceedings. Minutes of the proceedings are to be kept and signed by all voting members of the Jury. The decision requires a majority of all voting members of the Jury, not just of those present. In case of a tie, the TD's vote is decisive.

The principle of a free evaluation of the evidence is maintained. The rules on which the decision is to be based must be applied and interpreted in such a way that fair proceedings are guaranteed.

646.4 The decision is to be made public immediately after the proceedings by posting on the official notice board with the publication time stated.

647 Right of Appeals

647.1 The Appeal

647.1.1 Can be made:

- Against the decisions of the Jury regarding monetary fines as per art. 224.11;
- Against the decision of the Jury to terminate a race (art. 625);

领队或教练员参加会议。

此外，还应检查其他任何需要的证据，如录像带、照片、电影胶片等。

646.3 投票表决关于抗议的处理决定时，只有仲裁委员会成员可以在场。技术代表主持投票程序。投票过程记录经所有有表决权的仲裁委员成员签名后留存。决定根据有表决权的仲裁委员会成员的简单多数作出，而不仅仅是根据出席会议人员的多数。如果投票出现平局，技术代表拥有最终决定权。
在证据的采信上要坚持自由心证原则。在法律适用上要以保证程序公平的方式适用和解释作出决定所依据的规则。

646.4 在投票程序结束后，决定要立即公布，并在官方公告板上张贴，注明发布时间。

647 申诉的权利

647.1 申诉

647.1.1 申诉可以针对以下事由：
- 根据本规则第 224.11 条，不服仲裁委员会有关罚款的决定；
- 不服仲裁委员会终止比赛的决定（本规则第 625 条）；

- Against the recommendation of the Jury that a terminated race should count for FIS points;
- Against the official result. This appeal has to be directed exclusively against an obvious and proved calculation mistake.

647.1.2 Appeals must be submitted to the FIS Office only by the National Ski Association.

647.1.3 **Time Limits**

647.1.3.1 Appeals against Jury decisions must be submitted to the Appeals Commission within 48 hours of their announcement.

647.1.3.2 The official results may be appealed to the Council via the FIS Office within 30 days for matters that are outside the competence of the jury.

647.1.4 Decisions concerning appeals are taken by:
- The Appeals Commission;
- The FIS Court.

647.2 Postponing Effect

Evidence submitted (protest, appeal) will not cause a postponement of the sanction.

647.3 Submission

All appeals must be in writing. Proof and evidence are to

- 不服仲裁委员会作出的某一终止的比赛应计入国际雪联积分的建议；
- 对正式成绩的异议。该申诉必须直接专门针对某一明显且经证实的计算错误。

647.1.2 申诉只能由国家滑雪协会提交至国际雪联办公室。

647.1.3 申诉期限

647.1.3.1 对仲裁委员会的决定提出的申诉，必须在决定公布后 48 小时内提交到申诉委员会。

647.1.3.2 对正式成绩涉及的超出仲裁委员会权限的事项，可在 30 天内经国际雪联办公室向国际雪联理事会提出申诉。

647.1.4 下列组织对申诉作出处理决定：
- 申诉委员会；
- 国际雪联法庭。

647.2 救济不停止执行

提交证据（以及提起抗议、申诉）不会导致制裁延期。

647.3 提交

所有申诉必须以书面形式提交，包括据以申诉的理

be included.Appeals submitted after the deadlines (art. 647.1.3.1 and 647.1.3.2) will be declined by the FIS.

650 Rules regarding the Homologation of Competition Courses

650.1 General

All competitions must take place on FIS-approved (homologated) competition courses.

650.1.1 The competition courses proposed for homologation must comply with the technical requirements of the arts. 701, 801, 901 and 1001.

650.1.2 **Exceptions**

Exceptions may be granted on request.

Only the FIS Council can grant exceptions or deviations from the prescribed technical data.

The National Ski Association in question and the Sub-Committee for Alpine Courses submit the proposals for exceptions. If exceptions are granted the exception is valid from date of approval until revoked.

650.2 Request

The request for the homologation of a competition course is to be directed to the Sub-Committee for Alpine Courses through the appropriate National Ski Association and accompanied by the documents as per art. 650.3.

由和证据。最后期限（本规则第 647.1.3.1 条和第 647.1.3.2 条）之后提交的，国际雪联拒绝受理。

650　赛道认证相关规则

650.1　一般原则

所有比赛都必须在国际雪联批准（认证）的赛道上举行。

650.1.1　申请认证的赛道必须达到本规则第 701 条、第 801 条、第 901 条及第 1001 条规定的技术要求。

650.1.2　例外

依申请可以准予例外。

只有国际雪联理事会能够准予例外或者技术数据上与规定的偏差。

相关的国家滑雪协会和国际雪联高山滑雪场地分委员会可以共同提出请求批准例外的建议。经批准的特例自批准之日起生效，直到撤销批准为止。

650.2　请求

赛道认证的请求应通过相关的国家滑雪协会直接提交给高山滑雪场地分委员会，并随附本规则第 650.3 条规定的文件。

650.3 Documents

The request for the homologation of a competition course must be accompanied by the following six elements:

650.3.1 A description of the competition course, containing:

- Contact address with telephone number and e-mail;
- The name of the competition course;
- The location of the competition course;
- The type of alpine event(s) for which the homologation is requested (see art. 201.6.2);
- In case of re-homologation, the old homologation number and the name of the inspector that approved it;
- The start point expressed in meters above sea level;
- The finish point expressed in meters above sea level;
- The vertical drop expressed in meters;
- The surface length of the competition course expressed in meters (real developed length);
- The average gradient, the maximum gradient, the minimum gradient (in percentages);
- Emergency evacuation arrangements for injured competitors;
- Possible helicopter landing sites evacuation distance to the nearest hospital in kilometres and time, in winter conditions, and medical facilities available on site;
- Possible water supply for the competition course;
- Artificial snow-making installations;
- A description of the access facilities to the start and finish areas, and of the uphill transport with the turnaround time (time necessary from Finish to Start);

650.3 **文件**

赛道认证请求必须随附以下 6 份要素文件。

650.3.1 对赛道的说明，包括：

- 联系地址及电话号码、电子邮箱；
- 赛道名称；
- 赛道位置；
- 认证拟举办的比赛项目的类别（另见本规则第 201.6.2 条）；
- 属于重新认证的，原认证号码及批准该认证的认证官的姓名；
- 用米表示的起点海拔高度；
- 用米表示的终点海拔高度；
- 用米表示的垂直落差；
- 用米表示的赛道表面长度（实际展开长度）；
- 平均坡度、最大坡度、最小坡度（用百分比表示）；
- 受伤运动员的紧急转运安排；
- 可能的直升机停靠点，在冬季以公里数和时间计的转运至最近医院的距离，场地现有医疗设施；
- 赛道的可用水源；
- 人工造雪设备；
- 前往起点和终点区域的运输设施的说明，上山运输以及周转时间（从终点到起点的必要时间）的说明；

- A description of the start and finish areas including details of the terrain, aspect and facilities for spectators, and description of the shelters for the competitors at the start and finish;
- A description of the communication system and the available number of lines for Timing (pairs) showing type and number of underground/permanent or temporary cables including number of outlets along the competition course;
- Details about available radio apparatus.

650.3.2 A map with the competition course shown on it: this document should show the course's location within the rest of the ski resort, lifts, other courses, parking lots, etc.

650.3.3 A profile indicating the vertical drop and the lengths (horizontal and actual (slope) measured on site) of the competition course (contours at the same scale) including gradients.

650.3.4 A large and comprehensive image on which the competition course is marked. The size shall be at least 900 × 900 pixels. The image should be taken preferably from an opposite slope. If that is not possible, then an oblique aerial image will be acceptable.

650.3.5 A plan of the entire competition course with all details and data indicated, such as lift towers, groups of trees, snow-making hydrants, snow fences, steep sections,

- 起点终点区域包括地形、地貌以及服务观众的设施的详细说明，以及起点和终点运动员休息棚的说明；

- 通信系统及其赛道上可供计时系统使用的线路的数量（多少对）的说明，显示地下或者永久、临时的电缆的型号及数量，包括沿赛道部署的接线端口的数量；

- 可用对讲机设备的详细说明。

650.3.2　一张显示赛道位置的地图：该文件应当显示赛道在滑雪场中区位，以及缆车、其他雪道、停车场等的位置。

650.3.3　表示垂直落差和赛道（同一比例等高线）长度（水平长度及实际坡道长度）、坡度的剖面图。

650.3.4　一张上面标出赛道的全景大幅照片，像素至少达到900×900。照片应从赛道对面的山坡上拍摄。如果无法做到这一点，那么倾斜的航空照片也可以接受。

650.3.5　整条赛道的草图，标示出所有的细节和数据，如缆车塔台、树林、造雪机、雪道防护网、陡峭区段、弯道、雪道交叉口等，以及海拔、段面和滑雪场名

curves, trail intersections, etc. and information on elevations, section and resort names. The purpose of the plan is primarily to provide the inspector with condensed information on the actual state of the competition course, any improvements planned and also the potential location of permanent safety nets (A nets).

650.3.6 A certification that any development/improvement work on the ski slopes subject to approval or re-approval has been made in accordance with the existing national laws and with local and national regulations relating to the environment.

The environmental certification shall be provided only in case of:

- A first homologation, except if it is an already existing track or on land that needs no modification;
- A re-approval, only if additional, substantial work has been done.

650.4 The Homologation Inspector

650.4.1 Description

To be proposed to FIS for consideration as International Homologation Inspector, individuals must first be recognised within their National Ski Association as having completed the National Ski Association education and training process (if any) and as having been active and competent as a National Ski Association inspector, for both Speed (DH, SG) and Technical (GS, SL) events.

称等信息。提供草图的目的主要是为认证官提供有关赛道实际状态、所有改进规划及永久性安全网（A网）可能位置等的简明信息。

650.3.6　根据现行的国家法律以及与环境有关的当地和国家的法规，已经对需要批准或重新批准的滑雪坡道的全部开发 / 改进工作进行了认证。

环境认证仅在以下情况下应当提供：

- 赛道是第一次认证，但既有雪道或位于无须修改的土地上者除外；

- 重新批准，只有在完成了额外的实质性工作的情况下才需要提供。

650.4　认证官

650.4.1　说明

任何个人被推荐给国际雪联，并由其认证为国际认证官，必须先完成其所属国家滑雪协会举办的教育和培训课程，并被所属国家滑雪协会认可，并作为该国家滑雪协会的认证官在其国内的速度项目（滑降、超级大回转）和技术项目（回转、大回转）比赛中积极而称职地工作。

To hold a valid FIS Homologation Inspector licence the inspector must have a solid experience of several years in Alpine Skiing competitions like, as an example, National Ski Association Homologation Inspector or FIS TD/Referee or Chief of Race/Course or high level Team Coach/Athlete, and should have skills such as engineering, GIS, architecture, forestry, relevant computer skills and to be physically capable.
This experience allows the inspector to assess correctly the suitability of the competition courses with FIS technical requirements of the requested event (vertical drop, gradient, width, etc) and especially assess correctly the risks of a given competition course; the inspector must inform the Homologation Applicant about technical issues and mainly about safety issues for which the inspector must be able to propose solutions.

650.4.2 Nomination, Education and Development

Candidates must participate in at least 3 inspections with favourable recommendation of experienced Inspectors (in agreement with the Sub-Committee Chair) and submit their own documentation and Inspection Report to the Chair. Candidates should also participate at the bi-annual Update and attend the annual Sub-Committee meeting session.
After successful completion of previous necessary steps, candidates obtain a valid Homologation Inspector license and can be assigned to individual missions.
The Sub-Committee may decide not to issue an Inspector

要获得国际雪联的认证官执照，认证官必须有多年在高山滑雪比赛方面的丰富经验，例如作为国家滑雪协会的认证官或者国际雪联的技术代表、裁判长、竞赛长或者赛道长，或者优秀代表队的教练员、运动员，并具备工程、地理、建筑、林业和相关计算机技能等，并且有良好的身体素质。

上述经验使认证官得以正确地评估赛道是否具备国际雪联有关举办相应比赛的技术要求（垂直落差、坡度、宽度等），特别是要正确评估使用该赛道举办比赛的风险。认证官必须告知赛道认证申请人有关的技术问题和主要的安全问题，并能够向其提出解决方案。

650.4.2 提名、教育与发展

认证官候选人必须参加至少 3 次认证并得到有经验的认证官的有利建议（与国际雪联高山滑雪场地分委员会主任达成一致）并向国际雪联高山滑雪场地分委员会主任提交其文件材料和认证报告。认证官候选人还必须参加每 2 年举行一次的进修培训及认证分委员会的年会。

在成功完成前述必需的步骤后，认证官候选人获得有效的赛道认证执照并可以受指派独立执行任务。

认证官候选人未满足起码要求或者被认定还不称职

license if the candidate has not fulfilled all necessary requirements or is deemed to be unsuitable and needs to continue to train.

650.4.3 **Appointment**

The Chair of the Sub-Committee for Alpine Courses will study the homologation request and appoint an inspector to examine the competition course. The Inspector for Downhill and Super-G courses (including Downhill courses to be used for Entry League races) should not belong to the country requesting a first homologation.

Sufficient space must be provided on Downhill, Giant Slalom and Super-G courses, or on an emergency track or road or on the competition course itself, for the evacuation of competitors injured during the competition or training.

650.5 Homologation Procedure

650.5.1 **The Applicant**

The Applicant (ski resort, owner, organiser, club) will send the request for homologation through its National Ski Association to the Chair of the Sub-Committee for Alpine Courses and will deliver copy of the required documents submitted with the request, before the on-site inspection, to the assigned Inspector. In the request the Applicant and the National Ski Association must clearly recognise that the directed improvements of the competition course and the instructions for safety are mandatory for

并需要继续培训的，国际雪联高山滑雪场地分委员会可以决定不授予认证官执照。

650.4.3 认证官的任命

国际雪联高山滑雪场地分委员会主任初步研究认证请求后，任命一名认证官前往检查该赛道。滑降或者超级大回转赛道（包括用于入门级比赛的滑降赛道）的认证官不应来自首次申请认证的国家。

在滑降、大回转和超级大回转赛道上，或在应急用的雪道、道路上，必须留有充足的空地以便转运在比赛或训练中受伤的运动员。

650.5 认证程序

650.5.1 申请方

申请方（滑雪场、所有者、组织方、俱乐部）要通过国家滑雪协会向国际雪联高山滑雪场地分委员会主任发出认证请求，在现场视察之前，向指定的认证官发出随认证申请一并递交的所要求的申请材料的副本。在申请认证时，申请方及其国家滑雪协会必须明确认识到，对赛道改进的指示及安全方面的指令申请方必须严格遵循。如有违反（在后续的比赛中），被委任的比赛技术代表有权取消比赛(参见601.4.9.1)。申请方须直接为认证官报销全部差旅费

the Applicant. In case of non-compliance, the appointed TD has full right to cancel the race (see art. 601.4.9.1). The Applicant must reimburse travel and accommodation (full board) expenses directly to the Inspector.
The travel from the Applicant's home to the competition course site and back may be calculated as follows:
- Per travel day, CHF 100;
- Train fare: first-class;
- Travel in the Applicant's own car: CHF 0.70 per kilometre;
- Air travel: economy.

650.5.1.1 The Applicant (ski resort, owner, organiser, club) is responsible for the observance of applicable environmental regulations during development of the competition course including completion of any improvement required by the Inspector.

650.5.1.2 The Applicant must accompany the Inspector during the inspection, and for DH and SG the usual course setter of the race should be present as well. If the Inspector orders only minor improvements, the condition of the competition courses after completion of these improvements must be reported to the Inspector as soon as possible. For more extensive work, the Inspector will decide whether an additional inspection is necessary.

650.5.1.3 If necessary, the Applicant has the responsibility to translate the Homologation Report so that the requirements

和食宿费。

从认证官家里到比赛场地的往返旅费可按下列方式计算：

- 每个差旅日 100 瑞士法郎；
- 火车费：一等车厢；
- 自驾车：每公里 0.70 瑞士法郎；

- 飞机票：经济舱。

650.5.1.1 申请方（滑雪场、所有者、组织方、俱乐部）在开发赛道时有义务注意并遵守相应的环境规范，包括按照认证官的要求作出改进。

650.5.1.2 在认证视察期间，申请方必须陪同认证官，对于滑降和超级大回转赛道，日常的旗门设计员也必须到场。认证官只要求对赛道作较小改进的，完成这些改进后的赛道情况须尽快报告认证官。需要进行大范围整改工作的，认证官视情况决定是否需要再安排一次现场视察。

650.5.1.3 必要时，申请方有义务翻译认证报告，以便阅读及使用该报告者能够更准确地理解其要求。

are clearly understood by those reading and using the report.

650.5.2 **The National Ski Association**

The request for homologation prepared by the Applicant must be submitted by its National Ski Association to the Chair of the Sub-Committee for Alpine Courses. The National Ski Association will check if the Applicant has reimbursed the Inspector's expenses and if not will require the Applicant to meet this obligation.

650.5.3 **The Inspector**

After the request for homologation has been received by the Chair of the Sub-Committee for Alpine Courses, from the Applicant via the National Ski Association, the Chair will appoint an Inspector. The Inspector immediately contacts the Applicant about the time for the inspection and receives a copy of the homologation documents before the inspection.

After the inspection, if no further work is needed, the Inspector writes the Inspection Report. In case improvements are required on the competition course, the Inspector directs these to the Applicant and makes sure that those works have been carried out before filling the final on-line Inspection Report. After checking all other documents, the Inspector uploads the complete set of documents on the FIS Website through the "Homologation On Line System".

It is left to the discretion of the Inspector to decide

650.5.2 国家滑雪协会

由申请方准备的认证请求须由其所属的国家滑雪协会转交国际雪联高山滑雪场地分委员会主任。国家滑雪协会要检查申请方是否已经报销了认证官的支出，并责令违者履行此项义务。

650.5.3 认证官

国际雪联高山滑雪场地分委员会主任收到申请方通过国家滑雪协会提出的认证请求后，即指派认证官。认证官立即联系申请方确定视察时间，并在视察前收到认证申请文件的副本。

视察后，赛道不需要作进一步的整改工作的，认证官撰写《视察报告》。要求对赛道采取改进措施的，认证官向申请方指出并确保这些改进工作在线上最终完成《视察报告》时已经切实整改到位。在检查完所有其他文件后，认证官将已经完成的整套文件通过“赛道在线认证系统”上传至国际雪联官网。

考虑到冬天情况有所不同，在夏季视察后是否需要

whether, in addition to the summer inspection, a second inspection in winter will be necessary in consideration of different conditions in winter. This applies especially to safety regulations and the placing of nets. In case the competition course is not suitable for international races or for the given event, the Inspector writes the Inspection Report and sends it to the Chair of the Sub Committee for Alpine Courses. The request will then be deleted and the National Ski Association will be informed.

650.5.4 **Issue and Publication of the FIS Homologation Certificate**

The Chair of the Sub-Committee for Alpine Courses will examine and ratify the documents received via the "Homologation On Line System" . The Chair may ask the Inspector for further clarifications or amendments as the Chair has the right to refuse the Certificate's issue if the Chair considers that the race competition course or the documentation are not compliant with FIS rules or FIS standards. If the inspection report is positive then the Homologation Certificate will be issued and immediately published on the FIS website, together with the complete set of documents (Homologation Booklet) that will be visible to the authorised FIS Members (TDs, Inspectors, etc) having a valid FIS Member access.

The FIS System will automatically send a digital copy of the Homologation Certificate and Booklet to the Applicant, to its National Ski Association and to the Inspector, while the original 'paper' copy of the Homologation Certificate will be sent by standard mail only to the Applicant.

在冬季再视察一次，由认证官酌情决定。安全规则的遵守和安全网的置放尤其要注意。赛道不适宜举办国际比赛或指定赛事的，认证官撰写《视察报告》并将其发送给国际雪联高山滑雪场地分委员会主任。认证请求遂被否决并通知国家滑雪协会。

650.5.4 **国际雪联认证证书的颁发和公布**

国际雪联高山滑雪场地分委员会主任审查并正式批准通过“赛道在线认证系统”接受的整套认证文件。主任可以要求认证官进一步澄清或者修改。主任认为申请认证的赛道或者认证文件不符合国际雪联的规则或者标准的，有权拒绝颁发认证证书。《视察报告》得到批准，即颁发认证证书并立即在国际雪联官网上公布，随附整套认证文件（《认证文档》）获得国际雪联成员有效访问授权的国际雪联成员（技术代表、认证官等）都可以看到。

国际雪联的信息系统自动将《认证证书》及《认证文档》的数字文件副本发送给申请方、其所属国家滑雪协会和认证官。《认证证书》的原始“纸质”文本以标准邮件形式只发送给申请方。

650.5.4.1 The Homologation Certificate itself sets out the name and event of the competition course and its technical data. The registration number of the certificate indicates the total number of homologated competition courses, the month and year in which the Certificate was issued. The expiration date is indicated.

650.5.4.2 The Applicant's National Ski Association will be invoiced for the relative Homologation Fee (depending on how many competition courses and how many alpine events on the same competition course), to cover the administrative costs.

650.5.5 Expiration of the Application

If the requested work has not been completed within four years after the inspection is carried out and the homologation cannot be granted, the competition course will be deleted from the list of pending homologation applications. For further consideration a new application is required.

650.5.6 Validity of the FIS Homologation Certificate

650.5.6.1 Downhill and Super-G

The certificate is valid from the date of issue: it will expire on 1st July*, five (5) years later. A re-homologation must be carried out before a new certificate is issued.

*) = For the Southern Hemisphere 1st November.

650.5.4.1 《认证证书》会注明赛道名称、比赛项目类型及技术数据。证书的注册号显示认证赛道总数、认证证书的签发年月。失效日期也会注明。

650.5.4.2 申请方的国家滑雪协会会收到认证费的相关发票（取决于多少条赛道以及同一赛道上有多少项高山滑雪比赛项目），以支付赛道认证的管理费用。

650.5.5 申请的失效

视察结束后 4 年内要求申请方整改的工作未完成，且认证请求未获得批准的，该赛道将从待认证申请名单中删除。希望国际雪联再做考虑的，需要重新申请。

650.5.6 国际雪联认证证书的有效性

650.5.6.1 滑降和超级大回转

证书自签发之日起生效：有效期至 5 年后的 7 月 1 日 *。签发新证书之前必须重新进行认证。

* 南半球为 11 月 1 日。

650.5.6.2 Slalom and Giant Slalom

The certificate is valid from the date of issue: it will expire on 1st July*, ten (10) years later. A re-homologation must be carried out before a new certificate is issued.

*) = For the Southern Hemisphere 1st November.

650.5.6.3 For all Events

Homologation certificates are valid (within periods in art. 650.5.6.1 and 650.5.6.2) as long as no natural or artificial changes or changes in the regulations or technical requirements have occurred.

Natural changes can consist of:

- Erosion, land slides or the terrain becoming overgrown.

Artificial changes are:

- The construction of buildings, lifts;
- The construction of shelters, parks, roads or tracks etc;
- The installation of snow-making hydrants, snow retention fences or other significant hardware.

650.5.7 Compulsory Report

The National Ski Association which has obtained the homologation of a competition course is responsible to report to the Sub-Committee for Alpine Courses when any natural or artificial changes have occurred (see art. 650.5.6.3). The Chair is then allowed to investigate and if necessary order a new inspection.

650.5.8 Additional TD Report

Technical Delegates may submit Additional Reports

650.5.6.2 回转和大回转

证书自签发之日起生效：有效期至 10 年后的 7 月 1 日 *。颁发新证书前必须重新进行认证。

* 南半球为 11 月 1 日。

650.5.6.3 针对所有项目

只要没有自然的或人为的变化、在规则或技术要求上也没有变化的，认证证书持续有效（在本规则第 650.5.6.1 条和第 650.5.6.2 条规定的期限内）。

自然变化包括：
- 侵蚀、滑坡或赛道被植物覆盖。

人为变化包括：
- 修建建筑物、缆车；
- 兴建屋棚、公园、道路或轨道等；
- 安装造雪机、雪道防护栏或其他重要硬件设施。

650.5.7 强制报告义务

获得赛道认证的国家滑雪协会有义务向国际雪联高山滑雪场地分委员会报告赛道上已发生的任何自然或者人为的变化 (参见本规则第 650.5.6.3 条)。主任随后可以要求调查，必要时可以指令进行现场视察。

650.5.8 技术代表的附加报告

技术代表无论何时发现与赛道有关的问题或者不遵

to the Chair of the Sub Committee for Alpine Courses whenever experiencing problems related to the competition courses or non-compliance with current FIS Rules and Regulations: it is duty of the Chair to investigate and in appropriate cases suspend the homologation.

650.5.9 Relationship between Homologation, Snow and Weather as well as Special Conditions

An organiser should not depend entirely on the homologation of a competition course by the FIS, but also take note of the prevailing snow and weather conditions e.g. a Downhill course homologated by the FIS may be unsuitable for holding Downhill races when there is insufficient snow depth, unfavourable surface snow conditions, dense fog, heavy snow fall, storm or rain.

655 Competitions under Artificial Light

655.1 Competitions under artificial lights are permitted.

655.2 Lighting must meet the following specifications:

655.2.1 The light level anywhere on the course must not be less than 80 lux, measured parallel to the surface. The lighting should be as uniform as Possible.

655.2.2 Floodlights must be placed so that the light does not alter the topography of the competition course. The light must enable the competitor to discern the terrain and

守现行《国际雪联竞赛规则》及规定的事项，都可以向国际雪联高山滑雪赛场地分委员会主任提交《附加报告》。主任有义务安排调查并可以在适当情形下暂停认证证书的效力。

650.5.9 认证、雪况、天气以及特殊条件之间的关系

组织方不应完全依靠国际雪联对赛道的认证，也应注意当时的雪况和天气情况，如由国际雪联认证的滑降赛道，当积雪深度不够、积雪表面的情况不适合比赛，有浓雾、暴雪、暴风或降雨时，则不适合举行滑降比赛。

655 人工灯光下的比赛

655.1 允许在人工灯光下进行比赛。

655.2 灯光照明须符合以下具体规定：

655.2.1 赛道上任何地方的光亮度在测量平行地面亮度时应不低于 80 勒克斯。各处灯光亮度应尽可能一致。

655.2.2 必须安装泛光灯，以避免灯光改变赛道的地势形态。光线必须能让参赛者辨别地形，并且不能改变深度感知或清晰度。

must not alter the depth perception or definition.

655.2.3 The lights should not cast the competitor's shadow into the racing line and should not blind the competitor by glare.

655.3 The TD together with the Jury must check in advance that the lighting conforms to the rules.

655.4 The TD must submit a supplementary report on the quality of the lighting.

660 Gate Judges' Instructions

661 Control of Passage (Explanation)

661.1 All gate judges must receive a check card, along with weatherproof covering where necessary, for each run that will show:
Name of the gate judge, Number(s) of the gate(s) for which they are responsible and designation of the run (1st or 2nd).

661.2 If a competitor fails to pass through a gate (or a gate marker) correctly according to art. 661.4 the Gate Judge must immediately record the competitor's bib number and the gate number(s) where the fault occurred.

661.2.1 A drawing of the fault committed is essential.

655.2.3 灯光不应将运动员的身影投射在赛道上，也不应使运动员感到炫目。

655.3 技术代表会同仲裁委员会须事先检查灯光照明是否符合规则。

655.4 技术代表必须提交关于照明质量的补充报告。

660 旗门裁判员工作指南

661 旗门监控（解释）

661.1 旗门裁判员必须人手一张检查卡，如有必要需配有防雨雪封皮，每轮滑行都会载明：

旗门裁判员姓名；旗门裁判员所负责的旗门号码，并且注明第几轮滑行（第一轮或第二轮）。

661.2 运动员没有遵照本规则第 661.4 条的规定正确通过旗门（或旗门标识）的，旗门裁判员必须立即记录运动员的出发号码和其出现失误的旗门号码。

661.2.1 须绘制造成失误的示意图。

661.3 Should a competitor receive outside help, for instance after a fall, the Gate Judge must record this on the check card. (art. 628.13).

661.4 Correct Passage

661.4.1 A gate has been passed correctly when both the competitor's ski tips and both feet have crossed the gate line. If a competitor loses a ski, without committing a fault, e.g. not by straddling a pole, then the tip of the remaining ski and both feet must have crossed the gate line. This rule also applies when a competitor has to climb back up to a gate. (art. 614.2.3).

661.4.1.1 The gate line in Downhill, Giant Slalom and Super-G, where a gate consists of two pairs of poles holding gate panels between them, is the shortest imaginary line between the turning pole and the outside gate at snow level (art. 661).

661.4.1.2 The gate line in Slalom is the shortest imaginary line between the turning pole and the outside pole.

661.4.1.3 If a competitor removes a pole from its vertical position before both the competitor's ski tips and both feet have passed the gate line, the ski tips and feet must still pass the original gate line (marks in the snow). This is also valid in the case of a missing turning pole (or gate).

661.3　运动员获得外力帮助的（如摔倒后），旗门裁判员必须将这类失误记录在检查卡上（本规则第628.13条）。

661.4　正确通过旗门

661.4.1　运动员两只滑雪板的尖端和双脚均越过旗门线的视为正确通过旗门。运动员一只滑雪板脱落但没有产生骑跨回转杆等失误的，所剩另一只滑雪板尖端和双脚必须均越过旗门线。当运动员必须登山回到旗门位置时，这一规则同样适用（本规则第614.2.3条）。

661.4.1.1　滑降、大回转、超级大回转的每个旗门由2对上面有旗门布的旗门杆组成。在雪面上旗门绕行杆和外侧旗门之间的最短假想线段为旗门线（本规则第661条）。

661.4.1.2　回转旗门线是绕行杆和外侧杆之间的最短的假想线段。

661.4.1.3　运动员的两只滑雪板尖端和双脚未通过旗门线前旗杆倒斜，运动员的滑雪板尖端和双脚仍必须通过原旗门线（雪中标识）。本条款在旗门杆（或旗门）缺失时也同样适用。

661.4.2 In Parallel, the passage is correct when both ski tips and both feet have passed the turning pole in the direction of the turn (art. 661, fig. B).

662 Importance of the Task of the Gate Judge

662.1 Each gate judge should have a thorough knowledge of the competition rules. Gate judges are required to follow instructions from the Jury.

662.2 The decision handed down by a gate judge must be clear and unbiased. Gate judges must declare a fault only when they are convinced that a fault has been committed.

662.3 Gate judges can consult the adjacent gate judge in order to confirm their opinion and can even demand via a member of the Jury that the race is briefly interrupted, so that the tracks on the course may be checked.

662.4 When an adjacent gate judge, a member of the Jury or an official video controller makes a report concerning a competitor which differs from the notes of the gate judge in question, the Jury may freely interpret these notes in view of a possible disqualification of a competitor or of a decision concerning a protest.

661.4.2 在平行式比赛中，两只滑雪板尖端和双脚在转弯方向通过转弯杆为正确通过（本规则第 661 条图 B）。

662 旗门裁判员的职责任务

662.1 各旗门裁判员均应对比赛规则有全面了解。规则要求旗门裁判员遵照仲裁委员会的指令行事。

662.2 旗门裁判员所作判决必须清楚公正，只有在确信失误确实发生后才能公布。

662.3 旗门裁判员也可与临近的旗门裁判员协商以确证自己的判断，甚至可以向仲裁委员会成员提出比赛暂时中断的要求，以便检查赛道上的痕迹。

662.4 当临近的旗门裁判员、仲裁委员会成员或官方视频监控员就某运动员作出的报告与当事的旗门裁判员作出的记录有出入时，仲裁委员会基于运动员有可能被取消资格或对仲裁委员会的决定提出抗议这两方面的考虑，自由裁量这些记录。

663 Giving Information to a Competitor

663.1 In the case of an error or a fall, competitors are permitted to ask the gate judge if a fault was committed and the gate judge, if asked, must inform the competitors if they have committed a fault that would lead to disqualification.

663.2 Competitors are fully responsible for their actions and cannot hold the gate judge responsible.

664 Immediate Announcement of Disqualifying Faults

664.1 The Jury may decide that the gate judge will signal a disqualifying fault immediately by raising a flag of a particular colour, by a sound signal, or by other means as provided by the organisers (art. 670).

664.2 The gate judge must record all infringements on the check card regardless of immediate announcements.

664.3 The gate judge is required to give information to Jury members on request.

665 Duties of the Gate Judge on completion of the 1st and 2nd run

665.1 The chief gate judge (or assistant) is required to collect

663 向运动员提供信息

663.1 运动员发生失误或摔倒的，可以向旗门裁判员询问是否犯规，如果被问及此事，旗门裁判员必须告知运动员是否出现了丧失比赛资格的失误。

663.2 运动员要对自己的行为负全部责任，不能要求旗门裁判员对此负责。

664 及时公布导致取消资格的失误

664.1 仲裁委员会可以决定，旗门裁判员应立即通过升起特定颜色的旗帜、发出声音信号或通过组织方提供的其他方式，发出判定取消资格的信号（参照本规则第 670 条。

664.2 无论是否立即宣布，旗门裁判员都必须将所有犯规行为记录在自己的检查卡上。

664.3 旗门裁判员应根据要求向仲裁委员会成员提供信息。

665 在第一轮滑行和第二轮滑行完成时旗门裁判员的职责

665.1 根据要求，旗门裁判长（或其助手）在每轮滑行结

all the check cards immediately after each run and to pass them on to the Referee in the finish.

666 Duties of the Gate Judge at the Conclusion of the Race

666.1 Each gate judge who has recorded a disqualifying fault or who has been witness to an incident leading to a rerun must be available to the Jury until after the settlement of any protests.

666.2 It is the responsibility of the Technical Delegate to dismiss a gate judge who is waiting to be called by the Jury.

667 Supplemental Duties of the Gate Judge

667.1 Gate judges may be asked to perform other duties after they perform their required function, including the replacement of gate poles, torn or missing panels.

667.2 They should assist in keeping the course clear and remove any markings made on the course by competitors or third parties.

667.3 Competitors who are obstructed during their run must stop immediately and report this to the nearest gate judge. The gate judge must enter the details of the incident on the check card and have the card available for the Jury at the end of the 1st or 2nd run. The competitor

束后均应立即收集所有的检查卡并转交给终点区的裁判长。

666 旗门裁判员在比赛结束时的职责

666.1 每位记录了导致取消资格失误或目睹了导致重滑事故的旗门裁判员，都必须做到仲裁委员会随叫随到，直到抗议解决为止。

666.2 技术代表有责任解除等候仲裁委员会传唤的旗门裁判员的职务。

667 旗门裁判员的其他职责

667.1 旗门裁判员完成指派任务之余还可能应要求履行其他职责，包括更换旗门杆或损坏、撕脱的旗门布。

667.2 旗门裁判员应当协助保持赛道畅通，协助清除由运动员或第三方在赛道上留下的任何标记。

667.3 运动员在滑行中受到阻碍时必须立即停止比赛，向最近的旗门裁判员报告。旗门裁判员必须在检查卡上记下这一事故的详细情况，并且在第一轮或第二轮滑行结束时向仲裁委员会提供有关这一情况的记录。运动员可以向仲裁委员会任一成员申请重滑。

may apply to any member of the Jury for a re-run.

668 Location and support of the Gate Judge

668.1 Gate judge must be so placed that they can safely but properly observe the terrain, gates and course sections for which they are responsible. They should be near enough to be able to take prompt action, but distant enough not to hinder the competitor.

668.2 Organisers are obliged to outfit gate judges so that they are readily identifiable. Identification or clothing should be of a colour that will not be confused with a gate panel.

668.3 Gate judges must be in their location well before the start of the run.Organisers should provide gate judges with protective clothing against adverse weather where necessary and should provide some form of nourishment during the run.

668.4 Any equipment necessary to permit the gate judges to perform their assigned duties should be provided.

669 Number of Gate Judges

669.1 The organiser is responsible for having a sufficient number of competent gate judges available.

669.2 The organiser must inform the Jury of the number of gate

668 旗门裁判员的位置和保障

668.1 旗门裁判员必须配备在安全且能清楚观察到其所负责的区域的地形、旗门和旗门组的地方。这个地方要距离赛道足够近以便于其迅速采取行动；同时还应有一定距离，不致妨碍运动员滑行。

668.2 组织方必须为旗门裁判员提供全套服装，使其很容易识别。识别标志和服装的颜色不能与旗门的颜色相混淆。

668.3 旗门裁判员必须在比赛开始前各就各位。组织方应为旗门裁判员提供抵御不利天气的防护服装，并且在比赛期间应该为他们提供一定种类的营养品。

668.4 应提供便于旗门裁判员履行其职责所需的任何设备。

669 旗门裁判员的人数

669.1 组织方有责任提供人数足够且称职的旗门裁判员。

669.2 组织方必须告知仲裁委员会，在训练时尤其在比赛

judges available for training and particularly for the race.

669.3 At Olympic Winter Games, FIS World Ski Championships and FIS World Cup competitions, the number of gate judges will be determined by the Jury.

670 Video control

When the organiser has the equipment for official video control, the Jury will appoint an official video controller. The duties of the video controller are to observe the competitors' passage through the course.

680 Poles

All poles used in alpine events are described as slalom poles and are either rigid poles or flex-poles.

680.1 Rigid Poles

Must be round, uniform poles without a bending device and should be of the same material and dimensions as the flex pole. Rigid poles may be used for the outside gate or pole and in exceptional cases (e.g. high wind) as the outside pole of the turning gate (see art. 680.2.1.2).

680.2 Flex poles

Flex poles are fitted with a bending device. They must conform to the FIS specifications.

680.2.1 Use of Flex-poles

Flex-poles must be used for all alpine competitions

时能提供多少旗门裁判员。

669.3 在冬季奥林匹克运动会、国际雪联世界锦标赛和国际雪联世界杯中，旗门裁判员的数量由仲裁委员会决定。

670 视频监控

组织方备有设备进行官方视频监控的，仲裁委员会将任命 1 名正式的视频监控员，其职责是在比赛过程中观察运动员通过赛道的情况。

680 旗门杆

所有用于高山滑雪比赛的旗门杆都称为回转旗门杆，分为硬直杆和弹力杆两种。

680.1 硬直杆

必须是圆的、样式统一、无弹簧铰链等弯曲装置的杆，应与弹力杆材料和直径相同。硬直杆可用于外侧旗门或者外侧杆，在例外的情形下（如大风）可用做转弯旗门的外侧杆（参见本规则第 680.2.1.2 条）。

680.2 弹力杆

弹力杆配有弹簧铰链等弯曲装置，必须符合国际雪联的具体规定。

680.2.1 弹力杆的使用

除滑降比赛外，其他所有已纳入《国际雪联竞赛日

published in the FIS Calendar except Downhill. The use of flex poles may be requested by the Jury for Downhill.

680.2.1.1 Slalom

Slalom poles must be coloured red or blue. The turning pole must be a flex-pole.

680.2.1.2 Giant Slalom and Super-G

In Giant Slalom and Super-G two pairs of slalom poles are used, each pair carrying a gate panel between them. The gate panels should be fixed or tied so they should tear or break away from one pole. The turning pole(s) must be flex-pole(s).

680.2.2 FIS Specifications for Flex Poles

All further details in regard to construction and functioning of the flex poles are regulated in the valid FIS Specifications for flex poles.

690 Gate Panels for Giant Slalom Super–G and Downhill

Gate panels which conform to the FIS Specifications must be used for all Giant Slalom, Super-G and Downhill competitions published in the FIS Calendar. A list of homologated panels is published on the FIS Website. Arts. 701.3.2, 901.2.2 and 1001.3.2 remain valid.

历》的高山滑雪比赛均应使用弹力杆。滑降仲裁委员会可能会要求使用弹力杆。

680.2.1.1 回转赛

回转旗门杆必须为红色或蓝色，绕行杆必须是弹力杆。

680.2.1.2 大回转和超级大回转

在大回转和超级大回转赛中，应使用两对回转旗门杆，每对旗门杆各挂一面旗门布。旗门布应固定、系好，且能从一个旗门杆上撕脱下来。绕行杆必须采用弹力杆。

680.2.2 国际雪联对弹力杆的具体规定

有关弹力杆结构和功能的更多全面细节信息，请参见现行有效的国际雪联规范弹力杆的具体规定。

690 大回转、超级大回转和滑降的旗门布

符合国际雪联具体规定的旗门布必须用于所有《国际雪联竞赛日历》公布的大回转、超级大回转和滑降比赛项目。经认证的旗门布列表公布在国际雪联官网上。本规则第 701.3.2 条、第 901.2.2 条和第 1001.3.2 条仍然有效。

690.1 Release in case of collision

Gate panels should release from the pole when a competitor gets caught by it. The gate panel must meet the test requirements for this as defined in the specifications for Gate Panel Homologation.

690.2 No removal during normal collision with the pole

During normal collisions, the gate panel should not release from the pole.The gate panel must meet the test requirements for this defined in the specifications for Gate Panel Homologation.

690.3 Wind permeability

The panel must be made of wind-permeable material.

690.4 Advertising on Panels

Advertising on panels should not reduce wind permeability and the release mechanism of the panels.

695 Colours

For Major Events (art. 201.3.1) and Cups (art. 201.3.2 and 201.3.3) different alternative colours for poles and panels may be used. Orange can be used instead of red at all FIS levels. Poles and panels should be the same colour.

690.1 **万一旗门布发生绞缠，应能从旗杆上顺利脱解下来**

运动员被旗门布缠住时，旗门布应能从旗杆上顺利脱解。旗门布必须达到旗门布认证的具体规定中就此提出的检测要求。

690.2 **旗门布在正常撞击旗杆时不致脱解**

运动员正常撞击旗杆时，旗门布不应从旗杆上脱解下来。旗门布必须达到旗门布认证具体规定中就此提出的检测要求。

690.3 **透风性**

旗门布制作材料必须透风性能好。

690.4 **旗门布上的广告**

旗门布上的广告不应减弱其透风性，也不得妨碍旗门布的脱解。

695 颜色

重大比赛（本规则第 201.3.1 条）和杯赛（本规则第 201.3.2 条和第 201.3.3 条）的旗门杆和旗门布可交替使用不同颜色。国际雪联所有级别赛事都可以用橙色代替红色。旗门杆和旗门布应采用相同颜色。

3rd Section

Particular Rules for the Different Events

第三部分

各比赛项目的特殊规则

700 Downhill

701 Technical Data

701.1 Vertical Drop

701.1.1 Men's Courses

For Olympic Winter Games, FIS World Ski Championships and FIS World Cups:

- 800 m (in exceptional cases 750 m) - 1100 m.

For Continental Cups:

- 500 m - 1100 m.

For all other FIS races:

- 450 m - 1100 m (U21-U18, 700 m).

2 Run race:

- 350 m - 450 m.

701.1.2 Women's Courses

For all competitions:

- 450 m - 800 m (U21-U18, 700 m).

2 Run race:

- 350 m - 450 m.

701.1.3 Entry League Races (ENL) Women's and Men's

1 Run race:

- 400 m - 500 m.

2 Run race:

- 300 m - 400 m.

700　滑降

701　技术数据

701.1　垂直落差

701.1.1　男子比赛线路
冬季奥林匹克运动会、国际雪联世界锦标赛和国际雪联世界杯：
- 800 米（特殊情况下 750 米）至 1100 米。
洲际杯：
- 500 米至 1100 米。
国际雪联其他各类比赛：
- 450 米至 1100 米（U21 至 U18，700 米）。
两轮滑行比赛：
- 350 米至 450 米。

701.1.2　女子比赛线路
所有比赛：
- 450 米至 800 米（U21 至 U18，700 米）。
两轮滑行比赛：
- 350 米至 450 米。

701.1.3　入门级别比赛（ENL）女子和男子
一轮滑行比赛：
- 400 米至 500 米。
两轮滑行比赛：
- 300 米至 400 米。

The competition course must be homologated for Downhill with the start and finish positions for ENL indicated.

701.2 Course Length

The course length has to be measured by a measuring tape, wheel or GPS and printed on the start and the results list.

701.3 Gates

701.3.1 A Downhill gate consists of 4 slalom poles and 2 gate panels.

701.3.1.1 Courses are marked with red or blue gates (see art. 701.3.2).

701.3.1.2 If men and women use the same competition course, the additional gates for women must be blue.

701.3.2 For gate panels, rectangular panels are to be used, approximately 0.75 m wide by 0.50 m high. They are to be fastened on the poles, so that they can be recognised as easily as possible by the competitors. In place of red a luminous orange colour may be used. If the safety netting is the same colour as the gate panels (usually red or blue), and where the gates cannot be seen properly against the backdrop of the safety netting, an alternative colour for the gate panels (usually blue or red) may be used on those gates.

滑降项目比赛的赛道必须经过认证，并标明入门级别比赛起点和终点的位置。

701.2 **比赛线路长度**

比赛线路长度应采用测量尺、轮尺、GPS 等工具测量，并打印在出发顺序表和成绩列表中。

701.3 **旗门**

701.3.1 滑降比赛旗门由 4 根回转杆和 2 面旗门布组成。

701.3.1.1 比赛线路用红色或蓝色旗门标明（参见本规则第 701.3.2 条）。

701.3.1.2 如果男女使用同一条比赛线路，则女子比赛额外的旗门布必须采用蓝色。

701.3.2 应采用长方形旗门布，宽约 0.75 米、高约 0.50 米。旗门布应系在旗门杆上，要尽可能便于运动员辨认。可使用亮橙色代替红色。在赛事中，如果安全网的颜色与旗门布的颜色（通常为蓝色或红色）一致，同色安全网背景下不易区分旗门时，应采用对比颜色（通常为蓝色或红色）的旗门布。

701.3.3 The width of the gates must be at least 8 m.

702 The Courses

702.1 Joint Regulations for Downhill Courses

Downhill courses for Olympic Winter Games, FIS World Ski Championships, and the FIS World Cup must be specifically inspected, in order that they not only comply with the technical requirements, but also are technically demanding.

702.2 General Characteristics of the Courses

A Downhill is characterised by the six components of technique, courage, speed, risk, physical condition and judgement. It must be possible to ski the Downhill course from the start to the finish with different speeds. Athletes adapt speed and performance to their ski technical skills and individual self-responsible judgement.

702.3 Particular Regulations for the Course Layout

Courses should normally be approx 30 m wide. The inspector assigned for competition course homologation decides whether this width is sufficient and if necessary, may order widening. The inspector can also permit a width of less than 30 m depending on the line and terrain requirements, as long as the areas of the competition course before and after the narrow part permit this. Fall zones should be planned, where necessary, on the

701.3.3 旗门宽度必须至少 8 米。

702 比赛线路

702.1 滑降比赛线路通则

对冬季奥林匹克运动会、国际雪联世界锦标赛和国际雪联世界杯的滑降比赛线路必须进行专门视察，确保比赛线路既符合一般技术要求，又满足技术上的更高标准。

702.2 比赛线路的一般特征

滑降比赛的特征体现在 6 个方面，即技术、勇气、速度、冒险、身体状况和判断力。比赛线路必须满足运动员以不同的速度从起点滑到终点的要求。运动员根据自己的滑行技术水平和对自我能力负责的判断来调整滑行速度和动作。

702.3 赛道布置的详细规定

赛道应通常为 30 米宽。受指派负责赛道认证的认证官有权决定这一宽度是否足够，在其认为必要时可要求加宽。根据赛道线型和地形的需要，只要赛道狭窄段前后的区域允许，认证官也可以允许宽度不足 30 米。必要时应在转弯外侧设置缓冲区。尤其应在接近赛道的边缘处、下落处和跳跃处做一些能够协助控制速度的设计。

outside of curves. Possibilities to control speed should be made specifically for the approach to lips, drop-offs and jumps.
Not all parts of the course need necessarily to be skied at full speed. Surfaces may be left in their natural state.
Obstacles against which competitors may be thrown if leaving the competition course should be as well protected as possible with high safety nets, safety fences, pads or similar means if necessary, together with slip-sheets.
The function of safety installations must withstand weather conditions typical for alpine skiing.

702.4 Means of Transport

Access to the start must be provided by lifts or shuttle service.

703 Course Setting

703.1 Setting of the Gates

703.1.1 Gates must be set to delineate the desired racing line.

703.1.2 Before difficult jumps and difficult passages the speed should be controlled by appropriate course setting where possible.

703.1.3 At places where the outside gate must be removed, in exceptional cases decided by the Jury, the turning gate serves as a gate (see art. 904.3).

并非比赛线路的所有部分都要全速滑行。赛道表面可以保持自然状态。
对于运动员滑出赛道后有可能撞到的障碍物，应该采用高安全网、安全护栏、垫子或其他类似手段尽可能加强隔离防护。如有必要，还应安设防摔网。

安全装置必须经受得住典型的高山滑雪天气状况而不致影响其防护功能。

702.4　**交通方式**
必须提供通达起点处的缆车或班车。

703　旗门设计

703.1　旗门的设计

703.1.1　设计的旗门要反映出预想的比赛路线。

703.1.2　在有难度的跳跃坡前和有难度的旗门绕行前，应尽可能通过适当的旗门设计来控制速度。

703.1.3　如遇仲裁委员会决定必须去掉外侧旗门杆的特殊情况，绕行杆将成为旗门（参见本规则第 904.3 条）。

703.2 Preparation and Inspection of the Course

703.2.1 For all Downhill competitions listed in the FIS Calendar, the competition course should be completely prepared and race-ready before the first Jury inspection. It should be available with all of the installations as set out in the technical advisor's or homologation report, or as determined between the organiser and the Technical Delegate (for Olympic Winter Games, FIS World Championships and World Cup Referee or Assistant Referee) prior to the arrival of the teams.

703.2.2 Before the start of the training on the first official training day, there must be an inspection by the Jury with the technical advisor, if present and generally also in the presence of the team captains or trainers.

703.2.3 Before the start of the first official training the competitors should conduct a complete inspection of the course.

703.2.4 The members of the Jury must be available to receive requests and suggestions regarding the course, training etc. from the competitors and trainers.

704 Official Training

Special regulations may be issued for Downhill training for the Olympic Winter Games, FIS World Ski Championships, FIS World Cup and FIS Continental Cup.

703.2　比赛线路的准备和视察

703.2.1　《国际雪联竞赛日历》中所有滑降比赛的线路，必须在仲裁委员会第一次视察时完全准备完毕并可用于比赛。技术顾问或认证报告中所列的所有装置均应做到随时可用，或按照组委会和技术代表（冬季奥林匹克运动会、国际雪联世界锦标赛和世界杯裁判长或助理裁判长）在参赛队伍到达前的决定备妥。

703.2.2　在第一个场地适应训练日开始训练之前，仲裁委员会必须会同技术顾问（如果在赛事现场）视察一次线路，视察时领队或教练通常也应在场。

703.2.3　场地适应训练开始前，运动员应对线路进行完整的视察。

703.2.4　仲裁委员会成员应随时听取运动员、教练员对赛道、训练等方面的要求和建议等。

704　场地适应训练

冬季奥林匹克运动会、国际雪联世界锦标赛、国际雪联世界杯赛和国际雪联洲际杯赛的滑降训练可颁布特别规定。

704.1 **Obligation to Participate**

Official training forms an integral part of the competition. Competitors are required to participate in the training. All qualified competitors entered for the competition must have been entered and drawn in all official training runs. This is also valid where substitutes are authorised by special rules.

704.2 **Duration**

Three days should be scheduled for the inspection and official training.

704.2.1 A reduction in the number of training days or at least one training run may be decided on by the Jury.

704.2.2 Official training need not necessarily be on consecutive days.

704.3 **Race–ready Preparation**

The entire facilities (start, course, and finish area) must be completely prepared and ready for racing by the first official training day.

704.3.1 All crowd control barriers must be completed.

704.4 **First Aid and Medical Service**

The first aid and medical service must be completely operational during all training. Details of the Medical Support Requirements are given in chapter 1 of the FIS Medical Guide.

704.1 **参加的义务**

场地适应训练是比赛的组成部分，要求运动员参加训练。所有有资格参加比赛的运动员都必须抽签并参加过场地适应训练的各轮滑行。此规则也同样适用于经特殊规则授权参赛的替补运动员。

704.2 **训练时间**

应安排 3 天时间用以视察线路和进行场地适应训练。

704.2.1 仲裁委员会可决定缩短训练天数或至少进行 1 轮训练滑行。

704.2.2 场地适应训练不一定要连续进行数天。

704.3 **赛前准备**

第一天场地适应训练时，整套设施（起点区、赛道、终点区）必须完全设置好并做好竞赛准备。

704.3.1 所有用于观众管理的栅栏都必须设置完成。

704.4 **急救和医疗服务**

在各项训练期间，急救和医疗服务必须全面运行。有关《医疗保障要求》的详细信息，参见《国际雪联医疗指南》第一章。

704.5 Priority on the Lift Facilities to the Start

Organisers must arrange for competitors and specifically accredited officials to have assured priority on the lift facilities to the start in order to use the training times without waiting.

704.6 Training Numbers

Competitors must wear training numbers (bibs) for all official training.

704.7 Start Order

The start referee, or an official appointed by the Jury, must verify from a start list that the competitors start training in the order of the training start list, and that start intervals are maintained.

704.8 Timed Training

704.8.1 During at least one of the last two training days the times must be taken.

704.8.2 Recorded times must be given to the team captains at latest at the team captains meeting but may also be announced over the loud speaker or published on the scoreboard after each competitor's run.

704.8.3 A competitor must participate in at least one timed training run.

704.5 **通往起点区缆车的优先使用权**

组织方必须安排运动员和特别注册的官员享有前往起点的缆车优先使用权，以便他们充分利用训练时间而无须等待。

704.6 **训练号码**

运动员参加所有场地适应训练时，必须佩戴训练号码布。

704.7 **出发顺序**

起点裁判长或 1 名由仲裁委员会任命的官员根据出发顺序表检查运动员在训练时是否按顺序出发，以及出发时是否保持出发间隔。

704.8 **计时训练**

704.8.1 最后两天的训练中，至少有 1 天必须计时。

704.8.2 记录的时间最迟必须在领队会上交给各领队，但也可以在运动员每轮滑行后通过扩音器公布，或在计分板上公布。

704.8.3 运动员必须参加至少一次计时训练。

704.8.4 In case of a fall, or stopping, or being overtaken during a training run, competitors must leave the race line. Continuing the Downhill training run is not permitted. They may, however, move along the edge of the course to the Finish.

704.8.5 In case of atmospheric changes (snowfall etc.) between the last training day and the day of the race, an inspection of the course may be organised for the competitors on the day of the race.

704.8.6 Whenever possible, one training run should take place at the same time as that scheduled for the race.

705 Yellow Flag

705.1 Inspection

The Jury may, define the position of the yellow flags for the training and for the race if required which can be waved to alert the next competitor.The flags must be positioned before the first inspection and should be recognisable by the competitors.

705.2 Training

When competitors are stopped in training by the yellow flag, they have the right to re-start from the point where they have been stopped.

At the request of the stopped competitors, a Jury member may allow them a re-run if this is possible from the

704.8.4 滑行训练中摔倒、停止或正在被超越的运动员必须离开赛道，不允许继续进行滑降训练，可以沿赛道边缘滑向终点。

704.8.5 训练日最后一天至比赛当日出现天气变化（如下雪等）的，可于比赛当日再安排运动员视察一次赛道。

704.8.6 只要有可能，要安排一轮开滑时间与比赛的秩序册中预定的开赛时间相同的训练滑行。

705 黄旗

705.1 视察

仲裁委员会可以确定训练和比赛的黄旗位置，需要时可以挥动以提醒下一位参赛者。旗帜必须在第一次视察前放置好，应做到为运动员所识别。

705.2 训练

训练中被黄旗拦下的运动员，有权从被拦下的地点重新开始滑行。

经运动员申请，如果不影响比赛组织，且导致延迟的原因确实情有可原，仲裁委员会的成员可以允许

point of view of the organisation and any delay resulting there from. If a re-run is approved it is the responsibility of the competitors to present themselves to the start referee before the last competitor has started, otherwise this approval will be withdrawn.

705.3 Race

When competitors are stopped during the race they have the right to a rerun provided that the Jury considers this possible from an organisational point of view. The Jury should ensure that the competitor's re-run takes place before the last competitor on the start list of the race.

705.4 Obligation

When competitors are waved down by a yellow flag they must stop immediately.

705.5 Commands

On the command "start stop!" or "start stop, yellow flag" the start referee must close the start and must respond immediately via radio confirming that the start is closed, and state the start number of the last competitor to have started as well of the start number of the competitor held at the start ("start stop confirmed, number 23 on course, number 24 at the start").

The Jury member who called the "start stop" is also responsible for requesting yellow flag(s) that are necessary to stop competitor(s) on course.

该运动员重滑。获准重滑的运动员须在最后一名运动员出发前向起点裁判长报到，否则撤销重滑。

705.3 **比赛**

运动员比赛期间被拦下，只要仲裁委员会从比赛组织角度考虑认为可以重滑，运动员有权重滑。但仲裁委员会应确保该名运动员在出发顺序表上的最后一名运动员出发前开始重滑。

705.4 **义务**

黄色旗帜挥动（示意运动员停下来），运动员必须立即停下来。

705.5 **命令**

听到“出发停止”或“出发停止，黄旗”指令，起点裁判长必须关闭起点，立即通过对讲机回应且确认出发门关闭，并报告已出发的最后 1 名运动员的出发号码，以及被拦在起点等待出发运动员的出发号码（如：出发停止确认，第 23 号已上赛道，第 24 号在起点）。

发出“出发停止”指令的仲裁委员会成员还负责在需要时要求挥黄旗让赛道上的运动员停下来。

706 Execution of the Downhill

706.1 Downhill in One Run

A Downhill will be carried out in one run.

706.2 Downhill in Two Runs

706.2.1 A Downhill in two runs can be organised with the required vertical drop as stated in the ICR.

706.2.2 The result will be determined by the addition of the two run times. The rule "Starting order for the 2nd run" (art. 621.11) will be used.

706.2.3 All the rules for the Downhill are valid for the race in two runs. The Jury will rule in case of problems caused by the course, the training and the two runs.

706.2.4 The two runs should be run on the same day.

706.2.5 Downhill races carried out in two runs must be identified as such in the FIS Calendar, provided the competition course has a vertical drop according to art. 701.1.

706.2.6 In exceptional cases where carrying out the original Downhill is jeopardized (unfavourable snow or atmospheric conditions), the Jury is permitted to conduct the Downhill in two runs.

706 滑降比赛的实施

706.1 一轮滑行的滑降比赛

滑降比赛仅进行一轮滑行。

706.2 二轮滑行的滑降比赛

706.2.1 可以按照《国际滑雪竞赛规则》要求的垂直落差来组织二轮滑行的滑降比赛。

706.2.2 比赛成绩为两次滑行时间之和，适用“第二轮滑行出发顺序”规则（本规则第 621.11 条）。

706.2.3 所有关于滑降比赛的规则对二轮滑行的比赛均适用。因赛道、训练和二轮滑行引发的问题，由仲裁委员会裁决。

706.2.4 二轮滑行应在同一天进行。

706.2.5 如果进行二轮滑行的滑降线路的垂直落差是按照本规则第 701.1 条确定的，则必须在《国际雪联竞赛日历》中如实标明。

706.2.6 在特殊情况下，如果实施最初预定的滑降比赛有危险（不利的雪况或者天气条件），允许仲裁委员会分两轮滑行组织滑降比赛。

707 Crash Helmet

All competitors and forerunners must wear a crash helmet for official training as well as for the race that meets the FIS Equipment Specifications.

Soft ear protection is only permitted for helmets used in Slalom.

800 Slalom

801 Technical Data

801.1 Vertical Drop

801.1.1 Men's Courses

For Olympic Winter Games, FIS World Ski Championships and FIS World Cup:

- 180 m - 220 m.

For all other races of the FIS:

- 140 m - 220 m.

801.1.2 Women's Courses

For Olympic Winter Games, FIS World Ski Championships and FIS World Cup:

- 140 m - 220 m.

For all other FIS races:

- 120 m - 200 m.

801.1.3 U16 - U14 Courses

- 100 m - 160 m.

707　防护头盔

所有运动员和试滑员在场地适应训练和比赛时均须穿戴符合《国际雪联竞赛器材具体规定》的防护头盔。

仅在回转比赛中允许使用带软护耳的头盔。

800　回转

801　技术数据

801.1　垂直落差

801.1.1　男子比赛线路
对于冬季奥林匹克运动会、国际雪联世界锦标赛和国际雪联世界杯赛：
- 180 米至 220 米。
其他所有国际雪联比赛：
- 140 米至 220 米。

801.1.2　女子比赛线路
对于冬季奥林匹克运动会、国际雪联世界锦标赛和国际雪联世界杯赛：
- 140 米至 220 米。
其他所有国际雪联比赛：
- 120 米至 200 米。

801.1.3　U16–U14 比赛线路
- 100 米至 160 米。

801.1.4 **Entry League Races (ENL) Women and Men**

- 80 m - 120 m (Men 140).

Races in 3 runs:

- Minimum 50 m.

801.2 Gates

801.2.1 A slalom gate consists of two poles (art. 680) or where there is no outside pole the gate will consist of a turning pole.

801.2.2 Consecutive gates must alternate in blue and red.

801.2.3 A gate must have a minimum width of 4 m and a maximum of 6 m.

The distance from turning pole to turning pole of successive gates must not be less than 6 m and not more than 13 m (valid for all categories).

Exception U16 - U14 competitions:

- Between 7 m and 11 m.

The distance between gates within combinations (hairpin or vertical) must be not less than 0.75 m and not more than 1 m. The gates in hairpin or vertical combinations must be set in a straight line. Delayed gates must have a minimum distance of 12 m and a maximum distance of 18 m (U16- U14 Competition 15 m) from turning pole to turning pole.

801.2.4 Number of Direction Changes: (number of direction

801.1.4 入门级比赛（ENL）女子和男子
- 80 米至 120 米（男子 140 米）。
三轮滑行赛：
- 至少 50 米。

801.2 旗门

801.2.1 1 个回转旗门由 2 根回转杆组成（本规则第 680 条），如果没有外侧旗门杆，则旗门由 1 个绕行杆组成。

801.2.2 连续的旗门必须交替使用蓝色和红色。

801.2.3 旗门宽度至少 4 米，至多 6 米。

相邻两个旗门回转杆之间的距离不得小于 6 米，不得大于 13 米（适用于所有级别比赛）。

U16—U14 比赛例外：
- 7 米到 11 米。
组合旗门（发卡门或垂直门）间的距离不得小于 0.75 米，同时不得大于 1.00 米。发卡门或垂直门组合旗门必须设置在一条直线上。延迟旗门从回转杆到回转杆的间距最小 12 米，最大 18 米（U16—U14 比赛 15 米）。

801.2.4 所有国际雪联比赛换向次数（通过四舍五入的换向

changes by rounding up or down of the decimals) for all FIS events:

- 30% to 35% of the vertical drop, +/- 3 direction changes.

Exception for U16 - U14 competitions:

- 32% to 38% +/- 3 direction changes.

801.2.4.1 Exception for cases where the number of direction changes cannot be fulfilled due to unusual terrain, the Homologation certificate will show that an exemption has been granted.

802 The Courses

802.1 General Characteristics of the Course

802.1.1 At Olympic Winter Games and FIS World Ski Championships the course must be set on slopes with a gradient of approximately 33% to 45%. It may even be below approximately 33%, but may exceed approximately 52% only in very short parts of the course.

802.1.2 The ideal slalom course, taking into consideration the drop and the gradient specified above, must include a series of turns designed to allow the competitors to combine speed with neat execution and precision of turns.

802.1.3 The Slalom should permit the rapid completion of all turns. The course should not require acrobatics incompatible with normal ski technique. It should be a technically

次数）：

- 垂直落差的 30% 至 35%，+/-3 次换向。
U16—U14 比赛例外：
- 垂直落差的 32% 至 38%，+/-3 次换向。

801.2.4.1 因不规则地形致使换向次数无法满足要求的，以认证证书显示的准予例外的情形为准。

802 比赛线路

802.1 比赛线路的一般特征

802.1.1 在冬季奥林匹克运动会和国际雪联世界锦标赛上，比赛线路必须设在坡度为 33% 至 45% 的雪道上。雪道坡度可以低于 33%，也可以超过 52%（仅限于比赛线路中很短的部分）。

802.1.2 考虑到上述落差和坡度限制，理想的回转比赛线路必须包括一系列转弯，其设置应使运动员将速度与干净利落的动作和准确的转弯结合起来。

802.1.3 回转比赛中应允许运动员快速地完成所有转弯。其比赛线路不应要求运动员采用与正常滑行技术不相适应的特技动作。比赛线路应因地制宜巧妙安排，

clever composition of figures suited to the terrain, linked by single and multiple gates, allowing a fluent run, but testing the widest variety of ski technique, including changes of direction with very different radius. Gates should never be set only down the fall-line, but so that some full turns are required, interspersed with traverses.

802.1.4 Preparation of the Course

Slalom competitions must be raced on a course surface that is as hard as possible. If snow falls during the race, the chief of course must ensure that it is packed or, if possible, removed from the course.

802.2 Width

The competition course should be approximately 40 m wide, if two runs are set on the same slope.

803 Course Setting

803.1 Course Setters

803.1.1 Pre-inspection

This inspection must be carried out by the course setter before the course is set. The Slalom should correspond to the average ability of the first 30 competitors.

803.2 Number of Gate Combinations

A Slalom must contain horizontal (open) and vertical (closed) gates as well as a minimum of one and a

由单个或多个旗门相连，保证运动员能流畅滑行，同时又可以最大限度地检验运动员的滑行技巧，包括滑行中进行转弯半径不等的变化方向动作。旗门不应总设计成引导运动员沿滚落线下降，而应设置一些完整的大弯间之字形的穿越滚落线。

802.1.4 赛道的准备

回转比赛应在尽可能坚硬的雪面上进行。如在比赛期间降雪，赛道长要么保证雪被压实，要么尽其所能清除掉赛道上的降雪。

802.2 宽度

如果两轮滑行都在同一坡道上进行，则赛道至少应为 40 米宽。

803 旗门设计

803.1 旗门设计员

803.1.1 预视察

预视察必须由旗门设计员在设计比赛线路前进行。回转比赛线路的难度设置应与前 30 名运动员平均水平相当。

803.2 组合旗门数量

回转线路必须包括水平横向旗门（开口旗门）和垂直竖向旗门（闭口旗门），至少 1 组至多 3 组垂直

maximum of three vertical combinations consisting of three to four gates and at least three hairpin-combinations consisting of two gates. It must also contain a minimum of one and a maximum of three delay gate combinations.

803.2.1 **U14 – U16**

- U14: minimum 2 and maximum 4 hairpin combinations and minimum 1 and maximum 2 vertical combination consisting of maximum 3 gates;
- U16: minimum 3 and maximum 6 hairpin combinations and minimum 1 and maximum 3 vertical combinations consisting of 3 - maximum 4 gates;
- It must also contain a minimum of one and a maximum of three delayed turns.

The course should have no special technical difficulties. Flex-poles must be light poles (25 - 28.9 mm).

803.3 Gates and Combinations of Gates

The most important types of gates and combinations of gates are:
horizontal (open) gates, vertical (closed) gates, vertical combinations, and hairpin combinations and delayed gates combinations.

803.4 Setting

In setting Slalom the following principles should be observed:

旗门组合（每组中包括 3~4 个旗门），以及至少 3 组由 2 个旗门构成的螺旋门。回转线路同时必须包含至少 1 组至多 3 组蛇形门组合旗门。

803.2.1　U14—U16

- U14：至少 2 组至多 4 组发卡门，至少 1 组至多 2 组垂直旗门组合，每组包括至多 3 个旗门；

- U16：至少 3 组至多 6 组发卡门，至少 1 组至多 3 组垂直旗门组合，每组包括 3 个至最多 4 个旗门；

- 还必须包括至少 1 组至多 3 组蛇形转弯。

线路不应有特殊的技术难度。

弹力杆必须为轻质杆（25 毫米至 28.9 毫米）。

803.3　旗门和旗门组合

最重要的旗门类型和旗门组合类型有：

水平横向旗门（开口旗门）、垂直竖向旗门（闭口旗门）、垂直旗门组合、发长门组合以及蛇形旗门组合。

803.4　设计

设计回转线路时应遵循以下原则：

803.4.1 Avoidance of monotonous series of standardised combinations of gates.

803.4.2 Gates, which impose too sudden sharp braking on competitors, should be avoided, as they spoil the fluency of the run without increasing the difficulties a modern Slalom should have.

803.4.3 It is advisable before difficult combinations of gates to set at least one gate which allows the competitor to ski through the difficult combination under control.

803.4.4 It is not advisable to set difficult gate passages either right at the beginning or end of the course. The last gates should be rather fast, so that the competitor passes the finish at a good speed.

803.4.5 Where possible the last gate should not be too close to the finish. It should direct competitors towards the middle part of the finish. If the width of the slope necessitates it, the last gate can be common to both courses, provided the prescribed alternation of blue and red gates is maintained.

803.4.6 The slalom poles should be fixed (screwed in) by the chief of course or the assistants immediately after they have been set, so that the course setter can supervise the operation.

803.4.1 避免单调不变地将一系列标准化旗门组合在一起。

803.4.2 避免设计迫使运动员必须突然急停的旗门，这会破坏滑行流畅性且不能增加回转赛应有的难度。

803.4.3 建议在有难度的旗门组合前至少应设置一个旗门，以使运动员在良好控制下滑过这一有难度的旗门组合。

803.4.4 不建议在非常靠近起点和终点处设计有难度的旗门。最后一个旗门应以能使运动员相当快速地通过终点为宜。

803.4.5 在可能的情况下，最后一个旗门不应离终点太近，该旗门应引导运动员滑向终点线的中间部分。若坡道宽度有此需求，最后一道旗门可以为两条线路共享，只要旗门颜色遵循红蓝交替即可。

803.4.6 赛道上的各旗门设计完成后，赛道长或其助手应立即把回转旗门杆固定（拧入）到位，以便旗门设计员能够监督操作过程。

803.5 Checking the Slalom Course

The Jury must check that the course is ready for racing once the course setter has set it, paying special attention that:

- The slalom poles are firmly fixed (screwed in);
- The gates are in the right colour order;
- If necessary the position of the poles is marked;
- The numbers are in the right order on the outside poles;
- The poles are high enough above the snow;
- The two slalom courses are far enough from each other to avoid misleading the competitors;
- The reserve poles are correctly placed not to mislead the competitors;
- Start and finish are in accordance with art. 613 and 615.

804 Single Pole Slalom

All rules of the ICR are valid, except as follows:

804.1 Single Pole Slalom is permitted in all International FIS Competitions.

804.2 A Single Pole Slalom has no outside pole except the first and the last gate, a delayed gate and combinations (hairpin, vertical).

804.3 Where there is no outside pole, both feet and ski tips must have passed the turning pole on the same side, following the normal race line of the slalom crossing the

803.5　**回转比赛线路的检查**

旗门设计员设计好比赛线路后仲裁委员会须立即检查，以确定线路是否可以进行比赛，检查时尤其应注意：

- 回转旗门杆牢固地固定（拧紧）；
- 旗门颜色顺序正确；
- 如有必要，标出旗门杆的位置；
- 外侧旗门杆的号码顺序正确；
- 旗门杆在雪面上方的高度足够；
- 两条回转比赛线路之间保持足够远的距离，以免误导运动员；
- 备用旗门杆放置正确，不致误导运动员；

- 起点、终点符合本规则第 613 条和第 615 条。

804　单杆回转比赛

除下述内容外，《国际雪联滑雪竞赛规则》的所有条款均有效：

804.1　国际雪联所有国际比赛都允许单杆回转比赛。

804.2　除第一道和最后一道旗门，以及蛇形旗门和旗门组合（发卡门、垂直旗门）外，单杆回转比赛不设外侧旗门杆。

804.3　在没有外侧旗门杆的情况下，双脚和滑雪板前端必须从同侧通过绕行杆，沿着正常回转赛道穿过绕行杆之间的假想线。如果运动员有一只滑雪板脱落，

imaginary line from turning pole to turning pole. If competitors lose a ski, without committing a fault, e.g. not by straddling a pole, then the tip of the remaining ski and both feet must meet both requirements. If competitors have not correctly crossed the imaginary line from turning pole to turning pole and does not follow the normal race line, they have to climb back up and pass around the missed turning pole.
Where there is an outside pole (first and last gate, delayed gate, and combinations (hairpin, vertical) art. 661.4.1. is valid.

805 The Start

805.1 Start Intervals

The start takes place at irregular intervals in Slalom. The chief of timing and calculations or assistant tells the starter when each competitor should start, in agreement with the Jury. The competitor on the course need not have passed the finish line before the next competitor starts.

805.2 Starting Order

805.2.1 In the first run in sequence of the start numbers.

805.2.2 For the second run see art. 621.11.

805.3 Start Signal

As soon as the order for the next start is received, the

但没有犯规（例如没有骑跨旗门杆），则余下那只滑雪板的板尖和双脚都必须同时满足这两项要求。如果运动员没有正确地穿过绕行杆之间的假想线，即没有按照正常的路线滑行，则必须退回以重新绕过错过的绕行杆。

在有外侧旗门杆的情况下［第一道和最后一道旗门，蛇形旗门和旗门组合（发卡门，垂直旗门）］，本规则第 661.4.1 条有效。

805　出发

805.1　出发间隔

在回转比赛中，出发间隔是不固定的。经商仲裁委员会，计时计算长或其助理通知发令员各运动员应出发的时间。下一位选手出发前，赛道上的运动员不一定必须已越过终点线。

805.2　出发顺序

805.2.1　第一轮滑行应按出发号码顺序出发。

805.2.2　第二轮滑行参见本规则第 621.11 条。

805.3　出发信号

发令员接到准予下一个运动员出发命令后将提醒运

starter gives the competitor the warning "Ready" , "Attention" , "Achtung" and a few seconds later the start signal "Go! Partez! Los!" . The competitor must start within about 10 seconds after this order.

805.3.1 A competitor must appear, at latest one minute, after being called by the official. Early start times caused by the non-arrival of preceding competitors have to be taken into account. The start referee may however, permit a delay which, in the start referee' s opinion is due to "force majeure" . In doubtful cases, the start referee' s may allow the competitor a provisional start, inserted in the normal starting order. The start referee will make the necessary decisions.

805.4 Valid Start and False Start

Competitors must start according to art. 805.3, otherwise they will be disqualified.

806 Execution of the Slalom

806.1 Two runs

A Slalom must always be decided by two runs on two different courses.

Both courses must be used one after the other in the order decided by the Jury. Division of the competitors into two groups starting simultaneously on both courses is not permitted. Whenever possible, both runs should be held on the same day.

动员“预备”，几秒钟后，再发出出发信号“出发！”运动员必须在这个信号发出后 10 秒内出发。

805.3.1 运动员在比赛官员点名后最迟 1 分钟内必须出现。必须考虑因前面运动员未到达而导致的提前出发时间。不过，起点裁判长根据自己的判断可以“不可抗力”为由，准予某次延误。如有疑问，可以允许运动员临时出发，插入正常的出发顺序。起点裁判长将作出必要的决定。

805.4 有效出发和错误出发

各运动员均应按照本规则第 805.3 条之规定出发，否则将被取消资格。

806 回转比赛的实施

806.1 两轮滑行

回转比赛必须由在两条不同线路上进行的两轮滑行来决定成绩。

两条线路必须按照仲裁委员会决定的顺序依次使用。不允许将运动员分成两组同时在两条线路上开始比赛。只要可能，两轮滑行应安排在同一天。

806.2 Limitations in the Second Run

The Jury has the right to reduce the number of competitors for the second run to half on the first run start list. The decision has to be made no later than one hour before the start of the first run.

806.3 Video and Film Control

At Olympic Winter Games, FIS World Ski Championships, FIS World Cup and FIS European Cup the Organising Committee must arrange for recordings on video, so that the whole Slalom can be recorded.
At the other FIS Calendar races, a video or film control is recommended.

807 Crash Helmet

All competitors and forerunners must wear a crash helmet for official training as well as for the race that meets the FIS Equipment Specifications.
Soft ear protection is only permitted for helmets used in Slalom.

900 Giant Slalom

901 Technical Data

901.1 Vertical Drop

901.1.1 Men's Courses

- 250 m - 450 m.

806.2 第二轮滑行的限制

仲裁委员会有权将参加第二轮滑行的运动员人数减少到第一轮滑行出发顺序表的一半。该决定必须在第一轮滑行开始一小时前作出。

806.3 录像与影片监控

在冬季奥林匹克运动会、国际雪联世界锦标赛、国际雪联世界杯和国际雪联欧洲杯中，组委会必须安排录像，以便记录整个回转比赛的过程。

《国际雪联竞赛日历》中的其他比赛建议采用录像或影片监控。

807 防护头盔

所有运动员和试滑员在场地适应训练和比赛时必须穿戴符合《国际雪联竞赛器材具体规定》的防护头盔。

仅在回转比赛中允许使用带软护耳的头盔。

900 大回转

901 技术数据

901.1 垂直落差

901.1.1 男子比赛线路

- 250 米至 450 米。

901.1.2 **Women's Courses**
- 250 m - 400 m.

901.1.3 For Olympic Winter Games, FIS World Ski Championships and FIS World Cup the minimum vertical drop is 300 m (Women and Men).

901.1.4 **U16 - U14 Courses**
- 200 m - 350 m.
Giant Slalom for U16 must consist of two runs. For U14 the organiser may choose either one or two runs.

901.1.5 **Entry League Races (ENL) Women and Men**
- 200 m - 250 m.

901.2 The Gates

901.2.1 A giant slalom gate consists of 4 slalom poles (art. 680.2.1.2) and 2 gate panels.

901.2.2 The gates must be alternately red and blue. The gate panels are to be approx. 75 cm wide and approx. 50 cm high. They are fastened between the poles so that the lower edge of the panel is approx. 1 m above the snow and should be capable of tearing or breaking away from the pole (see art. 690).

901.2.3 The gates must be at least 4 m and at most 8 m wide. The distance between the nearest turning poles of two

901.1.2 女子比赛线路
- 250 米至 400 米。

901.1.3 冬季奥林匹克运动会、国际雪联世界锦标赛和国际雪联世界杯赛中，最小垂直落差为 300 米（男子和女子）。

901.1.4 U16—U14 比赛线路
- 200 米至 350 米。
U16 的大回转比赛必须采用两轮滑行。U14 的大回转比赛，组织者可以选择采用一轮或者两轮滑行。

901.1.5 入门级比赛（ENL）女子和男子
- 200 米至 250 米。

901.2 旗门

901.2.1 大回转旗门由 4 根回转杆（参见本规则第 680.2.1.2 条）和 2 面旗门布组成。

901.2.2 旗门必须红色、蓝色交替。旗门布宽约 75 厘米，高约 50 厘米。旗门布应系在两旗门杆之间，其底边距离雪面 1 米左右，旗门布应可从旗杆上撕脱或拉下（见本规则第 690 条）。

901.2.3 旗门宽度必须至少 4 米，至多 8 米。相邻两旗门绕行杆的最小距离不得少于 10 米。在 U16—U14 比赛中，

successive gates must not be less than 10 m. In U16 - U14 competition the distance between turning pole and turning pole must be not more than 27 m.

901.2.4 The Giant Slalom has to be set as follows (number of direction changes by rounding up or down of the decimals):
- 11% - 15% of the vertical drop in meters;
- U16 - U14: 13% - 18% of the vertical drop;
- Entry League (ENL): 13% - 15% of the vertical drop.

902 The Courses

902.1 General Characteristics of the Courses

The terrain should preferably be undulating and hilly. The competition course should normally have a width of approximately 40 m.

The inspector authorised to homologate the competition course decides whether this width is adequate and if necessary can order it to be widened. The inspector can also permit a width of less than approximately 40 m depending on the line and terrain requirements, as long as the areas of the course before and after the narrow part enable this.

902.2 Preparation of the Course

The competition course must be prepared as for the Downhill race. The parts of the course where gates are set and where competitors have to turn must be prepared as for a Slalom.

绕行杆和绕行杆之间的距离不得超过 27 米。

901.2.4　大回转旗门应按以下数据设置（经四舍五入调整后的换向次数）：

- 垂直落差的 11% 至 15%（单位：米）；
- U16—U14：垂直落差的 13% 至 18%；
- 入门级别（ENL）：垂直落差的 13% 至 15%。

902　比赛线路

902.1　比赛线路的一般特征

地形以起伏的丘陵地带为佳。赛道宽度一般应在 40 米左右。

经授权认证赛道的认证官可以决定上述宽度是否足够，如有必要，可命令加宽。根据赛道线形和地形的需要，只要赛道狭窄段前后的区域允许，认证官也可以允许宽度不足 40 米。

902.2　比赛线路的准备

比赛线路必须比照滑降比赛线路做好准备。比赛线路中设置旗门的部分及运动员须转弯处必须比照回转比赛准备。

903 Course Setting

903.1 Setting

In setting a Giant Slalom the following principles should be observed:

903.1.1 The first run should be set the day before the race. Both runs can be set on the same course but the second run must be re-set.

903.1.2 The skilful use of the ground when setting a Giant Slalom is, in most cases, even more important than for a Slalom, since combinations play a less important role owing to the prescribed width of the gates and the greater distances between them. It is therefore better to set mainly single gates, while exploiting the ground to the utmost. Combinations can be set, but mainly on uninteresting terrain.

903.1.3 A Giant Slalom consists of a variety of long, medium and short turns.Competitor should be free to choose their own line between the gates.

The full width of a hill should be used wherever possible. At places where the outside gate must be removed in exceptional cases decided by the Jury the turning gate serves as a gate.

903.1.4 The course setter in setting the course for youth should take particular consideration of the physical ability of the competitors.

903　旗门设计

903.1　设计

设计大回转线路应遵循以下原则：

903.1.1　第一轮滑行的线路应在比赛前一天设计好。两轮滑行可设在同一条赛道上，但第二轮滑行线路必须重新设计。

903.1.2　在大多数情况下，设计大回转线路时，巧妙利用地面特点比设计回转线路更为重要，因为旗门的宽度和旗门之间的距离较大，组合旗门也就显得不太重要。因此，最好主要设计单个旗门并最大限度地利用场地。可以设置旗门组合，但主要在平坦的地形上设计。

903.1.3　大回转比赛线路由各种大、中、小转弯组成。在旗门间运动员可自由选择自己的路线。

应尽可能利用整座山坡的宽度。在由仲裁委员会决定的特殊情况下，在必须移除外侧旗门的地方由绕行门来充当旗门。

903.1.4　旗门设计员在设计青少年比赛的赛道时，应特别考虑到运动员的体能状况。

904 Single Gate Giant Slalom

All rules of the ICR are valid, except as follows:

904.1 Single Gate Giant Slalom is permitted only in International FIS level Competitions (see art. 201.3.4, 201.3.5 and 201.3.6).

904.2 A Single Gate Giant Slalom has no outside gate, except for the first and the last gate and delayed gates.

904.3 Where there is no outside gate, both feet and ski tips must have passed the turning pole of the turning gate on the same side, following the normal race line of the Giant Slalom crossing the imaginary line from turning pole to turning pole. If a competitor loses a ski, without committing a fault, e.g. not by straddling a pole, then the tip of the remaining ski and both feet must meet both requirements. Where there is an outside gate (first and last gate, delayed gate) art. 661.4.1. is valid.

904.4 All rules and regulations dealing with the width of the course should be considered, as if there is an imaginary outside gate.

905 The Start

905.1 In the first run according to the start numbers (art. 621.3 and 622).

904 单门大回转比赛

除下述内容外，《国际雪联滑雪竞赛规则》的所有其他条款均有效：

904.1 仅允许在国际雪联级别的国际比赛中设置单门大回转比赛（详见本规则第 201.3.4 条、第 201.3.5 条和第 201.3.6 条）。

904.2 除第一个、最后一个和蛇形旗门外，单门大回转线路不设外侧旗门。

904.3 在没有外侧旗门的旗门，双脚和滑雪板尖端必须从同一侧通过回转门的绕行杆，沿着正常大回转赛道穿过绕行杆之间的假想线。如果运动员一只滑雪板脱落但没有犯规（如没有骑跨旗门杆），余下那只滑雪板的尖端和双脚必须同时满足这两项要求。在有外侧旗门的旗门（第一个和最后一个旗门、蛇形旗门）适用本规则第 661.4.1 条。

904.4 所有涉及赛道宽度的规则和规定都应考虑，就好像有一道假想的外侧旗门一样。

905 出发

905.1 第一轮滑行按照出发号码（本规则第 621.3 条和第 622 条）出发。

905.2 Starting order for the second run see art. 621.11.

906 Execution of the Giant Slalom

906.1 A Giant Slalom must always be decided by two runs (women and men).

The second run may be held on the same course, but the gates must be reset. Whenever possible, both runs should be held on the same day.

906.2 Limitations in the Second Run

The Jury has the right to reduce the number of competitors for the second run to half on the first run start list. The decision has to be made no later than one hour before the start of the first run.

906.3 Video Control

Art. 806.3 is applied, if possible, also for Giant Slalom.

907 Crash Helmet

All competitors and forerunners must wear a crash helmet for official training as well as for the race that meets the FIS Equipment Specifications.

Soft ear protection is only permitted for helmets used in Slalom.

1000 Super–G

905.2 第二轮滑行的出发顺序参见本规则第 621.11 条。

906 大回转比赛的实施

906.1 大回转比赛的成绩必须由两轮滑行决定（男子、女子）。第二轮滑行可在同一场地进行，但旗门必须重新设计。只要可能，两轮滑行均安排在同一天。

906.2 第二轮滑行的限制
仲裁委员会有权将第二轮滑行的运动员人数减少到第一轮滑行出发顺序表的一半。该决定必须在第一轮滑行开始一小时前作出。

906.3 视频监控
如果可能，本规则第 806.3 条同样适用于大回转比赛。

907 防护头盔

所有运动员和试滑员在场地适应训练和比赛时必须穿戴符合《国际雪联竞赛器材具体规定》的防护头盔。
仅在回转比赛中允许使用带软护耳的头盔。

1000 超级大回转

1001 Technical Data

1001.1 Vertical Drop

1001.1.1 Men's Courses

For Olympic Winter Games, FIS World Ski Championships, FIS World Cups and Continental Cups:

- 400 m - 650 m;

For all other FIS competitions:

- 350 m - 650 m.

1001.1.2 Women's Courses

For Olympic Winter Games, FIS World Ski Championships and FIS World Cups:

- 400 m - 600 m;

For all other FIS competitions:

- 350 m - 600 m.

1001.1.3 U16 - U14 Courses

- 250 m - 450 m.

1001.1.4 Entry League Races (ENL)

- 300 m - 500 m.

1001.2 Course Length

The length of the course must be measured with either a measuring tape, a wheel or GPS and has to be published on the start list and the results.

1001 技术数据

1001.1 垂直落差

1001.1.1 男子比赛线路
冬季奥林匹克运动会、国际雪联世界锦标赛、国际雪联世界杯和洲际杯赛：
- 400 米至 650 米。
国际雪联其他所有比赛：
- 350 米至 650 米。

1001.1.2 女子比赛线路
冬季奥林匹克运动会、国际雪联世界锦标赛和国际雪联世界杯赛：
- 400 米至 600 米。
国际雪联其他所有比赛：
- 350 米至 600 米。

1001.1.3 U16—U14 赛道
- 250 米至 450 米。
1001.1.4 入门级比赛（ENL）
- 300 米至 500 米。

1001.2 比赛线路长度

比赛线路长度应由测量尺、轮尺或 GPS 等工具测量并公布在出发顺序表和成绩列表上。

1001.3 Gates

1001.3.1 A Super-G gate consists of four slalom poles (art. 680.2.1.2) and two gate panels.

1001.3.2 The gates must be alternately red and blue. The gate panels are to be approx. 75 cm wide and approx. 50 cm high. They are fastened between the poles so that the lower edge of the panel is approx. 1m above the snow and should be capable of tearing or breaking away (art. 690).

1001.3.3 The gates must be at least 6 m and at most 8 m wide for open gates and at least 8 m and at most 12 m for vertical gates.

1001.3.4 The Super-G must be set as follows(number of direction changes by rounding up or down of the decimals):
For FIS level events 7% of the vertical drop equals the minimum number of direction changes. For Olympic Winter Games, FIS World Ski Championships, FIS World Junior Championships and Continental Cup level events 6% of the vertical drop equals the minimum number of direction changes.
The distance between the turning poles of two successive gates must be at least 25 m (exception: art. 1003.1.1).
U16 - U14 competitions: minimum 8%, maximum 12% direction changes of the vertical drop.
Entry League (ENL): minimum 7% of the vertical drop.

1001.3 旗门

1001.3.1 超级大回转的旗门由 4 根回转旗门杆（本规则第 680.2.1.2 条）和 2 面旗门布组成。

1001.3.2 旗门必须红色、蓝色交替。旗门布宽约 75 厘米，高约 50 厘米。旗门布应系在两旗门杆之间，其底边至少应高出雪面 1 米左右，旗门布应可撕脱或可从旗杆上拉下（参见本规则第 690 条）。

1001.3.3 开口旗门必须至少宽 6 米，至多宽 8 米。垂直闭口旗门至少宽 8 米，至多宽 12 米。

1001.3.4 超级大回转必须按如下数据设置旗门（经四舍五入调整后的换向次数）：
对于国际雪联级别的比赛，换向次数最少为垂直落差的 7%。对于冬季奥林匹克运动会、国际雪联世界锦标赛、国际雪联世界青少年锦标赛和洲际杯级别的比赛，换向次数最少为垂直落差的 6%。

相邻两个旗门绕行杆间的距离至少应为 25 米（例外参见本规则第 1003.1.1 条）。
U16—U14 比赛：换向次数最小为垂直落差的 8%，最大为 12%。
入门级别（ENL）：至少为垂直落差的 7%。

1002 The Courses

1002.1 General Characteristics of the Courses

The terrain should be undulating and hilly if possible. The competition course should normally have a width of approximately 30 m.

The inspector authorised to homologate the competition course decides whether this width is adequate and if necessary can order it to be widened. The inspector can also permit a width of less than approximately 30 m depending on the line and terrain requirements, as long as the areas of the competition course before and after the narrow part enable this.

1002.2 Preparation of the Course

The competition course must be prepared like a Downhill course. The course sections on which there are gates and where the competitors alter their directions must be prepared for a Slalom.

1002.3 Free–skiing on the Competition Course

Competitors should be given the opportunity to free ski on the closed competition hill before the course is set if possible.

1002.4 Homologation of Youth Super–G Courses

All competition courses used for U16 - U14 Super-G must be homologated. If the course to be used is homologated for FIS Giant Slalom, then a safety inspection

1002　比赛线路

1002.1　比赛线路的一般特征

地形应选择起伏的丘陵地带。赛道宽度一般应在 30 米左右。

经授权认证赛道的认证官可以决定上述宽度是否足够，如有必要，可要求加宽。根据赛道线形和地形的需要，只要赛道狭窄段前后的区域允许，认证官也可以允许宽度不足 30 米。

1002.2　比赛线路的准备

比赛线路必须比照滑降比赛线路做好准备。比赛线路上设置旗门组的部分及运动员须转弯处必须比照回转比赛线路准备。

1002.3　比赛坡道上的自由滑行

如果可能的话，在线路设计前应为运动员提供在封闭的赛道上自由滑行的机会。

1002.4　青少年超级大回转赛道认证

所有用于 U16—U14 超级大回转的赛道都必须经过认证。如果所使用的赛道为国际雪联认证的大回转赛道，需要国际雪联技术顾问进行一次安全视察。

by a FIS Technical Advisor is required.

1003 Course Setting

1003.1 Setting

In setting a Super-G the following principles should be observed:

1003.1.1 It is recommended to set the gates to make the best use of the terrain; Gate combinations according to art. 803.3 are allowed only in small numbers. The distance between the successive turning poles can in this case be less than 25 m, but must be at least 15 m.

1003.1.2 A Super-G should contain a variety of long and medium turns.Competitors should be absolutely free to choose their own line between the gates. It is not permitted to set only down the fall-line of the slope.

1003.1.2.1 At places where outside gate must be removed, in exceptional cases decided by the Jury the turning gate serves as a gate.

1003.1.3 Where the terrain allows it jumps may be set.

1003.1.4 U16 - U14 Super-G should be carried out in a form of varied run. The basic form should consist of jumps and gliding elements. The choice of course and course setting has to follow the speed and the U16 - U14 level of

1003 旗门设计

1003.1 设计

超级大回转的比赛线路设计应遵循以下原则：

1003.1.1 建议充分利用地形来设计旗门。按照本规则第 803.3 条之规定，设计的旗门组合数量不宜过多。相邻两道旗门的绕行杆间距可少于25米，但至少应为15米。

1003.1.2 超级大回转应包括各种大中型转弯。运动员在旗门间应有绝对的自由选择自己的滑行路线。旗门不得仅沿着坡道的滚落线设置。

1003.1.2.1 在特殊情况下，在必须撤销外侧旗门的地方，仲裁委员会可决定由绕行门充当旗门。

1003.1.3 在地形允许的地方可以设置跳跃区。

1003.1.4 U16—U14 超级大回转赛应以多种形式的滑行进行，基本形式应包括跳跃和滑行元素。赛道的选择和设置必须充分适应速度和 U16—U14 的技能水平。运动员应学会掌控速度和滑行。

skill. They should learn controlled speed and gliding.

1003.1.5 Course Setting for U14

Different courses must be adapted for U14 and U16, which should have turning radiuses corresponding to their age. The ski to be used is the appropriate Giant Slalom skis for U14 events.

1005 Start

Starting order and start intervals according to art. 621.3 and 622.

1006 Execution of the Super–G

A Super-G will be carried out in one run.

1007 Crash Helmet

All competitors and forerunners must wear a crash helmet for official training as well as for the race that meets the FIS Equipment Specifications.

Soft ear protection is only permitted for helmets used in Slalom.

1008 Yellow Flag

Art. 705 also applies.

1100 Combined

1100.1 Common Rules

Based on art. 201.6.2 and 201.6.9 Alpine Combined

1003.1.5 U14 级别的旗门设计

U14 和 U16 级别应采用转弯半径适合其年龄段的不同线路。所用滑雪板应为 U14 级别比赛适用的大回转滑雪板。

1005 出发

出发顺序和出发间隔按照本规则第 621.3 条和第 622 条执行。

1006 超级大回转比赛的实施

超级大回转比赛应只进行 1 轮滑行。

1007 防护头盔

所有运动员和试滑员在场地适应训练和比赛时必须穿戴符合《国际雪联竞赛器材具体规定》的防护头盔。

仅在回转比赛中允许使用带软护耳的头盔。

1008 黄旗

适用本规则第 705 条。

1100 全能项目

1100.1 通则

依据本规则第 201.6.2 条和第 201.6.9 条，高山滑雪

competitions may be held according to the technical regulations of the events and special regulations approved by FIS.

1100.2 Combined competitions may be held at all levels. When special rules apply (for example, Olympic Winter Games, FIS World Ski Championships, World Cup, Continental Cups), these rules are considered an integral part of the ICR.

1100.3 The following possibilities of Combined events are possible:
- Alpine Combined;
- Classical Combined;
- Special forms of Combined events.

1100.4 Combined competitions may be held as single or team events.

1100.5 Starting numbers given to the competitors for the first run remain the same for all runs.

1100.6 The results of a Combined competition are only counted if the competitor takes part in each event of the Combined and appears in the intermediate results.

1100.7 The Combined results are calculated by adding the race times of the single events or runs. Special forms of Combined events (art. 1103) can be calculated according to other regulations.

全能赛可按照国际雪联批准的相应比赛项目的技术规则和特殊规定举办。

1100.2 全能赛可在任一级别赛事中举行。当特殊规则适用时（如冬季奥林匹克运动会、国际雪联世界锦标赛、世界杯、洲际杯赛），此类规则被视为《国际雪联滑雪竞赛规则》的一部分。

1100.3 下列比赛项目组合可列入全能项目：
- 高山滑雪全能；
- 传统全能；
- 特殊形式的全能项目。

1100.4 全能赛可作为单人或团队赛事举办。

1100.5 运动员在每轮滑行中延用第一轮滑行时的出发号码。

1100.6 只有参加了全能赛所有单项比赛且有中间成绩的运动员才有权取得全能成绩。

1100.7 全能成绩由各单项比赛时间或各轮次滑行时间相加而得。特殊形式全能项目（本规则第 1103 条）的成绩根据其他相关规定计算。

1100.8 The Organising Committee must state in the invitation how many competitors are qualified for the second and any subsequent runs. The Jury may change this number.

1100.9 The start order is determined for each event according to art. 621. For special forms of Combined events see art. 1103.2.

1100.10 Only interim results may be published for those events or runs already completed. The official results are only published when all events or runs have been completed.

1100.11 The sequence of the different races to be combined may be decided by the Organisers and must be announced in the race notice and the programme. Changes may be made by the Jury.

1101 Alpine Combined

1101.1 Is the result of a Downhill or Super-G run (speed event) and a single Slalom run held according to the technical regulations for Slalom and those for Downhill or Super-G. The Alpine Combined event consists of two runs. (see art. 621.3.3, 621.11.2, 627.7).

1101.2 Downhill and Super-G events of Alpine Combined must be held on courses specifically homologated for Downhill or Super-G respectively.
The Slalom may be held on these courses.

1100.8　组委会必须在邀请函中说明参赛者有资格参加第二轮及后续各轮比赛的人数。仲裁委员会可改变该人数。

1100.9　根据本规则第 621 条决定各单项的出发顺序。全能项目的特殊比赛形式请参见本规则第 1103.2 条。

1100.10　对已经完成的比赛项目或滑行只会发布中间成绩。所有项目比赛或滑行结束后才能公布正式成绩。

1100.11　不同比赛项目的比赛顺序可由组织方决定，必须在比赛通知及比赛秩序册中公布。仲裁委员会可作出变更。

1101　高山滑雪全能

1101.1　高山滑雪全能由两部分组成：体现速度性的一轮滑降或超级大回转滑行（竞速项目）和体现技巧的单轮回转滑行。其举办是根据回转和滑降或超级大回转的技术规则进行的，成绩也是这两类比赛项目之和。因此，高山滑雪全能赛包括两轮滑行（参见本规则第 621.3.3 条、第 621.11.2 条、第 627.7 条）。

1101.2　高山滑雪全能中的滑降和超级大回转单项比赛必须分别在取得滑降或超级大回转认证的赛道上进行。回转比赛可在此类场地中举行。

1101.3 If possible both runs should be held on one day (exceptions can only be decided by the Jury).

1102 Classical Combined

1102.1 Is the result of a Downhill and a Slalom. Each event is to be considered separately.

1102.2 If the Slalom is held as the second event, those competitors marked with K or ZK start last in the second run, if they are not qualified within the top 30 competitors.

1103 Special Forms of Combined Events

1103.1 Combined competitions which consist of three (Triple) or four (Quadruple) events held according to art. 700 to 1000 are also permitted.

1103.2 FIS may authorize Combined competitions which consist of one or several events according to art. 700 to 1000 and other FIS Disciplines or other types of sport (e.g. alpine skiing combined with a Nordic event or swimming or sailing event, etc.). FIS approval is necessary for such Combined events. Participation and general regulations must be in accordance with the regulations of the ICR.

1101.3 如果可能，两轮滑行均应在一天内进行（例外情况只能由仲裁委员会决定）。

1102 传统全能

1102.1 比赛成绩为 1 轮滑降比赛和 1 轮回转比赛的成绩之和。每个比赛项目的比赛成绩分别计算。

1102.2 如果将回转赛安排在第 2 轮，在第 1 轮比赛未进入前 30 名的选手在其名单上标注 K 或 ZK，并将排在第 2 轮比赛中后出发。

1103 特殊形式的全能赛事

1103.1 允许全能赛由三到四个比赛项目组成，并按照本规则第 700 条至第 1000 条举办。

1103.2 国际雪联可授权举办由单项或多项高山滑雪比赛项目组成的全能比赛。其中有的单项可以是符合本规则第 700 条至第 1000 条规定的高山滑雪比赛项目，也可以是其他国际雪联竞赛分项或其他体育项目（如混合了北欧两项、游泳或帆船等项目的高山滑雪比赛等）。举办这种全能比赛需要得到国际雪联的批准。这些比赛的参赛规则和总则规定必须遵循《国际雪联滑雪竞赛规则》。

1210 General Team Competitions

1210.1 The staging of team competitions is permitted.

1210.2 In absence of any agreement to the contrary, a team consists of five competitors of which the three best times count for the result.

1210.3 The competitors of the individual teams must be named before the draw.

1210.4 FIS points will be awarded only if the individual events are conducted according to the rules of the ICR.

1210.5 The placing of the teams will be determined by addition of the race points of the three best competitors of each team. In case of a tie, the placing is determined by the result of the best individual competitors.

1210.6 For combined placing, the team score for each event is calculated according to art. 1100.7. In case of a tie, the best team is determined by the team placing in the order of Downhill, Super-G, Giant Slalom, and Slalom.

1211 Combined Team Event

The Event consists of two runs (Super-G and Slalom) and four series in each run.

1210　一般团体比赛

1210.1　可以举行团体比赛。

1210.2　如果没有相反的约定，每队由 5 名运动员组成，计算其中 3 人最佳的比赛成绩。

1210.3　必须在抽签前指定各队的参赛运动员。

1210.4　各比赛项目只有按照《国际雪联滑雪竞赛规则》进行，参赛运动员才能获得国际雪联积分。

1210.5　各队名次将根据本队最佳的 3 名运动员在比赛中获得的国际雪联积分累计决定。出现平分的，平分的各队的名次将由其个人成绩最佳的运动员决定。

1210.6　全能赛名次将根据本规则第 1100.7 条计算的各比赛项目团体得分决定。出现平分的，将根据各队依次在滑降赛、超级大回转赛、大回转赛和回转赛的排名决定最佳团队。

1211　全能团体比赛

比赛由两轮滑行组成（超级大回转和回转），每轮滑行包含 4 个回合。

1211.1 Participation

All Teams with at least 4 competitors (2 Men and 2 Women) that are qualified to participate in respective events (Super-G and Slalom) are authorized to enter.

1211.1.2 Participants per Team

Per Team and run a maximum of 2 Women and 2 Men must start. The total team size is limited to a maximum of 6 competitors.

1211.2 Competition courses

Women and Men ski on the same course.

1211.3 Enrollment

The Teams are enrolled in the reverse order of total FIS points. Women will receive bibs from 1 to 4 and Men from 5 to 8, ordered alphabetically.

1211.4 Ranking

The sum of rank positions of the competitors per Team from each of the series (1 competitor per team is a series) of both runs establishes the Winner of the Team Event.

In case of a tie of the total sum of rank positions, the number of best rank positions from individual series (1L, 2M, 3L, 4M, 5L, 6M, 7L and 8M) is considered. Should there still be a tie; the total sum of the times of all Series will count.

1211.1 **参赛**

至少有 4 名运动员（2 男 2 女）具备参加各单项比赛（超级大回转和回转）资格的团队方可参赛。

1211.1.2 各队的参赛运动员

各队每轮滑行至多有 2 名女子和 2 名男子运动员必须参赛。每队参赛人数限制在最多 6 人。

1211.2 **比赛线路**

女子比赛和男子比赛在相同线路上进行。

1211.3 **登记**

各队按国际雪联积分的倒序进行登记。各队女子运动员的出发号码布从 1 号到 4 号，男子的出发号码布从 5 号到 8 号，按字母顺序排列。

1211.4 **排名**

各队运动员在两项比赛中取得的每个回合比赛排名（每队 1 名运动员滑行 1 次为 1 个回合）的总和，决定团体比赛的优胜者。

总排名相同的，应计算各队每一回合最好排名的数量（1L、2M、3L、4M、5L、6M、7L 和 8M）。仍出现平局的，计算所有回合的比赛总时间。

1211.5 Announcement of the competitors at the Start

For the Series 1 Women, 5 minutes before begin of the series.

For all other Series after the end of the preceding Series until 1 minute before begin of the next Series.

In case of non-announcement within the times fixed by the Jury, the competitor is not allowed to start = DNS.

1211.6 Start Limitation

One and the same competitor must only start once per run at the FIS Combined Team Event.

1212 Mixed Team Parallel

1212.1 Type of Event

A Mixed Team Parallel event will be conducted as a parallel using Giant Slalom gates and panels.

1212.2 Team Size

The total team size per Nation is limited to a maximum of 6 competitors; at least 2 competitors from one gender. A competitor can only start a run once.

1212.3 Team Entry

The entries for the Mixed Team Parallel (without names) must be within 24 hours before the scheduled start of the team event.

1211.5 **起点检录**

女子第 1 回合检录时间为该回合开始前 5 分钟。

其他各回合检录时间为前一回合结束后至当前回合比赛开始前 1 分钟。
运动员在上述规定及仲裁委员会确定的时间内未检录的，取消其出发资格，即未出发。

1211.6 **出发限制**
在国际雪联举办的团体全能比赛中，每名运动员每轮滑行只能出发 1 次。

1212 高山滑雪团体比赛

1212.1 **比赛类型**
高山滑雪团体比赛以平行式进行，采用大回转旗门和旗门布。

1212.2 **团队规模**
每个国家队的规模最多不超过 6 人，同一性别的运动员至少有 2 人。每位运动员每轮滑行只能出发 1 次。

1212.3 **团队报名**
高山滑雪团体比赛的报名（不记名）必须在秩序册预定的团体赛开始时间前 24 小时完成。

1212.4 Team Ranking

The teams will be ranked in accordance the sum of each entered competitors FIS points, from lowest total points to highest.

1212.5 Seeding of the Teams

The entered teams will be seeded into heats (4, 8 or 16) based upon their ranking. A bracket list will be arranged as follows (Example for 8 Heats):

Heat 1: Nation ranked 1 vs Nation ranked 16(last);

Heat 2: Nation ranked 8 vs Nation ranked 9;

Heat 3: Nation ranked 5 vs Nation ranked 12;

Heat 4; Nation ranked 4 vs Nation ranked 13;

Heat 5: Nation ranked 3 vs Nation ranked 14 (3rd last);

Heat 6: Nation ranked 6 vs Nation ranked 11;

Heat 7: Nation ranked 7 vs Nation ranked 10;

Heat 8: Nation ranked 2 vs Nation ranked 15 (2nd last).

The best nation, according to the team ranking, will receive bib number 1 and the last nation will receive the last bib number.

Women will receive bibs starting from 1 and then Men, starting from 5, in alphabetical order. If a heat is incomplete the remaining nation will automatically qualify for the next round (a bye).

1212.6 Running the Competition

Each individual leg between two opponents consists of one run.

The start order will be as follow (as an example for

1212.4 **团队排名**

团队排名将根据各队运动员在比赛中获得的国际雪联积分总和由低到高排列。

1212.5 **种子队**

参赛队伍将根据排名确定为各组(4 组、8 组或 16 组)的种子队，由此形成分组安排如下（以 8 组为例）:

第 1 组 : 排名第 1 国 vs 第 16 国（最后 1 名）;
第 2 组 : 排名第 8 国 vs 第 9 国 ;
第 3 组 : 排名第 5 国 vs 第 12 国 ;
第 4 组 : 排名第 4 国 vs 第 13 国 ;
第 5 组 : 排名第 3 国 vs 第 14 国（倒数第 3 名）;
第 6 组 : 排名第 6 国 vs 第 11 国 ;
第 7 组 : 排名第 7 国 vs 第 10 国 ;
第 8 组 : 排名第 2 国 vs 第 15 国（倒数第 2 名）。

按照队伍排名情况，排名最高的国家队出发号码布为 1 号，排名最低的国家出发号码布为最后 1 个号。

女子出发号码布从 1 号开始，男子从 5 号开始，按字母顺序排列。如果某个分组仅有 1 支队伍，则该国家将自动获得进入下一回合的资格（轮空）。

1212.6 **进行比赛**

以两个国家每一组个人对决作为一个回合。

出发顺序如下（以分组赛第 1 场为例）:

Heat 1):
"Course Red" Nation 1 W1 against "Course Blue" Nation last W1;
"Course Red" Nation 1 M1 against "Course Blue" Nation last M1;
"Course Blue" Nation 1 W2 against "Course Red" Nation last W2;
"Course Blue" Nation 1 M2 against "Course Red" Nation last M2;
The blue course will be located on the skier' s right.

1212.7 Points Scoring

The winners of each individual leg scores 1 point for their Nation. In case of a tie of an individual leg, both nations are awarded1 point.
If there is a tie at the end of the heat (example 2:2) the Nation with the lowest combined time of the best individual woman and the best individual man run time (or second best in case of a tie for the best time) will win the heat.
If both competitors fall in any leg, the first competitor to reach the finish successfully will be the winner. If both competitors fail to finish, the competitor who successfully skied the furthest distance will be the leg winner.

1212.8 Reasons for Disqualifications (Immediate and without Protest)

- Changing from one course to another;
- Interfering with the opponent, accidentally or not;
- Not passing through a gate correctly (art. 661.4.2);

“红道”排名第 1 国家 1 号女选手对阵“蓝道”排名最后 1 位国家 1 号女选手；
“红道”排名第 1 国家 1 号男选手对阵“蓝道”排名最后 1 名国家 1 号男选手；
“蓝道”排名第 1 国家 2 号女选手对阵“红道”排名最后 1 名国家 2 号女选手；
“蓝道”排名第 1 国家 2 号男选手对阵“红道”排名最后 1 名国家 2 号男选手。
蓝道位于运动员滑行方向的右侧。

1212.7 **获得积分**

每一轮个人对决的获胜者为他的国家赢得 1 分。若为平局，则双方各得 1 分。

如果小组赛最终平局（2∶2），则个人成绩最好的男子和女子滑行时间之和（如果个人成绩最好的男女滑行时间之和仍相同，则用个人成绩第二好的来计算）最短的国家胜出。
如果在个人对决中两国选手都中途摔倒，则最先到达终点的一方胜出。如果都没有到达终点，则成功滑行距离最远者胜出。

1212.8 **取消资格的原因（立即执行且不得提出抗议）**

- 从一条线路滑到另一条线路；
- 有意或无意地干扰对手；
- 未能正确通过旗门（本规则第 661.4.2 条）；

- Stepping back (art. 614.2.3).

1212.9 Awards

The OC can present awards to the competing teams and can award special prizes for individual competitors, such as fastest woman or man or persons winning most points.

1212.10 Cup points

Cup points can be distributed based upon the decision of the appropriate Cup Sub-Committee.

1213 Special Cup Rules

Special, limited events may be run, such as World Cup City Events in accordance with Rules specifically established for such events by the appropriate FIS Committee.

1220 Parallel

1221 Definition

The Parallel is a competition where two competitors race simultaneously side by side down two courses. The setting of the courses, the configuration of the ground and the preparation of the snow are to be as equal as possible.

1222 Technical data

Minimum vertical drop should be: 50 m (ENL: 35 m);
Minimum direction changes should be:15(ENL: 12);
Minimum length of the competition course should be:160 m (ENL: 120 m).

- 后退（本规则第 614.2.3 条）。

1212.9 **奖励**

组委会可为参赛队伍颁奖，也可为选手个人设置特殊奖项，如最快获得积分最多者。

1212.10 **杯赛积分**

可根据相关的杯赛分委员会的决定授予杯赛积分。

1213 特殊杯赛规则

某些特殊形式或者有限定性的比赛（如世界杯城市比赛），可参照国际雪联相关委员会为其制定的特殊规则进行比赛。

1220 平行式比赛

1221 定义

平行式比赛是两名运动员同时沿着两条相邻线路滑行的比赛。线路设计、地形和雪况要尽可能相同。

1222 技术数据

垂直落差最小 50 米（入门级比赛为 35 米）；
最少应有 15 次换向（入门级比赛为 12 次）；
比赛线路长度最少 160 米（入门级比赛为 120 米）。

1222.1 **Jumps**

Jumps are permitted.

Recommendation:

- for Level 0 and 1: 2 (two) jumps ;
- for all other Levels: 1 (one) jump.

1223 Choice and Preparation of the Course

1223.1 Choose a slope wide enough to permit two courses, preferably slightly concave (permitting a view of the whole course from any point). The terrain variations should be the same across the surface of the slope. The course layouts should have a similar profile.

1223.2 Over the full width of the competition course, the snow should be consistently hard, similar to course preparation for Slalom, so that it is possible to offer similar race conditions on both courses.

1223.3 The Organiser must provide transport for the athletes back to the Start in the shortest time possible.

1223.4 The competition course must be entirely closed off. It is recommended to fence off reserved places intended for coaches, competitors and servicemen.

1224 The Courses

1224.1 Each course is designated by a series of gates, each gate

1222.1 **跳跃**

可以设置跳跃区，建议如下：

- 对于 0 至 1 级别的比赛，设 2 次跳跃；
- 其他级别的比赛：设 1 次跳跃。

1223 比赛线路的选择与准备

1223.1 选择一处宽度应足够容纳下两条比赛线路的坡道，最好略有凹面（便于从任何一点观察整条赛道）。赛道表面的地形变化必须贯穿整个坡道，与其保持一致。比赛线路必须设计为有着相似的剖面。

1223.2 在赛道整个坡面宽度上，雪况必须始终坚实，并作类似于回转赛的比赛线路准备，以便在两条比赛线路上提供相似的比赛条件。

1223.3 组织方必须为运动员提供能够用最短时间回到起点的交通方式。

1223.4 赛道必须全部封闭。建议用安全网隔出为教练员、运动员、服务人员预留的场地。

1224 比赛线路

1224.1 每条比赛线路由一系列旗门确定，每道旗门由两根

is composed of two slalom poles with a Giant Slalom gate panel stretched between them and fastened in such a way so as to tear or break away (see also art.690). Poles and panels are red for the course on skier's left and blue for the course on skier's right. The bottom of the panel must be approx. 1 m above the snow. Not valid for PSL.

1224.2 The same course setter sets both courses and makes sure they are equal and parallel and must ensure that the courses flow is smooth and that there is variety in the turns and that the courses have rhythm changes.

1224.3 After the last gate, the separation between the two courses must be marked to direct each competitor towards the middle part of their respective finish.

1225 Distance between the Two Courses

The distance between two corresponding gates (from turning pole to turning pole) should be no less than 8 m. The distance between the centre of the start doors should be the same as between the two courses.

1226 Start

1226.1 Start Doors

Two start doors approved by the FIS must be used. The

回转旗门杆和一面大回转旗门布组成。在两根旗门杆之间拉上一块旗门布并套好,便于撕脱或扯下（另见本规则第 690 条）。滑行方向左侧线路的旗门杆和旗门布用红色，右侧线路的用蓝色。旗门布底部必须高出雪面 1 米左右。不适用回转赛规则。

1224.2　两条比赛线路由同一旗门设计员设计，并确保赛道相同且平行。必须保证线路流畅并有多种弯道和节奏变化。

1224.3　最后一个旗门后，两条比赛线路的分界线必须划分清楚，以指引运动员尽可能滑向其各自终点的中间部分。

1225　两条比赛线路间的距离

对应的两条比赛线路（从回转杆到回转杆）之间的距离不应小于 8 米。出发门中点间的距离应同两条比赛线路的间距相同。

1226　出发

1226.1　**出发门**

两座出发门都应采用国际雪联认证的出发门。出发

doors must be capable of simultaneous and/or delayed opening and connected to the timing devices.

1226.2 The start signal can only be given after the Jury has given permission to start.

1226.3 **Start Command**

The Starter ensures that the competitors are ready by asking “Red course ready – Blue course ready – Attention” , and then activates the starting signal which opens the start doors.

1226.4 If one or both start doors fail to open the start must be repeated.

1227 Finish

1227.1 The finish areas should be symmetrical. The finish line must be parallel with the start doors.

1227.2 The finish line is split in two parts and marked. Each of these must be at least 8 m wide.

1227.3 It is necessary to visually divide the finish to keep the competitors separated after the finish line.

1228 Jury and Course Setter

1228.1 The Jury is established according to art 601.4.

门必须能够同时或者按预定时差延时打开并与计时设备相连接。

1226.2 仲裁委员会允许运动员出发后，才可以发出出发信号。

1226.3 **出发指令**

发令员通过询问“红色赛道准备—蓝色赛道准备—预备”以确定运动员已准备就绪，随后发出打开出发门的出发信号。

1226.4 有一道出发门未开启的，必须重新出发。

1227 终点

1227.1 终点区必须对称。终点线要与出发门平行。

1227.2 终点线一分为二并分别标记，每个宽度不少 8 米。

1227.3 有必要明显区分终点区，以确保越过终点线的运动员彼此分开。

1228 仲裁委员会与旗门设计员

1228.1 仲裁委员会根据本规则 601.4 设立。

1228.2 The Course Setter is appointed by the Jury of the competition (if not chosen by the FIS). Before setting the parallel course, the course setter must conduct an inspection and study the competition course in the presence of the Jury.

1229 Timing

In Parallel it is possible to measure either the difference in time (at Finish) or the individual run times (Start to Finish). If run times are recorded, the difference in time has to be calculated from the run times (in 1/100th seconds). The Jury has to announce at the Team Captains Meeting, which timing method will be used.

1230 Execution of a Parallel

1230.1 All Parallels will take place in two parts.

1230.1.1 Qualification:

All Parallels must have a qualification for all eligible competitors. The starting order for the Qualification shall be determined by FIS points. Cups may establish a special order.

The fastest 32 competitors from the qualification will advance to the first round (round of 32) of the Elimination Heats. In case of a tie for the 32nd position, the competitor with the higher bib number qualifies . Exception for FIS/ENL where the Event programme may permit 64 competitors.

1228.2 旗门设计员如果不是由国际雪联选定的，由仲裁委员会指定。在设计平行式比赛线路前，旗门设计员必须在仲裁委员会陪同下视察并研究线路。

1229 计时

在平行式比赛中，可以测量时间差（在终点处）或各选手的滑行时间（从起点处到终点处）。记录了滑行时间的，必须根据滑行时间计算时间差（精确到1/100 秒）。仲裁委员会必须事先在相应的领队会议上宣布采用哪种计时方法。

1230 平行式比赛的实施

1230.1 所有平行式比赛都由 2 部分组成。

1230.1.1 选拔赛

所有平行式比赛都必须进行一轮由所有参赛运动员参加的选拔赛，运动员在选拔赛上的出发顺序由其国际雪联积分决定，各种杯赛可以实行特别的出发顺序。

选拔赛中最快的 32 名运动员进入第一轮（32 强赛）的各淘汰组，如果第 32 名上出现多人，则出发号码大的运动员晋级。国际雪联的比赛或者入门级比赛都允许有 64 名运动员参加比赛的例外。

1230.1.2 **Elimination Heats**

Each Elimination Heat between two competitors consists of two runs. The competitors change courses for the second run (run-rerun).

1230.1.3 The Jury decides the method of inspection.

1230.2 Formation into Heats

1230.2.1 The competitors receive bibs numbered 1 to 32 as classified from the Qualification run (rank 1 = Bib 1) and keep them until the end of the competition.

1230.2.2 In the round of 32, sixteen heats of competitors are formed according to the Brackets list (see art 1234).

1230.2.3 Start order: following the order of the Bracket list, from top to bottom. All heats race in succession their first run and then their second. For each pair the competitor, who is listed first or respectively on top of the pairing, will start on the red course for the first run. For the second run the competitors change courses.

The following rounds follow the Bracket list from top to bottom.

1230.2.4 The losing 16 competitors are ranked according to the total time of their run and rerun of the round of 32, followed by competitors without a total time ranked according to time from the Qualification run (17th – 32nd).

1230.1.2　淘汰组

每个淘汰组中的两名运动员的比赛都包括两轮滑行。第二轮滑行时运动员交换比赛线路（初滑–复滑）。

1230.1.3　仲裁委员会决定视察比赛线路的方法。

1230.2　分组

1230.2.1　运动员会收到从 1 到 32 的分类号码，该号码根据选拔赛成绩确定（第一名就是 1 号），并要保存到比赛结束。

1230.2.2　在 32 强赛中，要按照对阵列表，设立 16 个淘汰组（参见本规则第 1234 条）。

1230.2.3　出发顺序：按照对阵列表的顺序，从上到下。各组先依次进行第一轮滑行，然后是第二轮滑行。每一组的一对运动员，列在前面或者排在该对运动员名单上面的运动员先沿红色赛道进行第一轮滑行。第二轮滑行时改变滑行赛道。

随后各回合都按对阵列表从上到下比赛。

1230.2.4　在 32 强赛中被淘汰的 16 名运动员，将根据 32 强赛的初复赛滑行总时间进行排名，没有总时间的参赛者在上述参赛者之后根据资格赛以来的成绩排名（17~32 名）。

1230.2.5 Competitors having a bye must start.

1230.3 Round of Sixteen

1230.3.1 The sixteen qualified competitors start according the Bracket list in heats from top to bottom.

1230.3.2 There are eight that qualify for the quarter-finals.

1230.3.3 The losing eight competitors are ranked according to the total time of their run and rerun of the round of sixteen, followed by competitors without a total time ranked according to time from the Qualification (9th – 16th).

1230.4 Quarter–finals

1230.4.1 The eight qualified competitors start according to the Bracket list in heats from top to bottom.

1230.4.2 The losing four competitors are ranked according to the total time of their run and rerun of the Quarter-finals, followed by competitors without a total time ranked according to time from the Qualification (5th – 8th).

1230.5 Semi–finals and Final

1230.5.1 The four qualified competitors start according to the Bracket list in heats from top to bottom.

1230.5.2 The losers of the semi-finals race their first run before the

1230.2.5 轮空的运动员也必须出发。

1230.3 十六进八赛

1230.3.1 16 位晋级的运动员将按照对阵列表从上到下分组出发。

1230.3.2 8 名运动员有资格参加四分之一决赛。

1230.3.3 在 16 强赛中被淘汰的 8 名运动员，将根据 16 强赛的总时间进行排名，没有总时间的参赛者在上述参赛者之后根据资格赛以来的成绩排名（9~16 名）。

1230.4 四分之一决赛

1230.4.1 8 名晋级的运动员按照对阵列表从上到下分组出发。

1230.4.2 在 8 强赛中被淘汰的 4 名运动员，将根据 8 强赛的总时间进行排名，没有总时间的参赛者在上述参赛者之后根据资格赛以来的成绩排名（5~8 名）。

1230.5 半决赛和决赛

1230.5.1 4 名晋级的运动员按照对阵列表从上到下分组出发。

1230.5.2 参加决赛者第一轮滑行前，半决赛失败者首先进行

finalist's race their first run, then the semi-finalists race their second run and then the finalists race their final run.

1231 Control of the Runs

The Jury determines the method of control of the runs.

1232 Disqualifications / Did Not Finish

1232.1 Reasons for disqualification are the following:

- Changing from one course to another;
- Interfering with an opponent, accidentally or not;
- Not passing through a gate correctly (art. 661.4.2);
- Stepping back (art. 614.2.3).

1232.2 Penalty Time

The penalty time will be 0.50 sec. In all cases the time difference for the start of the second run of each pairing can never be higher than the penalty time.

1232.3 The competitor who is disqualified first or does not finish in the first run of a heat will start the second run with a penalty time. If both competitors are disqualified or did not finish in the first run the competitor who completed the most gates before disqualification or did not finish is the winner of the first run.

1232.4 If both competitors do not finish the second run, the result of the first run counts. If both competitors were tied

争夺第三四名的第一轮滑行，其次，在参加决赛者第一轮滑行之后再进行第二轮滑行；最后，参加决赛者进行最终角逐。

1231 滑行监控

仲裁委员会决定监控滑行的方法。

1232 取消资格与未完成

1232.1 取消资格的原因如下所述：
- 从一条线路滑到另一条线路；
- 有意或无意地干扰对手；
- 未能正确通过旗门（本规则第 661.4.2 条）；
- 后退（本规则第 614.2.3 条）。

1232.2 罚时
罚时为 0.50 秒。在任何情况下，各组第二轮出发的时间差均不得超过罚时。

1232.3 被取消资格或未完成淘汰赛第一轮滑行的运动员，在第二轮滑行出发时将有罚时。如果两名选手在第一轮滑行中都被取消资格或没有完成比赛，则在被取消资格或没有完成比赛前完成最多旗门的选手晋级。

1232.4 如果两名运动员都没有完成第二轮滑行，按照第一轮滑行计算成绩。如果两名运动员第一轮滑行后战

after the first run, the winner of the second run or the competitor who completed the most gates in the second run will advance to the next round. If only one competitor is disqualified or does not finish in the second run of a heat the competitor is eliminated.

If both competitors are tied after the second run the competitor who wins the second run advances to the next round.

1232.5 In case of a tie in both runs the competitor with the lower bib will advance to the next round. If this happens in the Final and/or the Small Final,competitors will be ranked equally (tie).

1233 Slalom (PSL) or Giant Slalom (PGS)

In the case of issues or items not covered in art. 1220 – 1232 the Rules for Slalom or Giant Slalom (art. 800 or 900) must be considered. The registration of the event in the FIS calendar must indicate whether Slalom or Giant Slalom rules are applied. Special Rules for Cups may also be applied.

1240 KO System

1240.1 Participation

All competitors are admitted to the Qualification run according to the corresponding Series Rules.

1241 Mode and Time Frame

Due to organisational reasons it should not be permitted

成平手，则第二轮滑行的胜者或者在第二轮比赛中完成最多旗门的运动员将晋级。如果在小组赛第二轮滑行中只有一名运动员被取消资格或未完成滑行，该运动员被淘汰。

如果两名选手在第二轮滑行后战成平手，则赢得第二轮比赛的选手晋级。

1232.5 如果运动员在两轮滑行中不分胜负，出发号码小的运动员晋级，如果这种情形出现在决赛或小决赛中，运动员成绩并列。

1233 回转赛或者大回转赛规则

若有本规则第 1220 条至第 1232 条没有提及的问题或项目，则必须参考回转赛或者超级大回转赛规则（本规则第 800 条或者第 900 条）。申请纳入《国际雪联竞赛日历》的比赛必须明确是否适用回转赛或者超级大回转赛规则。杯赛的特别规则也可适用。

1240 淘汰赛体系

1240.1 **参赛**

所有运动员均按相应的系列规则参加资格赛。

1241 模式与时间框架

由于组织方面的原因，同一天内不应举行其他比赛。

to hold another event on the same day.

1241.1 Preliminary Round (Qualification Run) – Course 1

- Classical execution, traditional course length and vertical drop;
- Starting order according to the corresponding Series Rules;
- Valid for FIS points with FIS adder;
- The starting numbers remain the same for the complete event.

1241.2 Intermediate Round, 1st Run – Course 2

The thirty fastest competitors from the Preliminary Round start in an elimination heat (the 30th against the 1st, etc.). The three best lucky-losers are qualified for the next run and are ranked in order of their race time after the 15 qualified competitors.

If two competitors from the same heat do not finish (DNF) or are disqualified (DSQ) in the 1st run, the lucky-loser option is adopted (the 4th best lucky-loser will be qualified for the 2nd run). In case of a tie, both competitors advance to the next run.

Break

1241.3 Intermediate Round, 2nd Run – Course 3

The fifteen qualified competitors plus the three fastest lucky-losers (only two lucky-losers in case of a tie in the 1st Intermediate Round) again compete in an elimination run (the 18th against the

1241.1 **初赛（资格赛）——线路 1**

- 传统比赛，传统比赛线路长度和垂直落差；

- 出发顺序依照相应系列规则；

- 用国际雪联积分法计算的国际雪联积分有效；
- 全部比赛采用相同的出发号码。

1241.2 **复赛，第 1 轮滑行——线路 2**

预赛中胜出的前 30 名最快的选手以淘汰赛分组的形式出发（第 30 名对第 1 名，依此类推）。在淘汰选手中选 3 名成绩最好的幸运者晋级进入下一轮滑行，依其比赛时间排在晋级的 15 名选手之后。

如果两名同组选手在第一轮比赛中未完成（DNF）或取消资格（DSQ），则采用“幸运输家”选项（第四名成绩最好的“幸运输家”晋级第二轮比赛）。如出现平局，两名运动员均晋级下一轮滑行。

休息

1241.3 **复赛，第 2 轮滑行——线路 3**

15 名晋级运动员加上 3 名最快的幸运输家运动员（若在复赛第一轮滑行中出现平局，则只选 2 名）再次进行淘汰赛角逐（第 18 名对第 1 名，依此类推）。

1st, etc.).
If two competitors from the same heat are DNF or DSQ in the 2nd run, the luckyloser from the 2nd run will be qualified for the 3rd run (final run) in order to have nine competitors. In case of a tie in one heat, both competitors advance to the final.
Break

1241.4 **Final Run – Course 3**
The nine qualified competitors (10 competitors in case of a tie in the 2nd Intermediate Round) start in the reversed order of their times in the 2nd run of the Intermediate Round.

1242 Results after the Intermediate Rounds and the Final

1242.1 After the 1st run of the Intermediate Round, ranks 19 - 30 are allocated (ranking according to times, in case of DNF, DNS or DSQ according to the time in the Qualification Round).

1242.2 After the 2nd run of the Intermediate Round, ranks 10 - 18 are allocated (ranking according to times, in case of DNF, DNS or DSQ according to the time of the 1st Intermediate Round).

1242.3 After the Final, ranks 1 - 9 are allocated (ranking according to times, in case of DNF, DNS or DSQ according to

若两名同组选手在第二轮中未完成（DNF）或取消资格（DSQ），则第二轮比赛幸运输家将有资格参加第三轮（最后一轮）比赛，以保持 9 名选手参赛格局。如有一组出现平局，两名选手都能进入决赛。

休息

1241.4 **决赛——线路 3**
9 名合格选手（如在第二轮复赛中打成平手，则为 10 名选手）按照在复赛中第二轮滑行的时间逆序出发。

1242 复赛和决赛后的成绩

1242.1 复赛第一轮滑行后决出第 19 名至第 30 名［若有未完成（DNF）、未出发（DNS）或取消资格（DSQ），则按资格赛轮次的时间排序］。

1242.2 复赛第二轮滑行后决出第 10 名至第 18 名［若有未出发（DNF）、未完成（DNS）或取消资格（DSQ），则按复赛第一轮时间排序］。

1242.3 决赛结束后决出第 1 名至第 9 名［按时间排序；若有未完成（DNF）、未出发（DNS）、取消资格（DSQ）， the time of the 2nd Intermediate Round).

1242.4 The Final result will be established by adding the 2nd and 3rd run = Winner.

1242.5 Protest time: 5 minutes after the last heat (after each run).

则按复赛第二轮时间排序]。

1242.4　决赛成绩=第二轮滑行成绩+第三轮滑行成绩，以此决定优胜者。

1242.5　抗议期限：（每轮滑行后）最后一组结束后的5分钟内。

垂直落差、旗门数和换向次数检查表

Check List for vertical drop (VD), number of gates (NG) and number of direction changes (DC)

比赛项目 EVENT			冬奥会 / 世锦赛 OWG/ WSC	世界杯 WC	洲际杯 COC	国际雪联赛事 FIS	青少年比赛 CHI	入门级比赛 ENL
滑降（第 700 条）DH (Art. 700) Downhill	女子 W	垂直落差 VD	450–800					一轮 1 Run：400–500m 两轮 2 Runs：400–500m
	女子 W	旗门布 Gate Panel	0.75 × 0.50// 旗门布颜色（参见第 701.3.2 条）//colour for gate panels (see art. 701.3.2)					
	男子 M	垂直落差 VD	350–450（2 轮比赛 2 Runs Race）					
	男子 M	旗门数 NG	按照规定进行 as required					
	男子 M	垂直落差 VD	800(750[1])–1100		500–1100	450–1100		一轮 1 Run：400–500m 两轮 2 Runs：400–500m
回转（第 800 条）SL (Art. 800) Slalom	女子 W	垂直落差 VD	140–220		120–200		100–160	80–120 3 轮：至少 50 3 Runs:50 min
	女子 W 男子 M	换向 DC	换向次数 Number of direction changes					
	女子 W 男子 M	换向 DC	30%–35%(+/–3)				32%–38% (+/–3)	30%–35%(+/–3)
	男子	垂直落差 VD	180–220		140–220		100–160	80–140 3 轮：至少 50 3 Runs: 50 min

续表

比赛项目 EVENT			冬奥会 / 世锦赛 OWG/WSC	世界杯 WC	洲际杯 COC	国际雪联赛事 FIS	青少年比赛 CHI	入门级比赛 ENL
大回转（第 900 条）GS (Art. 900) Giant Slalom	女子 W	垂直落差 VD	300–400		250–450		200–350[2]	200–250
	女子 W 男子 M	换向次数 DC	换向次数 Number of direction changes					
			11%–15%				13%–18%	13%–15%
		旗门布 Cate Panel	0.75 × 0.50 红色（橙色）和蓝色（参见第 695 条）red (orange) & blue (see art. 695)					
	男子 M	垂直落差 VD	300–450		250–450		200–350[2]	200–250
超级大回转（第 1000 条）SG (Art. 1000) Super-G	女子 W	垂直落差 VD	400–600		350–600		250–450	300–500
	女子 W 男子 M	换向 DC	换向次数 Number of direction changes					
			至少 6%（6% min）			至少 7%	8%–12%	至少 7%（7% min）
		旗门布 Gate Panel	0.75 × 0.50 红色（橙色）和蓝色（参见第 695 条）red (orange)& blue (see art. 695)					
	男子 M	垂直落差 VD	400–650			350–650	250–450	300–500
平行式比赛（第 1220 条）P (Art. 1220) Parallel	女子 W 男子 M	垂直落差 VD	至少 50m（min 50m）至少 160m 长（min length 160m）				至少 35m 至少 120m 长	至少 35m 至少 120m 长
		NG	至少 15（min 15）				至少 12	至少 12
		旗门布 Gate Panel	0.75 × 0.50 红色赛道 / 蓝色赛道 red course / blue course					

1) 例外情况参见第 701.1.1 条
2) 参见第 901.1.4 条

高山滑雪常用术语英汉对译表

Accreditation 注册。该术语广泛出现于本规则中，如第 604 条随队官员的注册。

Alpine Combined 高山滑雪全能(1101),即混合多项单一比赛项目(滑降、大回转等) 的比赛项目。

Announcement 检录，通常安排在起点，即对运动员的起点检录(Announcement of the competitors at the start) (1211.5)。在本规则中还有公告（ 214)、公布（ Announcement of Disqualifying Faults，664) 等意思，需要结合上下文领会。

Appeal 申诉。不同于抗议（ protest)，是对抗议的结果不服的进一步异议（ 647)。申诉只能由国家滑雪协会提交国际雪联办公室(647.1.2)。

Athletes Declaration 国际雪联《运动员宣言》。其中对运动员的行为举止提出了全面的要求，没有签署此项声明的运动员往往无法参加国际雪联的绝大多数活动。

Bibs 出发号码布，其上印着运动员的出发号码。比赛或者训练时必须佩戴。

Board/Snowboard 单板，通常与滑雪板（ 双板) 对称，如 skis/board (207.1.1)，Skis / Snowboards (207.1.2)。

By-laws 补充规定，在国际雪联的规范体系中属于中间层级的规范，其上有《国际雪联章程》(FIS Statutes)、规则(Rules)、规定(Regulations)，其下有工作指南(Instructions)、具体规定(Specifications)。

Calendar 《国际雪联竞赛日历》，即FIS Calendar，由国际雪联认可并公布的比赛的目录，其中包括举办日期、地点、组织方等。

Chief Gate Judge 旗门裁判长(601.3.5，665.1)。负责组织和监督旗门裁判员(gate judges)的工作。

Chief of Course 赛道长，根据仲裁委员会的指令和决定负责做好赛道的准备工作。

Chief of Course Equipment 设备长(不同于赛道长Chief of Course)，直译为赛道设备长。更为复杂的是赛道设备及技术设备长(Chief of Course Equipment and Technical Equipment)，二者可合并，也可分立，具体由组织方决定；许多比赛中不设设备长，其职能由赛道长兼任，但这不影响本规则单独规定设备长的职责(601.3.9.2)。

Chief of Medical and Rescue Services 医疗与救援主管(601.3.8)。

Chief of Race 竞赛长，指导比赛所有准备工作，并监督技术领域的活动，召集会议研究讨论技术问题，经商技术代表后主持领队会议(601.3.1)。

Chief of Timing and Calculations 计时计算长。负责计时与成绩计算，指挥下列官员：发令员starter，助理发令员assistant starter，起点记录员start recorder，计时长chief timekeeper，助理计时员assistant timekeepers，终点监督员 finish controller，计算长及其助理 chief of calculations and the assistants（601.3.6）。

Chief Race Director 即世界杯等赛事中的裁判长 Referee (Chief-Race-Director)（601.2.1）。

Coaches 教练 (220)，运动队主要官员（Team Officials）之一。
原文有 Coaches(220) 和 Trainers（604.2）两种表述,具体区别不详。原文所附索引中，也将二者并列，可见是有意区分二者。

Commercial Markings 商业标识。

Competition 竞赛。

Competitor 运动员，本规则中最常用的指代，不宜译为参赛运动员或者参赛选手，因为许多运动员虽然到了赛场甚至上到了起点，但因为各种原因并没有实际参加比赛。如第 217.4 条提到的已抽签但未到场参赛的运动员。
与此相关的概念还包括参赛许可（Licence）和参赛资格（Qualification），二者有所不同。

Complete the course 完赛，指运动员没有犯规地完成整个比赛线路的滑行。这个概念对于理解 course 的本义很有帮助：course 是运动员依规则真正需要完成的滑行路线；实际滑行路线与比赛线路不一致的，如错过或者过错旗门，都属于没有完赛。

Competition course 比赛用的线路。由旗门在赛道上确定的参赛运动员按照规则滑行的比赛线路，通常简称线路（course）。
在某些场合，译为赛道更好，如第 650.1 条规定：所有比赛都必须在国际雪联批准（认证）的赛道上举行。不译为线路的原因是，赛道是承载比赛线路的雪道，国际雪联的认证也仅限于赛道；线路则是比赛时的滑行轨迹，经旗门设计后才会出现，因此每场比赛都会不同，或者说同一赛道上会有多条比赛线路。

第 650.3.1 条提到的 description、containing，可以印证 competition course 的本义。

此外，本规则中许多情形下单独的 course 应视为 competition Course。此时，更需要识别其具体所指，如在第 623.1 条有关重滑的规定中提到：Competitors should make their way to the Finish along the side of the course，这里的 course 就必须译为赛道，如果译为比赛线路，则沿其边缘滑下就会撞到每个旗门的绕行杆。

Control 有三重意思：

1. 监督。第 200.5 条要求：《国际雪联竞赛日历》中的所有比赛均须接受国际雪联技术代表的监督。最主要的就是派 TD 到场。

2. 检查。如第 221.4 条中的兴奋剂检查 Doping controls，第 222.6 条对比赛器材是否合规的检查等。

3. 控制。如第 208.1.4 条中的 accreditation and access control。

Course 该词是本部分规则中出现频率最高、内容最关键、组词最丰富，相应的译法也最多的一个核心概念。结合上下文、该词参与构成的词组的含义并考虑构词词组的省略等因素，将该词译为以下译法：

1. 线路：这是 course 最核心的义项，指赛道上通过旗门设计结合旗门通过规则形成的指引运动员比赛时滑行的虚拟路线，旗门只是其外在表现，赛道则是其实地载体。对旗门与线路关系的最佳解释是第 615.1.2 条中的用旗门设计比赛线路（setting the course with gates），即旗门设计的重点是比赛的滑行线路，不是旗门本身。

2. 赛道：实为 competition course 的简写，是比赛时封闭的、包围线路及旗门等比赛设施的区域，是用于比赛的线路所在场地，即雪场中可以连续、顺利滑下的一段足够长、达到规定高度差的雪道。第 614.1.1 条对此有精确的定义：赛道是从某一特定雪道中围出的区域，其技术参数等由各自的国际雪联认定证书具体描述。第 623.2.1 条 中的 Blocking of the course，根据上下文，特别是 Blocking 的时态，显然是指整个赛道范围内出现了使正在滑行运动员受阻的情形，滑行线路上出现阻碍仅是其中的一种情形。

3. 旗门设计：第 703.1.1 条对旗门设计的界定（Gates must be set to delineate the desired racing line）间接印证了线路、赛道与旗门三者间的关系。

Course Length 比赛线路长度。比赛线路的长度不同于赛道的长度，因为同一赛道上设计的比赛线路，转向次数越多，线路就会越长。

Course Setter 旗门设计员，最具有技术含量的比赛官员，第 603 条专门规定其职责、权利等。

Course Setting 旗门设计，即通过确定旗门、旗杆在赛道上的位置，结合旗门通行规则，设计出比赛用的线路（desired racing line）。

Course Testers 线路检验员，不同于旗门设计员，而是与试滑员类似负责检验旗门设计员所设计的线路的适滑性（608.9.3.3）。没有专设时可由试滑员代责。

Court of Arbitration for Sport 体育仲裁法庭，这是一个常设机构，与每项比赛临时设立的仲裁委员会不同；享有对兴奋剂申诉案件的专属管辖权（203.2.1）。

Deadlines 截止期限（643）。通常会被译为截止日期，但本规则最短计时单位为毫秒，通常计时单位为小时、分、秒，日显然太长了。

Direction changes 换向次数。运动员在比赛线路上需要转换前进方向的次数，具体体现为旗门设计时需要设置的旗门数（801.2.4）。
一般情况下，换向次数 = 转弯（turns）数 = 旗门数。
如第 1001.3.4 条规定，国际雪联级别的超级大回转比赛，换向次数最少为垂直落差的 7%,则换向次数 = 高度差(以米为单位)× 7%(取整数)。

Discipline 国际雪联竞赛分项，高山滑雪、越野滑雪都是国际雪联竞赛分项（201.4）。

Disqualifying Faults 导致取消比赛资格的犯规（664）。

DNF 未完成 did not finish，常见违规 DNS\NPS\DNF\DSQ 之一。

DNS 未发出 did not start，常见违规 DNS\NPS\DNF\ DSQ 之一。

Doping 兴奋剂检测。

Downhill 滑降。

Draw 抽签（217）。在领队会上举行（604.3，604.4），关键是确定出发顺序：运动员在每一比赛项目和国际雪联竞赛分项中的出发顺序要根据特定程式通过抽签结合积分确定（217.1）。

DSQ 取消资格 disqualification，常见违规 DNS\NPS\DNF\DSQ 之一。

Entries 报名（604.4）。根据第 215.3 条，只有国家滑雪协会有资格经办国际比赛的参赛报名。

Equipment 竞赛器材（Competition Equipment）。“运动员参加国际雪联比赛只能携带符合国际雪联规定的竞赛器材”（221.1）。

Event 比赛项目（201.5, 218.3.4），其上位概念是 discipline 和 sport，

前者为国际雪联竞赛分项，后者为运动项目。就高山滑雪而言，滑雪是 sport，其下分为高山滑雪、越野滑雪等国际雪联竞赛分项；高山滑雪又包含多个比赛项目，如回转、大回转、超级大回转等，这些比赛项目统称 Alpine Events（国际雪联竞赛分项代码为 AL），纳入 FIS 比赛的就是国际雪联比赛 FIS Events（206.2）。

Fence 防护网，指圈定赛道的 ABC 网，不是过于强硬的栅栏（614.3.2）。

Finish line 终点线。在电子计时系统中，这条线即切光系统的多条光束标定，终点区地面施划的彩色粗实线只用于示意，不是计时用终点线。第 615.2 条对此有明确的解释：位于计时切光器之间的终点线须沿横向用彩色涂料清楚地标明。

Finish Referee 终点裁判长。从官方视察线路开始直至训练和比赛全部结束，终点裁判长必须始终坚守在终点，以便履行第 601.3.4 条规定的确保终点区、终点冲刺区和终点停止区的组织规定切实得到遵守等职责。

FIS 国际滑雪联合会（International Ski Federation），简称国际雪联。

FIS Congress 国际雪联代表大会，这是国际雪联的最高决策机构。

FIS Council 国际雪联理事会，这是国际雪联的执行机构。

Forerunner 试滑员，是组委会的成员，由组织者在已签署国际雪联《运动员宣言》的运动员中挑选，数量不少于 3 人（605.1）。试滑员应具备以比赛方式滑完全程的滑雪能力（605.3），但不得再参加相应比赛（605.4）。

Gate Fault 旗门失误，导致禁止继续比赛。运动员漏过 1 个旗门，不得继续通过后续旗门（614.2.2）。

Gate Judge 旗门裁判员。

Giant Slalom 大回转。

Homologation 认证。国际雪联的认证很多，包括 Gate Panels，Slalom poles，Timing Equipment，但最主要的是对赛道（course）的认证。需要注意的是，认证的是赛道，线路则要在每次比赛时另行设计在赛道上。

Horizontally 水平方向，第 615.2 条在规定终点线时明确要求其必须是水平的，因为滑行方向总是与滚落线同向，大致是垂直方向。

Inspection 视察。其中的关键任务是视察经设计的比赛线路 Inspection of the Course。因视察主体不同，分为 3 类（614）：

1.Inspection, Competitors：运动员视察以线路为主，译为运动员视察线路。

2.Inspection, Course Setter：旗门设计员视察的也主要是线路。

3.Inspection, Jury：仲裁委员会视察，不限于线路，而是赛道乃至整个场地。

Instructions 工作指南，在国际雪联的规范体系中属于最低层级的规范，其上有《国际雪联章程》（FIS Statutes）、规则（Rules）、规定（Regulations）、补充规定（By-laws），其下有具体规定（Specifications）。

除了上述抽象意义外，还可以指具体的指令，如 Gate Judges' Instructions（660），additional instructions of the Jury（205.1）。

International Ski Federation 国际滑雪联合会，简称国际雪联，FIS。

Interruption 暂停。比赛暂时停止，随后仍可继续 restart，此前已进行的比赛仍有效。注意 restart 是继续进行比赛，而不是重新比赛。

注意与 terminated 的区别，终止就是比赛结束，即使没有赛完（601.4.6.2，624）。

Jury 仲裁委员会，负责封闭的比赛场地内的技术性事务。其成员（由同时是组委会成员的下列人员兼任）包括：技术代表，裁判长，竞赛长，速降和超级大回转比赛项目的副裁判长（回转和大回转比赛项目的副裁判长），起点裁判长，终点裁判长（601.4），这些成员除竞赛长外，均由国际雪联理事会任命（601.4.1.1）。

仲裁委员会由出席会议成员按简单多数制作出决定（601.4.5.3），但对抗议（protest）的处理决定，以仲裁委全员为基数取多数票决定（646.3）。

KO System 淘汰赛（1240）。

Kombi 组合赛，规定在国际青少年高山滑雪比赛（608）中。其中，U16–U14 组合赛是一项国际承认的比赛，由一系列不同标准弯道和旗门组合而成，这项比赛满足了这一年龄段的发展需要（608.9）。

Licence/FIS Licence 全称为国际雪联参赛许可证（Licence to participate in FIS Races），简称国际雪联许可证（FIS Licence）。

国家滑雪协会为运动员在相应的国际雪联竞赛分项中进行注册，并向符合参赛标准的运动员核发参加国际雪联比赛许可证。

Medical examination 医学检查，不同于与兴奋剂有关的药检。本规则第 221 条中就是将健康评估（evaluation，221.1）、医学检查（221.2）和反兴奋剂（anti-doping，221.3）分别规定的。

National Ski Association 国家滑雪协会，是国际雪联的成员单位。从第 202.2 条的规定看，国际雪联只与各国家滑雪协会打交道，与国家无关。

NPS 禁止出发 Not Permitted to Start（627），常见违规 DNS\NPS\DNF\ DSQ 之一。

Official Training 场地适应训练，在许多项目中是比赛的一个组成部分（704）。
旧译法译为公开训练，但这种训练实际上与公开与否无关。
另有 training run，也属于赛道适用训练，但可以进行计时。

Organisers 组织方，负责组织国际雪联比赛者，通常为某个国家的滑雪协会，但不一定是滑雪比赛实际举办地的国家的滑雪协会（202.2）。

Organising Committee（**OC**） 全称组织委员会，但组委会显然更通用。与组织方（Organisers）不同，组委会由组织方和国际雪联委派的成员组成，享有组织方的权利、承担组织方的义务和履行组织方的职责（211.2）。

Parallel Events 平行式比赛，是两名运动员同时沿着两条相邻线路滑行的比赛，比赛线路、地形和雪况要尽可能相同（1221）。

Photocell system 切光系统，比赛计时用电子感光计时触发系统。当规则规定的运动员的身体的特定部门遮挡切光系统光束时，计时系统开始（切入起点线）或者结束（切入终点线）计时，在此之间的时间，即为该运动员的比赛用时。

Points 积分，主要指国际雪联积分（FIS Points，FIS Race Points ）。

Protest 抗议。不同于申诉（appeal），是对判罚不服提出的异议（640）。

Qualification （运动员）参赛资格。与参赛许可有关联，但二者不完全等同。

Quotas 配额，是根据参赛运动员人数等确定的随队官员、医务、技术等人员数额（604.1），故不是名额。仲裁委员会有权根据比赛情况压缩有关参赛队上述人员的配额，以此作为其纪律处分手段的一部分。

Race course 赛道，即 competition course，从有关关闭赛道（closed race course，604.1；closed course，614.1.4）的表述看，由于比赛线路是一条假想的虚拟线，无所谓封闭，能够关闭的只有赛道，即比赛线路所依托的实体的雪道。因此，赛道的范围确实大于线路，赛道是比赛线路的载体。

此外，从第 903.1.1 条的表述看，两轮滑行可设在同一赛道，但第二轮滑行线路必须重新设计（Both runs can be set on the same course but the second run must be re-set），也可以得出同样结论。

Race Secretary 负责整个比赛的竞赛技术方面的所有秘书工作，如做好抽签准备，负责技术官员、仲裁委员会和领队的会议记录等（601.3.7）。

Re-run 重滑：仅针对在已经开始的滑行被阻碍的运动员个人。

注意：本规则只有重滑，没有比赛从头开始的重赛。

Referee 裁判长，是比赛中仅次于 TD 的技术官员，其职责和权利见第 601.4.10 条。单独使用时指裁判长，组成词组的还有副裁判长 Assistant Referee、起点裁判长 Start Referee、终点裁判长 Finish Referee，注意区分。

Registered time 登记时间，由助理计时员记录的运动员比赛时间。登记时间只是计算成绩的素材，是用于计算比赛时间的，不是正式的比赛用时。

Regulations 规定，这是国际雪联较高位阶的规范。在其之上有《国际雪联章程》（FIS Statutes）、规则（Rules），在其之下有补充规定（By-laws）、工作指南（Instructions）、具体规定（Specifications）。

Restart 比赛暂停后继续比赛，此前进行的比赛仍然有效，故不是重赛。

Result list/Result lists/Results list 意思都是正式成绩列表。result list（最集中出现在 621.11.2 中），results list（701.2）和 result lists（601.4.9.3），但没有 results lists，这显然是原文在语法上不太规整之处。这三个表述的原中文译法有成绩列表（最普遍）、成绩单、成绩公告等。将这些内容一一搜罗并校正为规范统一的译法，是本次译制工作最突出的特点。

Rules/FIS Rules 规则，这是国际雪联较高位阶的规范。在其之上有《国际雪联章程》（FIS Statutes），在其之下有规定（Regulations）、补充规定（By-laws）、工作指南（Instructions）、具体规定（Specifications），共同构成国际雪联的规范体系。

在本规则中，FIS Rules 特指《国际雪联滑雪竞赛规则》，即本规则。

Run（*n.*） 滑行（名词），比赛中参赛运动员从起点滑行至终点称为一次滑行，所有参赛运动员依次完成一次滑行称为一轮滑行。本规则第 611.2.1 条禁止在任何一轮滑行期间重新同步计时系统的规定，很好地说明了滑行的“次”与“轮”的关系：比赛中的每一轮，都会有多个运动员各滑行 1 次，故必须区分人次与轮次，以避免引起混淆。

Sanction 制裁。第 200.6 条特别强调：对运动员、官员或者教练员实施并公布的法律制裁，应当取得国际雪联和相应国家滑雪协会的双重确认。

Service Personnel 服务人员。

Slalom 回转。

Slope 雪道。容纳赛道及其内的比赛线路、可用于训练的有雪坡道（614.1.3）。

Specifications 具体规定，在国际雪联的规范体系中属于最低层级的规范，其上有《国际雪联章程》（FIS Statutes）、规则（Rules）、规定（Regulations）、补充规定（By-laws）、工作指南（Instructions）。

Speed event 竞速项目，包括滑降 Downhill 或超级大回转 Super-G。与之对应的是竞技项目（1101）。

Speed orientation 竞速偏好，组合赛两种模式之一，即大回转 / 超级大回转组合模式。与之对应的是竞技偏好。

Start 出发。本规则中指出发的动作及其名词化，但也有起点的意思。为了便于区分，与狭义的出发运作有关的场合，包括由 start 构成的词组，都译为“出发”，如出发线（Start Line）、出发程序（Start Procedure）、出发信号（Start Signals）；将地点等位置概念有关的，译为起点。

Start Area 出发区（狭义）、起点区（广义）。本规则原文中并没有区分这两层含义，但其实际用法却有这两层意思的区别：根据 613.1，出发区在起点区范围内，只有包括起点线（starting line）及与之毗连的出发坡道（start ramp）构成的区域，才是严格意义上的出发区。

起点区内依距离出发线由远及近，至少可以分为 4 个区域：隔离区（special roped off area）—遮蔽棚（shelter for the competitors waiting for the call to start）—出发棚（start hut）—出发区。本规则中没有给隔离区具体的概念化命名，而是笼统地用 special roped off area 指代，该区域用于隔离公众与教练、领队等服务人员（be provided for trainers, team captains, service personnel etc., in which they may take care of the waiting competitors without being interrupted by the public），故名。

Start interval 出发间隔，比较有意义的是固定出发间隔（fixed start interval），指滑降、超级大回转等比赛中使用的出发方式。

Start Number 出发号码。写在出发号码布（bibs）上，比赛或者训练时必须佩戴。

Start order 出发顺序（608.5），与运动员分组和本人排名有关。

Start ramp 出发台，其关键是出发线后的坡道，这是运动员出发后最先进入的滑行线路，供迅速提速用，是起点区内从起点线（starting line）开始延伸至比赛线路的区域。不译为起点坡道是因为起点只是一个点或者一条线，出发坡道则是数以千平方米计的一个大坡面（613.2）。

Start Referee 起点裁判长。从官方视察线路开始直至当天的训练或比赛全部结束，起点裁判长都必须始终坚守在起点，以便履行第 601.3.3 条规定的确保有关出发和组织出发方面的规定切实得到遵守等职责。

Start Recorder 出发记录员。

Starter 发令员。受计时计算长指挥的起点官员，往往还配有助理发令员（assistant starter）作助手。

Statutes 《国际雪联章程》（FIS Statutes），这是国际雪联最高位阶的规则。在此之下有规则（Rules）、规定（Regulations）、补充规定（By-laws）、工作指南（Instructions）、具体规定（Specifications），共同构成国际雪联的规范体系。

Sub-Committee for Alpine Courses 国际雪联高山滑雪场地分委员会。这种译法在国内已经约定俗成，但考虑到原文中出现了 Course，译为赛道也许更为贴切。

Super-G 超级大回转。

TD 技术代表（Technical Delegate）。国际雪联为所有比赛任命技术代表及其他比赛官员（601.2）；其中，冬奥会、国际雪联世锦赛和国际雪联世青赛的技术代表由高山滑雪委员会推荐，国际雪联理事会任命（602.2.1），其他比赛的技术代表由高山滑雪技术代表分委员会任命（602.2.2）。

技术代表任命裁判长、速降和超级大回转比赛项目的副裁判长，以及遇有不可抗力情势时仲裁委员会成员的替换人选（601.4.2.2）。

Technical Adviser 技术顾问，不同于 TD。高山滑雪委员会任命的支持仲裁委员会工作的技术顾问，其在仲裁委员会中有权发表意见，但无权表决（601.4.11）。

Team Captain 领队。指参赛队的领队。由于国际雪联的国际及以上比赛通常以国家为单位组队，因此，领队通常就是国家队的领队。但原文的表述上，通常用国家滑雪协会领队（National Ski Association team captain，603.1.1）指称，不用国家队领队的称谓。

Team Captains Meetings 领队会议。这个会议很重要，决定并传达许多与具体比赛有关的大事，特别是抽签（Draw），详见第 604.3 条。

Technical orientation 竞技偏好，组合赛两种模式之一，即回转 / 大回转组合模式。与之对应的是竞速偏好。

Terminated/Termination 终止比赛，即 Termination of a Competition，指比赛彻底结束，以后不再补赛或重赛（601.4.6.2，625）。

Trainers 教练员，与领队搭档。领队和教练员必须根据配额由组织方注册，注册后赋予第 604.2 条规定的权利和义务。

Sportsmanlike 运动员风范。like 更主要地表达可外显的修养，故 unsportsmanlike 有不绅士之意，但只是不得体，并非不道德；故不宜译为违反体育道德，因为内在的道德是看不见的。

Vertical drop 垂直落差，即线路在垂直高度上的落差，用米表示的数值乘以适当的百分比，即为换向次数 Number of Direction changes（608.9.4.3）。

Yellow Flag 黄旗（705）。